E–Government Interoperability and Information Resource Integration:
Frameworks for Aligned Development

Petter Gottschalk
Norwegian School of Management, Norway

Hans Solli-Sæther
Norwegian School of Management, Norway

INFORMATION SCIENCE REFERENCE

Hershey · New York

Director of Editorial Content:	Kristin Klinger
Senior Managing Editor:	Jamie Snavely
Managing Editor:	Jeff Ash
Assistant Managing Editor:	Carole Coulson
Typesetter:	Carole Coulson
Cover Design:	Lisa Tosheff
Printed at:	Yurchak Printing Inc.

Published in the United States of America by
 Information Science Reference (an imprint of IGI Global)
 701 E. Chocolate Avenue, Suite 200
 Hershey PA 17033
 Tel: 717-533-8845
 Fax: 717-533-8661
 E-mail: cust@igi-global.com
 Web site: http://www.igi-global.com/reference

and in the United Kingdom by
 Information Science Reference (an imprint of IGI Global)
 3 Henrietta Street
 Covent Garden
 London WC2E 8LU
 Tel: 44 20 7240 0856
 Fax: 44 20 7379 0609
 Web site: http://www.eurospanbookstore.com

Library of Congress Cataloging-in-Publication Data

Gottschalk, Petter, 1950-
E-government interoperability and information resource integration : frameworks for aligned development / by Petter Gottschalk and Hans Solli-Sæther.
  p. cm.
Includes bibliographical references and index.
Summary: "This book focuses on the integration of new technologies into digital government, generating new insights into e-government interoperability"--Provided by publisher.

ISBN 978-1-60566-648-8 (hardcover) -- ISBN 978-1-60566-649-5 (ebook)
1. Internet in public administration. I. Solli-Sæther, Hans. II. Title.
JF1525.A8G675 2009
352.3'802854678--dc22

                          2008051167

British Cataloguing in Publication Data
A Cataloguing in Publication record for this book is available from the British Library.

All work contributed to this encyclopedia set is new, previously-unpublished material. The views expressed in this encyclopedia set are those of the authors, but not necessarily of the publisher.

Table of Contents

Chapter XII

Foreword

In this well-timed book Petter Gottschalk and Hans Solli-Sæther present popular e-government interoperability practices. They use several organization and management theories as a means of understanding the underlying factors of interoperability. Improved interoperability at all levels of public sector and between public and private sector is of critical importance to make electronic government more successful. The authors bring together their expertise as academics and researchers, along with their professional experience as Chief Information Officers of several organizations.

This book covers a range of important topics such as barriers of interoperability and solutions to overcome them, value configuration for interoperability, alignment of information resources to government tasks, defining stages of E-Government interoperability, strategic planning for alignment of E-Government initiatives. Interoperability represents an import issue for all governments, yet not many executives are quite clear about the various aspects of interoperability and therefore run the risk of missing opportunities in integration projects.

Semicolon (Semantic and Organisational Interoperability in Communicating and Collaborating Organisations) is a research and development project partly funded by the Norwegian Research Council. The main goal of Semicolon is to develop and test ICT-based methods, tools, and metrics to obtain faster and cheaper semantic and organizational interoperability both with and within the public sector. This book serves as a valuable literature review establishing a common ground for research into organizational interoperability. A number of cases are included to provide additional help to the reader better understand the subject matter, and relate it to real-world scenarios. Further it adds academic rigor to its arguments with theoretical aspects of organizational interoperability.

This book is a most comprehensive guide on all the aspects of interoperability, and is highly commendable for practitioners, researchers, policy makers, and consultants alike.

Terje Grimstad
General manager, Karde AS
Project manager, Semicolon
Oslo, Norway

Preface

The mobilization of electronic information across organizations has the potential of modernizing and transforming information exchanges. The current information exchange is, however, often inefficient and error-prone (Eckman, Bennet, Kaufman, & Tenner, 2007). Exchanges of information and services are often fragmented and complex, dominated by technical as well as organizational problems.

High-ranking issues among the defining purposes of e-government are highly agile, citizen-centric, accountable, transparent, effective, and efficient government operations and services (Scholl & Klischewski, 2007). For reaching such goals, the integration of government information resources and processes, and thus the inter-operation of independent information systems are essential. Yet, most integration and interoperation efforts meet serious challenges and limitations.

Improved interoperability between public organizations as well as between public and private organizations is of critical importance to make electronic government more successful. In this book, stages of E-Government interoperability is identified and discussed. In one of the stage models, four stages are presented: work process stage, knowledge sharing stage, value creation stage, and strategy alignment stage.

This book is about electronic government interoperability, focusing on integration and interoperability in digital government. In addition to stages of interoperability, a number of other important topics and areas are covered in this book to shed light and generate new insights into the way forward for E-Government interoperability. For example, value configurations may differ between co-operating agencies, creating challenges in connecting primary and secondary activities.

The mission of this book is to:

- Identify barriers to interoperability and solutions to overcome such barriers. As will become evident and practitioners already know, there are surprisingly many and high barriers to move on to achieve benefits from E-Government.
- Classify government activities into value configurations for interoperability. As people in the strategy field already know, the contingent approach to strategy implies that value chains, value shops, and value networks have very different value creation logic.
- Align and integrate information resources to government tasks. Information as a valuable resource is enabling work processes to be carried out.
- Define stages of E-Government interoperability, which can be used by agencies to learn the path to improved interoperability. By identifying development stages, scholars, and practitioners have a framework within which they can diagnose the current situation and plan for future improvements in interoperability.
- Identify frameworks for aligned development to establish effective interoperability. A number of frameworks are presented in this book, enabling the reader to select one or a few that seem appropriate for the situation.
- Provide a model for strategic planning for alignment of E-Government initiatives. The Y-model describes the current situation and the desired situation, thereby evaluating a gap between current and desired that should be reduced and closed by means of a new strategy.

The generalizability of the findings in this book to the entire E-Government might be found problematic by some readers. We as authors have mainly used case studies in the end from law enforcement, and we have used those case studies to generalize it to entire E-Government. Some readers may have a problem with that, primarily because not all government functions are enforcement. As we are very well aware, governments also provide transaction services; in fact, those transaction services are a more sizeable part of some governments. Therefore, early chapters in the book are mainly applying examples from transaction services. We justify our law enforcement focus in terms of very high demands on interoperability to solve crimes committed by transnational organized crime group. Only if local police gets access to information from hospitals, customs, municipalities, schools and so forth, both domestic and abroad, are some of the trafficking cases possible to solve. The findings from law enforcement are very well generalizable to other government sectors, where interoperability contributes to improved service.

The audience for this book includes (but is not limited to):

- Information systems designers, developers and programmers in public and private software organizations, who want to think in the big picture of interoperability when solving technical problems.
- Project managers in IT projects, who are responsible for all aspects including interoperability of systems.
- CIOs and IT managers, who are responsible for operations of interoperable systems and information sharing.
- Undergraduate students in systems development, who should learn about the intricacies of not only technical interoperability, but semantic and organizational interoperability as well.
- Graduate students in management information systems, who will typically become project managers for IT projects and CIOs in both private and public organizations.

Introduction to Chapters

This book is concerned with all the problems preventing governments all over the world from gaining the potential benefits of interoperability. It shows how governments can move out of these problems by addressing issues such as information resources, alignment projects and governance structure. At the most advanced level of interoperability, organizational interoperability, this books shows that it is more about politics and top management ambitions than it is about technical or technology options.

First, Chapter I starts out by defining and describing electronic government interoperability. Based on the concept of E-Government (or digital government), the extent of interoperability is measured in terms of transaction costs. When interoperability improves, then transaction costs drop. Transaction cost theory is important to understand interoperability in financial terms.

Chapter II introduces the concept of value configurations. A value configuration is the way an organization creates value for its stakeholders and clients. Three alternative value configurations exist for organizations. First, the value chain is a value configuration for sequential operations producing goods and services. Next, the value shop is a problem solving entity working in a cyclical fashion. Finally, the value network is connecting parties that exchange with each other. Interoperability between different value configurations requires connections into different primary activities.

In Chapter III, the resource-based theory is introduced. The main resource in more and more organizations is knowledge, and the representation of knowledge in systems is information. Therefore, interoperable information systems support inter-organizational knowledge management. Strategic knowledge resources are characterized by being valuable, non-imitable, non-transferable, combinable, exploitable, and rare.

Chapter IV builds on the previous chapter by discussing ways of information resource integration. It discusses information asymmetry and information sharing, identity management in information resources, inter-organizational information integration, and managing integration projects. An example of geographic information systems is introduced, where geographic information from several sources are needed to provide a useful and complete picture of demographics, business, crime and weather in a geographic region.

Chapter V introduces the evolutionary perspective of stages of growth models. Such models are helpful to determine where an organization is, where it came from, and in what direction it is moving in terms of interoperability with other organizations. Stages of growth imply that there is a cumulative improvement over time, where continuous struggle and successes are more important than paradigm shifts.

A number of frameworks for aligned development have been proposed, and some of them are presented in Chapter VI. The frameworks for improved interoperability vary in breath and depth, and there is so far no single framework covering all dimensions and aspects of interoperability in electronic government available. Instead, interoperability projects have to choose elements from several frameworks that seem suited for their specific situation. By selecting elements and ordering them in a useful way, an organization applies the contingent approach to organizational development.

Strategic planning for alignment is introduced in Chapter VII. The Y-model for IS/IT strategy includes steps for gap analysis, action planning, and implementation evaluation. Implementation of an information systems interoperability strategy is important for several reasons. Firstly, the failure to carry out strategy can cause lost opportunities, duplicated efforts, incompatible organizational and inter-organizational units and wasted resources. As well, the extent to which a strategy meets its objectives is determined by implementation. Further, the lack of implementation leaves users and managers dissatisfied and reluctant to continue doing strategic planning work. Finally, the lack of implementation creates problems establishing and maintaining priorities in future strategic planning.

When inter-organizational systems and information exchanges are introduced, who should then make decisions? In this case, several organizations are stakeholders in systems and exchanges and hence need to have a say when the system is modified, replaced or expanded. To organize decision rights in a professional way,

IT governance is introduced in Chapter VIII. IT governance defines key areas and accompanying decision rights for collaborating organizations.

In most organizations, the IT manager has a key role in all initiatives to improve interoperability. The IT manager, typically in the position of chief information officer (CIO), is involved in both strategic planning and strategy implementation. Therefore, Chapter IX introduces the role of CIO to shed light on what kind of position is important for success.

Chapter X introduces the case of police investigations. Many police investigations need information from other organizations to identify victims, suspects and criminal markets. In serious crime cases, often carried out by organized crime groups, information from law enforcement agencies in other countries is often required. When a Moroccan drug dealer in the city of Oslo receives his orders from an Albanian smuggler in Berlin, narcotics may have traveled through several countries on its way from Afghanistan or Colombia to the market in Norway. Policing organizations such as Europol and Interpol have systems that Norwegian Police is connected to, such as Schengen Information System (SIS).

Chapter XI returns to stages of growth for operability, focusing on the most challenging task of organizational interoperability. Organizational interoperability is dependent on executives who are willing to cooperate with executives in other organizations for mutual benefits. Levels of organizational interoperability are labeled business process interoperability, knowledge management interoperability, value configuration interoperability, and strategy position interoperability.

Finally, Chapter XII presents system dynamics modeling as a powerful tool for managers to identify, conceptualize, represent, and analyze operational, tactical and strategic business issues.

REFERENCES

Eckman, B. A., Bennet, C. A., Kaufman, J. H., & Tenner, J. W. (2007). Varieties of interoperability in the transformation of the health-care information infrastructure. *IBM Systems Journal, 46*(1), 19-41.

Scholl, H. J., & Klischewski, R. (2007). E-Government Integration and Interoperability: Framing the Research Agenda. *International Journal of Public Administration, 30*(8), 889-920.

Acknowledgment

This research was part of the Semicolon project supported by the Norwegian Research Council, contract no 183260.

Chapter I
Electronic Government Interoperability

1.   ELECTRONIC GOVERNMENT INTEROPERABILITY

Digital government, E-Government, and E-governance: all are terms that have become synonymous with the use of information and communications technologies in government agencies. Regardless of the label, digital government has become a prominent strategy for government administrative reform. E-Government projects can potentially increase the quality of government services, generate financial savings, and improve the effectiveness of government policies and programs (Pardo & Tayi, 2007).

First in this chapter, the concept of E-Government is introduced followed by a description of the global assessment of E-Government readiness. The chapter continues discussing interoperability in electronic government. A list of nine constraining influences electronic government interoperability is presented. Benefits of interoperability are identified, and an introduction to transaction cost theory is given as a means to understand benefits of interoperability. Then a distinction is made between interoperability and integration, and the difference between technical, Semantic and organizational interoperability is discussed. At the end of the chapter a case of Geographic Information Systems is presented.

1.1   The Concept of E-Government

The term "electronic government" or "E-Government" or "digital government" appeared about a decade ago, and there is no commonly accepted definition. Some see E-Government as the migration of government information and services to an on-line delivery mode, where the scope of E-Government covers the interaction between government and citizens (G2C), government and business enterprises (G2B), and inter-agency dealing (G2G). Others see E-Government as the provision of routine government information and transactions using electronic means, most notably those using Internet technology, whether delivery at home, at work, or through public kiosks.

It is an underlying assumption in this book that Internet technologies and specifically E-Government should have as their main purpose the improvement of the ways in which government serves its citizens and the ways in which citizens interact with public institutions. This philosophy of E-Government implies that for E-Government to be anything more than automated service provision, it needs to reach far beyond the conduct of routine government business to embrace social, economic and political change.

Some stress that successful E-Government programs should not only be based on the perceived efficiency gains for government itself, but rather on the satisfaction of consumers. For example, the UK's "techno-centric model" has been criticized for failing to engage citizens as anticipated, underplaying the importance of knowledge management and clashing with traditional values of public service.

Some factors which seem important from the perspective of the suppliers of E-Government include: the capacity for significant organizational change, the development of leadership skills, a grasp of the distinction between "hard" (technological factors) versus "soft" (human factors), and understanding of the differences in catering for the private and public sectors, and for citizens in developed and developing nations.

From the perspective of citizens' needs (the "demand side" in economic terms), it might be stressed the vital role of factors such as the impact on citizens of transaction costs, an understanding of cultural barriers, for example social exclusion caused by the problem of unequal access to the Internet, citizens' expectations of government services and their degrees of acceptance of technological innovations, and possible mismatches between governmental and social uses of the Internet.

For example, Vietnam is transforming into a networked society where more people are becoming connected, and more advanced applications, such as E-Government, are becoming available. From 2000, the Government of Vietnam determined that, with Vietnam integrating more comprehensively into the global economy, the building of an effective E-Government would help to facilitate its capacity to manage resources, implement sound policies and better satisfy the needs of citizens. Vietnam has a government official (an E-Government champion) in charge of all E-Government activities who liaises with other departments and ministries to ensure interoperability and interconnectivity (United Nations, 2008). Statistical data suggested that in May 2007 there were about 16 million Internet users, and 70 million others were living and working without the use of computers in Vietnam. This has to be taken into account when developing digital government in the nation.

E-Government implies fundamental knowledge redistribution and requires a careful rethinking of the management of information resources and knowledge bases. E-Government strategies include; information dissemination on searchable databases, customer satisfaction, online translations, implementing the use of e-checks and be able to measure government systems. It aims to offer accessibility to government information and services for citizens, businesses and government agencies thereby improving the quality of e-services and providing greater opportunities for participation in democratic institutions and processes.

Electronic government is the delivery of services to citizens via the Internet. The goal of E-Government is to capture benefits of the electronic economy. Although there is sparse information about the quality and efficiency of E-Government initiatives, an increasing number of governmental units are incorporating or expanding the use of information technologies into many of their activities (Esteves & Joseph, 2008).

Digital government has been considered a powerful strategy for administrative reform. However, projects looking for benefits to service quality or more effective and efficient government programs face a plethora of technical, organizational, and institutional challenges. As the organizational complexity of the projects increases and more agencies collaborate and share information both potential benefits and challenges increase (Luna-Reyes, Gil-Garcia, & Cruz, 2007).

The emerging IT-for-development approach towards public sector transformation is creating new perceptions about government and governance. The twin objective of achieving further improvements in service delivery and efficacy in government functioning is bringing about a rethinking of the role of IT. Governments are increasingly looking towards E-Government-as-a-whole concept, which focuses on the provision of services at the front-end, supported by integration, consolidation and innovation in back-end processes and systems to achieve maximum cost savings and improved service delivery (United Nations, 2008).

Governments all over the world are recognizing E-Government as a strategic option to fine-tune their internal and external operations. In order to foster citizen-centric services, they need to integrate themselves as well as stakeholders vertically and horizontally. This can be achieved by bringing the efficiencies and experiences of e-business to E-Government. That requires new e-business models for government solutions that reduce cost and improve service effectiveness (Papazoglou & Ribbers, 2006).

Digital government, E-Government, and e-governance are all terms that have become synonymous with the use of information and communication technologies in government agencies. Inter-organizational information integration has become a key enabler for E-Government. Integrating and sharing information across traditional government boundaries involves complex interactions among and with technical and organizational processes. From a technical perspective, systems designers and developers must regularly overcome problems related to the existence of multiple platforms, diverse database designs and data structures, highly variable data quality, and incompatible network infrastructure. From an organizational perspective, these technical processes often involve new work processes, mobilization of limited resources, and evolving inter-organizational relationships. These necessary changes are influenced by specific types of social interaction, which take the form of group decision-making, learning, understanding, trust building, and conflict resolution (Pardo & Tayi, 2007).

E-Government or digital government has become a global theme in governments pursuing an agenda of providing citizen services and increasing agency efficiency using IT. E-commerce and e-business is considered a trigger of E-Government. Citizens have acquired competence in handling and operating e-commerce applications (net banking, e-ticketing, e-shopping) but most governments have not offered public digital self-service to the same degree and the public digital services that have been introduced are generally used to a lesser degree than private services. A government needs to consider markets for differentiated products and services to satisfy the variation of needs among its citizens. Electronic markets may be just that kind of application that will trigger requisite information from citizens in order to offer them the relevant government services (Pedersen, Fountain, & Loukis, 2006).

Electronic markets for the allocation, financing and distribution of public goods were identified by Vragov and Kumar (2006). For example, electronic markets might be connecting citizens to pension reform (Ranerup, 2006). Salleh, Rohde and Green (2006) studied the effect of enacted capabilities on adoption of a government electronic procurement system by Malaysian SMEs, while Cui, Zhang, Zhang and Huan (2006) explored E-Government impact on Shanghai organizations' informatization process.

1.2   Global Assessment of E-Government Readiness

The United Nations E-Government survey (United Nations, 2008) presented a comparative assessment of the 192 United Nations member states' response to the pressing demands of entrepreneurs for quality government service and administra-

Table 1.1. Top 20 countries in the 2008 E-Government readiness index (United Nations, 2008)

Rank	Country
1	Sweden
2	Denmark
3	Norway
4	United States
5	Netherlands
6	Republic of Korea
7	Canada
8	Australia
9	France
10	United Kingdom
11	Japan
12	Switzerland
13	Estonia
14	Luxembourg
15	Finland
16	Austria
17	Israel
18	New Zealand
19	Ireland
20	Spain

tion. The survey evaluated the application of IT by governments. Survey results indicate that the aims to which IT is put to use vary, but include: better access and delivery of services to citizens, improved interaction with citizens and businesses, and the empowerment of citizens through access to information.

The United Nations (2008) survey of E-Government readiness represents a comparative assessment of the member states' ability to transform their governments by using IT internally and externally. The top 20 countries are listed in the Table 1.1. It is worth noting that in this survey, there were no countries in the top 20 from the African, Caribbean, Central American, Central Asian, South American, and Southern Asian regions. United Nations (2008) believes the high cost of deploying a robust infrastructure is one reason for this discrepancy. In addition, many developing countries have been unable to fully implement their E-Government policies, mainly due to other competing pressing social issues that need to be dealt with in the context of tight budget constraints, such as health, education and employment.

The creation of one administrative Europe is realized primarily by the national E-Government programs. According to Wilson, Van Engers and Peeters (2007), national, regional and municipal government agencies struggle with interoperability, standardization, collaboration, service integration and ICT. Within the European Union, there are agreements made on new services in areas such as tax interoperability, spatial planning standards, and best practices in urban management.

1.3   Interoperability in Electronic Government

Interoperability is referring to a property of diverse systems and organizations enabling them to work together (Cabinet Office, 2005a; Office of the Government Chief Information Officer, 2007). Interoperability is the ability of government organizations to share information and integrate information and business processes by use of common standards (State Services Commission, 2007).

Interoperability is the ability of ICT systems to communicate, interpret and interchange data in a meaningful way (Archmann & Kudlacek, 2008). Interoperability is the ability of government organizations to share and integrate information by using common standards. Successful service innovation and multi-channel service delivery depend on strategies, policies and architectures that allow data, IT systems, business processes and delivery channels to operate, so that services can be properly integrated. If channels and back office processes are integrated, different channels can complement each other, improving the quality of both services and the delivery to government and citizens simultaneously. The ideal is to create an environment in which data, systems and processes are fully integrated and channels become interoperable instead of merely coexisting (United Nations, 2008).

When systems and organizations are able to inter-operate then information and services are provided and accepted between them. In a narrow sense, the term interoperability is often used to describe technical systems. In a broad sense, social, political, and organizational factors influencing systems and systems performance are also taken into account.

For example, new technologies are being introduced in hospitals and labs at an ever-increasing rate, and many of these innovations have the potential to interact synergistically if they can be integrated effectively. However, as pointed out by Eckman, Bennet, Kaufman and Tenner (2007), the current health-care information exchange is inefficient and error-prone; it is largely paper-based in most countries, fragmented, and therefore overly complex, often relying on antiquated information technology. E-health is an important part of E-Government. At the same time, health care costs are rising dramatically. Errors in medical delivery are associated with an alarming number of preventable, often fatal adverse events. A promising strategy for reversing such a trend is to modernize and transform the health-care information exchange, that is, the mobilization of health-care information electronically across organizations within a region or community (Eckman et al., 2007).

However, in the case of hospitals, there are limitations to free flow of information. Information systems often handle sensitive information about individuals and other organizations. Collection and sharing of such information is affected by privacy concerns (Otjacques, Hitzelberger, & Feltz, 2007).

In the business world, where electronic commerce and electronic business relies on interoperability, and which has inspired electronic government, enterprise interoperability might be defined as follows (Doumeingts, Müller, Morel, & Vallespir, 2007, p. 1):

Interoperability in the context of enterprises and enterprise applications can be defined as the ability of a system or a product to work seamlessly with other systems or products without requiring special effort from the customer or user. The possibility to interact and exchange information internally and with external organizations is a key issue in the enterprise sector. It is fundamental in order to produce goods and services quickly, at lower cost, while maintaining higher levels of quality and customization. Interoperability is considered to be achieved if interaction can, at least, take place at the three levels: data, applications and business enterprise through the architecture of the enterprise model and taking into account the Semantics issues. It is not only a problem of software and information technologies. It implies support of communication and transactions between different organizations that must be based on shared process models and business references.

As electronic government refers to the delivery of government services (information, interaction and transaction) through the use of information technology, a distinction can be made between the front and back offices of public service delivery organizations. The interaction between citizens and civil servants occurs in the front office, while registration and other activities take place in the back office. Bekkers (2007) found that back-office co-operation is a serious bottleneck in E-Government due to different interoperability problems.

One important action to improve information sharing is standardization in information systems. It is necessary to define the compatibility standards to be adopted among systems (Santos & Reinhard, 2007). Some organizations will have to change their technical and organizational processes and make accommodations in response to standardization initiatives (Gogan, Williams, & Fedorowicz, 2007).

From a technology perspective, the pursuit of greater interoperability across enterprise-wide architectures (important elements of a platform for service delivery) for the public sector as a whole has often become a centralized force. Yet a significant novelty in this digital environment is the manner by which centralization and collaboration are viewed as complementary (United Nations, 2008).

A recent line of E-Government research has emphasized the importance of inter-organizational information sharing in the public domain. For example, Schooley and Horan (2007) explored information sharing relative to service performance. They utilized a time-critical information services conceptual framework as analytical lens.

In the European Union, Archmann and Kudlacek (2008) finds that the interoperability challenges at local and regional levels are formidable. Based on an analysis of European good practice in the area, they recommend deploying open standards on a large scale in order to avoid the blockage of legacy systems that cannot work together with new technology. They argue that the ability of ICT systems to communicate, interpret and interchange data in a meaningful way is dependent on open standards. Interoperability requires the use of metadata and technical standards in order for different infrastructures to be linked together and data to be exchanged.

Inter-organizational systems concepts provide a targeted means to look at the cross-organizational features of a socio-technical system. Examples are criminal justice and services to citizens. Such examples demonstrate a need to improve capabilities to share data, information and knowledge across departmental, organizational, geographic, and institutional boundaries. Such inter-organizational improvements in information sharing will improve the performance of public sector services (Schooley & Horan, 2007).

Scholl and Klischewski (2007) list a number of constraints that influence government integration and interoperability. These constraints have to be considered at different stages in our model. First Scholl and Klischewski mention constitutional and legal constraints, where integration and interoperation may be outright unconstitutional because the democratic constitution requires powers to be divided into separate levels and branches of government. The US constitution, for example, separates government into federal, state, and local government levels and into legislative, judicial, and executive branches. Total interoperability between levels and branches might offset that constitutional imperative of checks and balances. Scholl and Klischewski list eight more constraints: jurisdictional constraints, collaborative constraints, organizational constraints, informational constraints, managerial constraints, cost constraints, technological constraints, and performance constraints. While several of these constraints can be handled and solved, others should be considered when identifying the optimal stage of interoperability.

Each of the nine constraining influences on electronic government integration and interoperability are described by Scholl and Klischewski (2007, p. 893) as follows:

1. **Constitutional/legal constraints:** Integration and interoperation may be outright unconstitutional because the democratic constitution requires powers to be divided into separate levels and branches of government. The US constitution, for example, separates government into federal, state, and local government levels and into legislative, judicial, and executive branches. Total integration and interoperability between and among branches and levels would virtually offset that constitutional imperative of checks and balances. On the other hand, the constitution also affords and sanctions integration and interoperation within certain boundaries.
2. **Jurisdictional constraints:** Since under the constitution, governmental and non-governmental constituencies operate independently from each other and own their information and business processes, neither integration, nor interoperation, nor information sharing can be imposed on them, rather as an independent entity each constituency's participation in any interaction is voluntary. However, by means of jurisdictional authority, the government entity can engage in integration and interoperation with other entities.
3. **Collaborative constraints:** Organizations are distinct in terms of their disposition and readiness for collaboration and interoperation with others. Past experience, socio-political organization, and leadership style influence the degree of proneness and adeptness of potential interoperation. However, in cases of compatible leadership styles, adequate socio-political organization, and positive past experiences, integration and interoperation might flourish.
4. **Organizational constraints:** Organizational processes and resources may differ between organizations to such an extent that integration and interoperation might prove exceedingly difficult to achieve without standardizing on processes, systems, and policies. Yet, where organizations align their organizational context they enable themselves to enjoy increased degrees of integration and interoperation.
5. **Informational constraints:** While transactional information might be more readily shared, strategic and organizational information might be not; also, information quality issues arise when integrating information sources across various domains of control and quality standards. Still, information stewardship fosters use of shared information, which in turn fosters stewardship for sharing information.
6. **Managerial constraints:** Interoperation becomes inherently more complex the more parties with incongruent interests and needs become involved. As

a result, the demands of the respective management task might exceed the management capacity of interoperating partners. However, along the lines of shared interests, interoperation and integration can materialize.

7. **Cost constraints:** Integration and interoperation between diverse constituencies might be limited to the lowest common denominator in terms of availability of funds: also, unexpected budget constraints might pose serious challenges to long-term interoperation projects over time. On the other hand, information-sharing initiatives have reportedly helped contain cost. Within the cost boundaries of the respective partners, certain projects appear to be sustainable.

8. **Technological constraints:** The heterogeneity of E-Government platform and network capabilities might limit the interoperation of systems to relatively low standards. On the other hand, an increasing number of E-Government information systems might adhere to higher standards over time, such that increased interoperation becomes possible.

9. **Performance constraints:** As performance tests suggest, the higher the number of interoperating partners, the lower is the overall system performance in terms of response time. Yet, the focus on prioritized needs might enable fewer but more effective interoperations.

These nine constraints represent a complex environment for electronic government interoperation.

1.4   Benefits of Interoperability

Benefits of interoperability might be identified in terms of the defining purposes of digital government. High-ranking issues among the defining purposes of E-Government are highly agile, citizen-centric, accountable, transparent, effective, and efficient government operations and services (Scholl & Klischewski, 2007). For reaching such goals, the integration of government information resources and processes, and thus the interoperation of independent information systems are essential. Yet, most integration and interoperation efforts meet serious challenges and limitations. Legner and Lebreton (2007) phrased the following questions concerning present achievements and upcoming challenges in interoperability research:

• *What is the medium to long- term impact of the suggested interoperability concepts?* Despite the tremendous research efforts that have been spent on developing solutions to improve the interoperability of information systems, very little work has been done in analyzing to what extent organizations, i.e. the real victims of interoperability gaps, would benefit from the innovative concepts that have been presented in the last five years. The applications that have been developed are generally presented in pilot form and thus represent an idealized form of the business problem addressed. Pilots are generally functionally tested in an isolated environment, thus leaving integration issues out of the scope.

- *What is the optimal level of interoperability from an organization-level perspective?* Stating that organizations suffer under a lack of interoperability means that business interoperability research efforts should be spent in finding out which level of interoperability a organization should strive for. The optimal level of IT supported interoperability varies between the different types of suppliers so that full operability does not automatically mean optimal interoperability. Logically, the first step toward improving interoperability is to define where a organization currently is and where it should be.
- *Which factors impact the optimal level of interoperability?* Characteristics of value chain collaboration, such as the planned duration of the relationship between partners and their interdependence is one of many factors identified in prior research on networked organizations and inter-organizational systems.

Gouscos, Kalikakis, Legal and Papadopoulou (2007) introduced a framework and methodology for establishing indicators and metrics in order to assess the quality and performance of one-stop E-Government service offerings. The set of quality and performance indicators and metrics proposed was derived in an outcomes assessment approach, based on the perspectives of E-Government service providers and end-users and following a goal-question-metric line of work that depart from some key quality and performance benefits.

1.5   Transaction Cost Theory

Another approach to identify benefits of interoperability is in terms of transaction cost reduction. In his seminal paper, Coase (1937) suggested transaction costs as the primary determinant of the boundaries of the organization. Ideally, contracts between buyers and sellers provide adaptation strategies for all possible contingencies. However, this requires either certainty regarding the future economic environment or unbounded rational reasoning (knowing all possible future states). Transaction costs arise because complete contracting is often impossible, and incomplete contracts give rise to subsequent renegotiations when the balance of power between the transacting parties shifts (Williamson, 1979). Transaction costs include the costs associated with writing contracts as well as the costs of opportunistic holdup at a later date. Although internal organization or hierarchies are posited to offer lower costs of coordination and control and to avert subsequent opportunistic behavior, related problems can occur in decentralized organizations. A major concern is the loss of high-powered incentives when the pay-for-performance link is attenuated by internal production (Anderson, Glenn, & Sedatole, 2000).

In our perspective of digital government, transaction cost focus has two implications. First, the organization of government into agencies might be determined by transaction costs, where the number of agencies and the tasks of each agency should be such that transaction costs are minimized. Next, inter-organizational arrangements, such as information systems interoperability, should be such that transactions costs are minimized.

Based on transaction cost theory, we might assume that when the degree of systems interoperability is high between two cooperating agencies, then transaction costs are low. Opposite, when the degree of systems interoperability is low between two cooperating agencies, then transaction costs are high. Therefore, benefits of interoperability can be measured in terms of transaction costs and changes in transaction costs over time.

Generally, organizations are hypothesized to choose organizational boundaries to minimize the sum of production and transaction cost (Williamson, 1979). Five attributes of business exchange are positively associated with transaction costs: (1) the necessity of investments in durable, specific assets; (2) infrequency of transacting; (3) task complexity and uncertainty; (4) difficulty in measuring task performance; and, (5) interdependencies with other transactions. The necessity of early investments in durable, transactions-specific assets (e.g. human and physical capital) shifts the balance of power between transaction participants, because in later renegotiations these costs are sunk costs of the party that incurs them. Infrequent transactions increase the likelihood of opportunistic behavior in later periods by reducing the threat of retribution. In situations where broader market reputations are at stake, infrequent transactions may be sustainable. However, even long-term contracts often do not provide sufficient adaptation mechanisms, and inflexibility may actually induce holdup. Task complexity, uncertainty and measurement problems exacerbate the problem of identifying and contracting for contingencies. Interdependencies introduce contingencies among transactions that suggest co-location (e.g. system-level sourcing) or that require high-level coordination (Anderson et al., 2000).

Transaction cost theory thus tells us that interoperability in digital government is influenced by (1) the need for specific hardware and software; (2) the frequency of information transacting; (3) task complexity and uncertainty; (4) difficulty in measuring task performance; and, (5) interdependencies with other transactions.

The five transaction attributes indicate settings in which opportunistic behavior is likely. If transactions costs offset production cost advantages of the external supplier of information and knowledge, the organization subsumes the activity - an outcome termed vertical integration, where the agency takes over or duplicates the information processing.

Empirical research indirectly tests transaction cost theory by relating observed information sourcing decisions to transaction attributes that proxy for transaction costs. Evidence on the relation between transaction-specific investments, contract duration, and technological uncertainty generally supports the theory. However, because production costs are objectively calculated by the accounting system, while transaction costs are assessed subjectively through indirect indicators, functional managers are likely to differ in the importance that they assign to reducing transaction costs. For example, managers sometimes seem more reluctant to outsource when investments in specific assets are necessary; and contrary to theory, managers sometimes consider previous internal investments in specific assets a reason to insource. In certain circumstances decision-makers systematically misestimate (or fail to consider) transaction costs (Anderson et al., 2000).

In E-Government, sourcing alternatives are not always present. For example, tax statements for individuals can only be obtained from the tax authority. Hence, production costs have to be set to infinite, making them always lower than transaction costs.

Organizations are turning in increasing number to strategic alliances to help them compete. Yet, a number of researchers argue that the costs of coordinating activities outweigh the benefits that these alliances can provide. A crucial question to be addressed then is; what are the factors that determine these coordination costs? Artz and Brush (2000) examined supplier relationships that were governed by relational contracts, and they found support for the transaction cost theory. Asset specificity and environmental uncertainty directly increased coordination costs.

In transaction cost economics, an organization chooses to source via its own hierarchy or via the market, based on relative cost, which has two components: production costs and co-ordination (transaction) costs. Economies of scale, via the market, can reduce production costs. Transaction costs are determined by several factors: asset specificity, transaction frequency and uncertainty. Asset specificity is the degree to which an asset can be redeployed to alternative uses and by alternative users without sacrifice of productive value (Hancox & Hackney, 2000).

Williamson (1979) identified three types of transaction according to specificity. Non-specific transactions have low asset specificity and are associated with the acquisition of commodities. Idiosyncratic transactions have high specificity. Mixed transactions have elements of both commodity and customization. Transaction specificity can be viewed alongside transaction frequency, a second major construct of transaction cost economics, which distinguishes occasional from recurrent transactions. Two frequency categories multiplied by three specificity types produce six discrete transaction types. It can be argued that the market is better for all but transactions, which are both recurrent and idiosyncratic. The third major determinant of transaction costs is uncertainty, compounded by the bounded rationality of humans and often associated with the complexity of the product to be acquired. Rather than developing specialized client-specific products, vendors may find it cheaper and safer to provide a standard product, whereas organizations may prefer to acquire complex products via the internal hierarchy rather than the market. Throughout market usage, there is also the danger of opportunism – lack of candor or honesty in transactions (Hancox & Hackney, 2000).

Opportunism is self-interest seeking with guile, and includes overt behaviors such as lying, cheating and stealing, as well as subtle behaviors such as dishonoring an implicit contract, shirking, failing to fulfill promises, and obligations. It is the equivalent of bad faith, the implication being that the party who is opportunistic is not trustworthy. In an outsourcing setting, opportunism may involve misrepresentations, unresponsiveness, unreasonable demands, and lying. The notion of opportunism is what differentiates transaction cost theory from alternative conceptualizations of the organization, such as agency theory, relational exchange theory, or resource view. The transaction cost economics presumption is that economic actors attempt to forecast the potential for opportunism as a function of unfolding circumstances, and then take preventive actions in transactions where opportunism is likely to be high. Opportunism is an explanatory mechanism, not readily observable, and typically empirically untested. However, it is important because it has potential for enormous impact on economic performance (Jap, 2001).

Opportunism is likely to increase if there are only a small number of vendors as only a few are able and willing to contract. Transaction costs appear to be difficult to avoid and may be unavoidably greater in some settings than in others. For example, it can be argued that in the public sector contract creation and monitoring are more difficult because of the sector's complexity and because there are costs associated with bureaucracy and democracy which are hard to allocate to specific functions (Hancox & Hackney, 2000).

Transaction cost economics has emerged as a common framework for understanding how managers craft governance arrangements. The general proposition of this literature is that managers align the governance features of inter-organizational relationships to match known exchange hazards, particularly those associated with specialized asset investments, difficult performance measurement, or uncertainty. In response to exchange hazards, managers may craft complex contracts that define remedies for foreseeable contingencies or specify processes for resolving unforeseeable outcomes. When such contracts are too costly to craft and enforce, managers may choose to vertically integrate. Many have argued, however, that transaction cost economics overstates the desirability of either integration or contractual safeguards in exchange settings commonly labeled as hazardous. This view recognizes that in many industries managers engage in complex, collaborative market exchanges that involve rather high levels of asset specificity and that are characterized by other known hazards. Cooperation and relational governance are often viewed in this literature as substitutes for complex, explicit contracts or vertical integration (Poppo & Zenger, 2002).

According to Henisz and Williamson (1999), transaction cost economics is a comparative contractual approach to economic organization in which the action resides in the details of transactions on the one hand and governance on the other. Given that all complex contracts are unavoidably incomplete (by reason of bounded rationality) and that contract as mere promise, unsupported by credible commitments, is not self-enforcing (by reason of opportunism), the question is which transactions should be organized how. Much of the predictive content of transaction cost economics works through the discriminating alignment hypothesis, according to which transactions, which differ in their attributes, are aligned with governance structures, which differ in their costs and competences, so as to effect a (mainly) transaction cost economizing result. Implementing this requires that transactions, governance structures, and transaction cost economizing all be described.

Transaction cost economics concurs that the transaction is the basic unit of analysis and regards governance as the means by which order is accomplished in a relation in which potential conflict threatens to undo or upset opportunities to realize mutual gains (Henisz & Williamson, 1999). The problem of conflict on which transaction cost economics originally focused is that of bilateral dependency. The organization of transactions that are supported by generic investments is easy: classical market contracting works well because each party can go its own way with minimal cost to the other. Specific investments are where the problems arise. Contracts that are supported by durable investments in non-redeployable assets pose contractual hazards, in that one or both parties can defect from the letter of spirit of an agreement. That is true even if property rights are well defined, contract laws are well conceived, and the judiciary enforces the laws in a principled way. Thus, even if property rights are well defined in general, some property rights are very hard to describe (it is not cost effective to describe them with greater precision) and hard to enforce (it is difficult for a court to be apprised of true underlying conditions). Property rights ambiguities thus remain even in a regime where best efforts to define and enforce property rights through the courts have been made. Similar considerations apply to contract law: there are limits on how exacting the law can be and how effectively the courts can enforce the law.

Transaction cost economics is located on the branch of the new institutional economics that is mainly concerned with governance. The new institutional economics argues that institutions are both important and susceptible to analysis. It is based on the assumption that human actors have limited cognitive competence – often referred to as bounded rationality. Given such cognitive limits, complex contracts such as IT outsourcing contracts are unavoidable incomplete. Contractual incompleteness poses problems when paired with the condition of opportunism – which manifests itself as adverse selection, moral hazard, shirking, sub goal pursuit, and other forms of strategic behavior. Because human actors will not reliably disclose true conditions upon request or self-fulfill all promises, contract as mere promise, unsupported by credible commitments, will not be self-enforcing (Williamson, 2000).

Saarinen and Vepsäläinen (1994) applied transaction cost economics to procurement strategies for information systems. Procurement means the choice among suppliers (in-house personnel, outside experts, consultants, software contractors, or package dealers) and contracting forms (salary, project contract, package price, lease or rent) for acquiring an asset. In applying transaction cost economics to the procurement methods of information systems, Saarinen and Vepsäläinen (1994) first identified the most important characteristics of the desired transactions (information systems projects) and alternative governance structures (project organization) in order to find the effective strategies. They conclude that systems that are company-specific and involve high uncertainty have to be internally developed because they require both the specific knowledge and intensive interaction between developers and users. More standard requirements indicate the use of outside consultants or software contractors who have experience and knowledge about a similar type of systems. For routine systems common in many organizations, acquisition and tailoring of a software package provides the most efficient procurement strategy.

Transaction cost economics describes the organization not in technological terms (as a production function) but in organizational terms (as a governance structure). Organization and market are alternative modes of governance that differ in discrete structural ways. Chief among the attributes that describe a mode of governance are (1) incentive intensity, (2) administrative controls, and (3) the legal rules regime. These in turn give rise to differential adaptive capacity - in both autonomous and cooperative adaptation respects. Alternative modes of governance are internally consistent syndromes of these attributes – which is to say each has distinctive strengths and weaknesses (Williamson, 1999).

Legner and Lebreton (2007) argue that transaction cost theory seems to be an appropriate approach to quantify interoperability as interoperability issues are the result of the division of work and occur in the context of exchanges between organizational actors. Transaction cost theory concurs that the transaction between interoperating organizations is the basic unit of analysis and regards governance as the means by which order is accomplished in a relation in which potential conflict threatens to undo or upset opportunities to realize mutual gains.

Transaction cost theory allows the quantification of interoperability improvements, but empirical results on the pertinence of transaction cost theory for assessing interoperability investments are still missing. Next to the operational dimension, the impact of interoperability improvements on the strategic positioning of a company still remains unstructured. In this context, it would be very valuable to know whether superior interoperability levels contribute to the creation or extension of a competitive edge. Since very few strategic interoperability investigations are known, reliable conclusions cannot be drawn on the contribution of interoperability in the achievement of a competitive advantage (Legner & Lebreton, 2007).

1.6   Interoperability and Systems Integration

A distinction should be made between interoperability and integration. Integration is the forming of a larger unit of government entities, temporary or permanent, for the purpose of merging processes and/or sharing information. Interoperation in E-Government occurs whenever independent or heterogeneous information systems or their components controlled by different jurisdictions/administrations or by external partners smoothly and effectively work together in a predefined and agreed upon fashion. E-Government interoperability is the technical capability for E-Government interoperation (Scholl & Klischewski, 2007).

The issues that arise when attempting to integrate disparate systems within and across organizations continue to plague not only large enterprise alliances, but also most businesses across all industries, according to Papazoglou and Ribbers (2006). They argue that there exist today several products and technical solutions that deal with the challenges relating to actual physical connectivity and communication of the systems involved in a given exchange by sharing messages or using tightly coupled workflows. However, what is lacking from most available technology solutions that would improve the odds for integration success is the ability to exchange meaningful, context-driven data, messages and business processes between autonomous systems. The challenges of enabling each system to appropriately understand the information that is being shared relates to the logical aspects of using and sharing data and business processes based on their intended meaning. This is part of a broader problem known as the Semantic interoperability problem. The Semantic interoperability problem needs to be examined and solved both at the data and the process-level.

According to Papazoglou and Ribbers (2006), interoperability requires standardization in four dimensions: technology, syntax, Semantics, and pragmatics. Technology standards concern middleware, network protocols, security protocols, and the like. Syntax standardization means that the network organization has to agree on how to integrate heterogeneous applications based on the structure or language of the messages exchanged. Normally, commonly acceptable data structures are chosen to represent well-known constructs, e.g. invoice descriptions. Semantic standards constitute agreements in extension to syntactic agreements on the meanings of the terms used for an enterprise's information systems. Pragmatic standards, finally, are agreements on practices and protocols triggered by specific messages, such as orders and delivery notifications.

The integration of back offices implies the integration of information domains. An information domain is a unique sphere of influence, ownership and control over information in terms of specification, format, exploitation and interpretation. However, domain integration evokes interoperability problems, such as (Bekkers, 2007, p. 379):

- Conflicting, exclusive or overlapping jurisdictions and accountability
- Different legal regimes with conflicting rights and obligations, e.g. in relation to privacy and safety regulations
- Different working process and information processing process, routines and procedures
- Incompatibility of specific 'legacy' information and communication technology infrastructure
- Conflicting information specifications and lack of common data definitions
- Conflicting organizational norms and values, communication patterns, and growth practices

Integration models are being introduced and applied to overcome these problems. The governance of back-office integration is critical to E-Government interoperability, and its criticality rises at higher stages in the development model suggested in this book. Understanding intrapreneurship by means of state-of-the-art integration technologies as well as organizational learning (Drejer, Christensen, & Ulhoi, 2004) is required for success.

In an exploratory study of the European Union, (Otjacques et al., 2007) found considerable cross-country differences in legal and administrative provisions and technical standards. These differences cause particular challenges for information systems in digital government, as there is a growing mobility of goods, persons, and related data within the European Union.

In a research agenda for E-Government integration and interoperability, Scholl and Klischewski (2007) suggest future research projects to study the foci and purposes, limitations and constraints, as well as processes and outcomes of integration and interoperation in electronic government. In such future research projects, the stages of growth model presented in this book might prove helpful in organizing findings. Scholl and Klischewski (2007) list a number of constraints that influence government integration and interoperability, as described in Chapter 1.3. These constraints have to be considered at different stages in our model. Among the basic constraints that have to be handled early in the stage model is the challenge of Semantics. Semantic interoperability is part of the interoperability challenge for networked E-Government organizations. Inter-organizational information systems can only work if they are able to communicate and work with other such systems and interact with people. This requirement can only be met if communication standards are applied. A standards-based technology platform allows partners to execute a traditional business function in a digitally enhanced way. A necessary common information systems platform is a set of standards that allows network participants to communicate and conduct business processes electronically (Papazoglou & Ribbers, 2006).

Depending on process types to be supported in inter-organizational relationships, various types of transactional characteristics of processes have to be specified at the conceptual level: atomicity requirements of parts of a process, isolation requirements of parts of a process, and integrity constraints with respect to a process. Atomicity requirements can be of two kinds: strict atomicity and loose atomicity requirements (Grefen, Ludwig, & Angelov, 2003). To specify strict atomicity, parts of a process are indicated that are to be executed in an atomic (all-or-nothing) fashion. A first approach is to strictly partition a business process into atomic sub processes, which may be referred to as business transactions. This means that every process step is part of a business transaction. A second approach is to annotate arbitrary (non-overlapping) sub processes as atomic, which may be called atomicity spheres. This means that not all process steps are part of atomic sub processes (Grefen et al., 2003).

The roles of an interoperability solution represent the stakeholders or potential users. According to Archman and Kudlacek (2008), interoperability is not an end to itself, but a tool to solve the problems of different stakeholders. To be successful, integration and interoperability projects have to satisfy stakeholder needs. Furthermore, such projects need to be guided by a direction. One directional approach is suggested in this book in terms of stages of growth for E-Government interoperability. By systematically developing interoperability in terms of work process, knowledge sharing, value creation, and ultimately strategy alignment, long-wanted benefits from E-Government might be expected.

1.7   Technical, Semantic and Organizational Interoperability

Interoperability of systems enables interoperability of organizations. Systems interoperability is concerned with the ability of two or more systems or components to exchange information and to use the information that has been exchanged. A data-level integration technique must focus on a complete picture that delivers more than data, objects or messages. It needs to focus on conveying meaning to create fluency. Meaning, in a practical sense, is about meta-data, business rules and user supplied application context to facilitate robust information transformation between disparate systems and applications (Papazoglou & Ribbers, 2006).

Archmann and Kudlacek (2008) found that key success factors for technical interoperability include the application of already existing technologies, common understanding and use of data. Data schemes, common syntax, accessibility, security and privacy are important issues when working on technical interoperability.

Semantic interoperability is part of the interoperability challenge for networked organizations. Inter-organizational information systems can only work if they are able to communicate and work with other such systems and interact with people. This requirement is called interoperability, and it can only be met if communication standards are applied. A standards-based technology platform allows partners to execute a traditional business function in a digitally enhanced way. A common information systems platform, then, basically is a set of standards that allows network participants to communicate and conduct business processes electronically (Papazoglou & Ribbers, 2006).

A Semantic network is a directed graph in which concepts are represented as nodes, and relations between concepts are represented as links. It is a map of the cognitive terrain that surrounds and gives meaning to a concept and through which each concept is ultimately understood. A concept is a unit of information that can be represented by a word or phrase, and the meaning of which is embodied in its relations to other concepts. On the other hand, relations are a special category of concepts that depict the linkages between and among concepts. An instance, or sometimes termed a proposition, is a unit composed of two concepts and their relationship. As each concept can be linked to many other concepts, Semantic networks can be complex and multidimensional (Khalifa & Liu, 2008).

Khalifa and Liu (2008) studied a Semantic network applied in computer-mediated discussions. The Semantic network was the discussion representation for computer-mediated discussions. Computer-mediated discussions have become an integral component of many knowledge management systems used to support knowledge management activities. In communities of practice, for example, computer-mediated discussions support the externalization, communication and internalization processes of knowledge sharing among members.

As Semantic interoperability is broader than the technology, syntax and practice levels, and encompasses elements of them, it deserves to be discussed further. According to Papazoglou and Ribbers (2006), Semantic issues at the data level are concerned with the actual meaning of data found in one system, and how it relates to data found in each and every one of the other partners' systems. Addressing these Semantic concerns involves discovering how information is used differently by each the cooperating organizations, and how that information maps to the normative alliance view. Semantic issues at the business process level are concerned with mutual agreement about how business processes are defined and managed. A need for process re-engineering, corresponding implementation efforts and organizational changes are often needed. These efforts are often more about redesigning business processes than about making them easy to change and combine with those of cooperating organizations (Papazoglou & Ribbers, 2006).

Archmann and Kudlacek (2008) found that key success factors for Semantic interoperability are drafting, agreeing and using common definitions. Therefore, a wide and extensive commitment and support from all organizational levels is essential. The promotion and dissemination of these common definitions are further steps in the process to attract other agencies as well as the public's interest.

Organizational interoperability is concerned with the ability of two or more units to provide services to and accept services from other units, and to use the services so exchanged to enable them to operate effectively together (Legner & Lebreton, 2007). Interoperability represents a dynamic capability for transacting organizations. Teece, Pisano and Shuen (1997) define dynamic capabilities as the organization's ability to integrate, build, and reconfigure internal and external competences to address rapidly changing environments. Dynamic capabilities thus reflect an organization's ability to achieve new and innovative forms of competitive advantage given path dependencies and market positions. Dynamic capabilities are identifiable, specific processes. Some dynamic capabilities integrate resources. For example, product development routines by which managers combine their varied skills and functional backgrounds to create revenue-producing products and services are such dynamic capability (Eisenhardt & Martin, 2000).

1.8   Interoperability Frameworks

New Zealand E-Government interoperability framework (NZ e-GIF) is a set of policies, technical standards, and guidelines. It covers ways to achieve interoperability of public sector data and information resources, information and communications technology (ICT), and electronic business processes. It enables any agency to join its information, ICT or processes with those of any other agency using a predetermined framework based on "open" (i.e. non-proprietary) international standards (State Services Commission, 2007).

Hong Kong special administrative region interoperability framework supports the government's strategy of providing client-centric joined up services by facilitating the interoperability of technical systems between government departments, as well as between government systems and systems used by the public. The interoperability framework defines a collection of specifications aimed at facilitating the interoperability of government systems and services. By bringing together the relevant specifications under an overall framework, IT management and developers can have a single point of reference when there is a need to identify the required interoperability specifications that should be followed for a specific project (Office of the Government Chief Information Officer, 2007).

It is increasingly important for government agencies to collaborate across jurisdictional and functional boundaries. Inter-organizational systems supporting interagency collaboration must accommodate a wide range of factors from the external environment and participating organizations as part of their design and operation (Fedorowicz, Gogan, & Williams, 2007).

In order to enjoy some of the greatest benefits of digital government, the integration of information across organizational boundaries is necessary. However, these digital government initiatives face serious challenges, since the required level of inter-organizational collaboration and trust is often not supported by existing institutional arrangements, organizational structures, and management processes (Luna-Reyes et al., 2007).

Although much digital divide research focuses on access to technology, another cause of the divide is the lack of information awareness that we call information asymmetry. Information asymmetry often stems from inadequate information sharing and can result in negative consequences for both the information poor and the information rich (Clarkson, Jacobsen, & Batcheller, 2007).

1.9   The Case of GIS Interoperability

Geographic Information Systems (GIS) are applied in a variety of electronic government situations, from tracing the origins and spread of foot and mouth disease on farms to locating crime hot spots for law enforcement. GIS have become indispensable to effective knowledge transfer within both the public and private sector. However, as pointed out by Gottschalk and Tolloczko (2007) the level of sophistication varies among agencies applying GIS. Furthermore, the extent to which GIS interoperate with each other are subject to substantial variation.

A survey on interoperability for GIS in the UK was conducted by the E-Government unit of the Cabinet Office (2005b). According to this survey, 49% of the surveyed government organizations participated in data sharing projects for GIS, indicating that half of the organizations were working on Stage 1 of the stage model for E-Government interoperability (which will be presented later in Chapter 5). The fractions at higher levels were not identifiable from the survey. Many different application packages were in use, such as ESRI, Mapinfo, Intergraph, GGP, CadCorp, INNOgistic and Autodesk.

To improve interoperability of such systems for GIS and other E-Government systems, the UK Cabinet Office (2005b) developed an E-Government interoperability framework. The framework is mostly technical in nature, stressing alignment with the Internet and adoption of the browser as the key interface. The framework intends to stimulate government agencies to work more easily together electronically, make systems, knowledge and experience reusable from one agency to another, and reduce the effort needed to deal with government online by encouraging consistency of approach. In terms of our suggested stage model for E-Government interoperability, the framework seems only to cover Stages 1 and 2. For example, urban planning is a complex task requiring multidimensional urban information (spatial, social, economic, crime, etc.). The need for assistance in performing urban planning tasks has led to the rapid development of urban information systems (Wang, Song, Hamilton, & Curwell, 2007).

Geographic information systems have become an important tool for crime measures and spatial analysis of criminal activity. Classical and spatial statistics have been merged to form more comprehensive approaches in understanding how crime is related to social problems. According to National Institute of Justice (2006), these methods allow for the measurement of proximity effects on places by neighboring areas that lead to a multi-dimensional and less static understanding of factors that contribute to or repel crime across space.

Geographic information systems in law enforcement represent digital repositories for E-Government. Crime mapping is concerned with knowledge management in E-Government for change management in policing. The diffusion of information technology (IT) in policing is accelerating as technology to support knowledge work in law enforcement is improving. The diffusion of computerized crime mapping in policing is part of this IT revolution in law enforcement.

The theoretical framework for crime mapping in law enforcement is often based on the theory of problem-oriented policing. A broad and popular definition of problem-oriented policing is as follows: Problem-oriented policing is designed to identify and remove the causes of recurring crime and disorder problems that harm communities. The concept of problem-oriented policing places a high value on developing, within that strategy, new responses that are preventive in nature, that are not dependent on the use of the criminal justice system, and that draw on the potential contributions of other public agencies, the community, and the private sector. Problem-oriented policing can be associated with police effectiveness and crime prevention. Crime prevention, as well as crime, is hard to define, but problem-oriented policing is most closely related, but not limited, to situational crime prevention. Since problem-oriented policing is more of a theoretical concept, not a theory of crime, it is suitable for the use of the study of processes in crime prevention initiatives in the police and their effectiveness. Still this concept needs a more practical and manageable framework to be used in the research.

The well-known SARA model has been widely used as a framework for problem-oriented policing and has almost become synonymous with problem-oriented policing. Research studies by Home Office Research (2000) in the UK have applied the SARA model for assessing problem-oriented initiatives. Norwegian police literature also uses the SARA model as a framework for carrying out problem-oriented policing.

Scanning, analysis, response, and assessment are the four stages in the SARA model (Policing, 2005). It is important to have a clear understanding of what these stages imply.

1.   **Scanning.** The scanning stage includes the following activities:
     o   Identifying recurring problems of concern to the public and the police,
     o   Identifying the consequences of the problem for the community and the police,
     o   Prioritizing those problems,
     o   Developing broad goals,
     o   Confirming that the problems exist,
     o   Determining how frequently the problem occurs,
     o   How long it has been taking place, and
     o   Selecting problems for closer examination

In what ways these problems are identified is crucial. Crime mapping is a technique widely used. However, as Hough and Tilley (1998) state, identifying problems in a manner that paves the way to their solution is an art as much as technology. Management may use performance indicators within crime prevention to identify these problems. In order to address important issues at this stage in the SARA model, findings from weaknesses in problem-solving initiatives from the UK may be used to give a more understandable perspective of quality and efficiency at this stage. The weaknesses were found to be (Home Office Research, 2000): failure to check that a nationally identified problem exists locally, failure to check out systematically whether perceptions of existing problems are accurate, and failure to check the scale of a problem.

2.   **Analysis.** Distinguishing the analysis stage from the scanning may seem hard, and the analysis is quite a challenging phase that involves the following activities:
     o   Identifying and understanding the events and conditions that precede and accompany the problem,
     o   Identifying relevant data to be collected,
     o   Investigating what is already known about the specific problem,

- o   Taking inventory of how the problem is currently addressed,
- o   Identifying strengths and limitations of the current response,
- o   Narrowing the scope of the problem as specifically as possible,
- o   Identifying a variety of resources that may be of assistance in developing a deeper understanding of the problem, and
- o   Developing a working hypothesis about why the problem is occurring

The weaknesses found in the UK were (Home Office Research, 2000): acceptance of definition of problem at face value, use of only very short-term data, and failure to examine the genesis of problems.

3.   **Response.** The response phase includes the following activities:
- o   Brainstorming for new interventions,
- o   Searching for what other communities with similar problems have done,
- o   Choosing among the alternative interventions,
- o   Outlining a response plan,
- o   Identifying responsible parties,
- o   Stating the specific objectives for the response plan, and
- o   Carrying out the planned activities.

Weaknesses found in the response stage in the UK were (Home Office Research, 2000): short term focus, failure to read relevant literature, picking the solution prior to, or in spite of, analysis, failure to plan how the measures could in practice be made operational, failure to think through the mechanisms by which the measure could have its impact, and failure to think through needs for sustained reduction, specifically failure to consolidate following crackdown.

4.   **Assessment.** The importance of assessment or evaluation of crime prevention initiatives cannot be stressed enough regardless of the type of initiatives. Without evaluation, crime prevention practice cannot be improved and without hard evidence about effectiveness, reliable information about best practice cannot be disseminated, and it is widely recognized that evaluation and assessment is the most deficient aspect of crime prevention. In the SARA-model the assessment stage includes the following activities:
- o   Determining whether the plan was implemented (a process evaluation),
- o   Collecting pre- and post-response qualitative and quantitative data,
- o   Determining whether broad goals and specific objectives were attained,

   o   Identifying any new strategies needed to augment the original plan, and

   o   Conducting ongoing assessment to ensure continued effectiveness.

Most of these issues correspond with terms listed by Hough and Tilley (1998) for evaluation of crime prevention initiatives. Weaknesses found in the UK were (Home Office Research, 2000): shortage of good evaluations, and uncritical transfer of responses used elsewhere.

Problem-oriented policing relies on collaboration with partners at the various stages in the SARA model. Some of the weaknesses in the UK were failure to involve partners and insensitivity to others' agendas, styles, constraints or ideologies (Home Office Research, 2000).

Crime is not spread evenly across maps. It clumps in some areas and is absent in others. People use this knowledge in their daily activities. According to National Institute of Justice (2005), they avoid some places and seek out others. Their choices of neighborhoods, schools, stores, streets, and recreation are governed partially by the understanding that their chances of being a victim are greater in some of these places than in others. In some places people lock their cars and secure their belongings. In other places they do not.

Crime mapping is concerned with advancing spatial understanding. Areas of concentrated crime are often referred to as hot spots. National Institute of Justice (2005) identified several crime hot spot theories. For example, place theories explain why crime events occur at specific locations. Street theories deal with crimes at slightly larger geographic areas than specific places; that is, over small, stretched areas such as streets or blocks. Neighborhood theories attempt to explain neighborhood differences. Still other theories attempt to explain differences in crime patterns at much higher levels of aggregation. For example, theories of crime differ among cities and among regions. On the city level, suggested actions may include citywide changes in economic, transportation, education, welfare, and recreation policies.

There are many GIS that are applied in law enforcement organizations. Here are some examples of systems in the UK that were reviewed by (Chainey & Smith, 2006):

- Amethyst: Devon and Cornwall
- CADDIE: Sussex
- COSMOS: Birmingham
- GMAC: Greater Manchester
- JUPITER: East Midlands Government Office region
- LASS: London Government Office region
- NERISS: North East Government Office region

- North West Regional Crime Mapping System: North West Government Office region
- Project DRAGON: Welsh Assembly
- SCaDIS: Surrey.

Ashby and Longley (2005) conducted an empirical study of the Devon and Cornwall Constabulary. They found that geo-demographic analyses including people and places of local policing environments, crime profiles, and police performance provided a significantly increased level of community intelligence for police use. This was supplemented and further enhanced by the use of penetration ranking reports where neighborhood types were ranked by standardized crime rates, and cumulative percentage of the crime was compared with the corresponding population at risk.

An example of GIS in Norway is illustrated in Figure 1.1. In the centre of Oslo, pocket thieves were becoming very active. Application of GIS revealed a pattern, and one of the hot spots was identified. The hot spot was the restaurant Uncle Donald in the University Street. Police officers contacted the owner of the restaurant as well as the doormen. One action taken was to install hangers for clothes underneath each guest table. Another action was a wardrobe for guest clothes. In

Figure 1.1. Geographic information system applied to pocket theft in Oslo

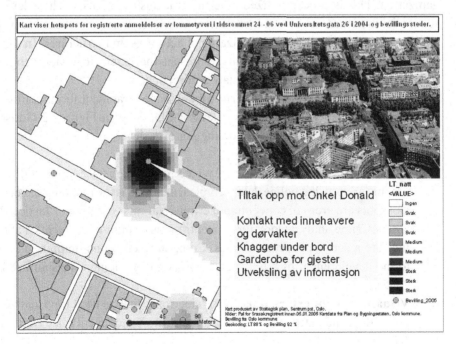

addition, policing information was shared with people employed in the restaurant. As a consequence, the number of pocket thefts dropped in this restaurant as well as in the city as a whole.

National Institute of justice (2005) argues that moving beyond the manual pin-mapping approaches of the past, desktop GIS technologies have introduced crime analysts to new ways of visualizing and mapping crime. Specifically, tools for dynamic visualization and mapping in a GIS environment make it possible to inductively describe and visualize spatial distributions, identify unusual observations or spatial outliers, and discover patterns of spatial association, including clusters and hot spots.

Weisburd and Lum (2005) studied diffusion of computerized crime mapping in policing. They found that diffusion is dependent on the importance of hot spots policing approaches, and is linked strongly to those approaches in police agencies with computerized crime mapping capabilities. We will organize such research findings into the stages of growth model. The diffusion of an innovation such as crime mapping can be conceptualized as a process in each law enforcement agency. In the following, we conceptualize the process in terms of maturity levels as suggested by Gottschalk and Tolloczko (2007). The purpose of this maturity model is to help practitioners and researchers study organizational evolution and determine future direction in a police organization's use of electronic systems when mapping crime.

Maturity models assume that predictable patterns exist in the growth of an organization. This is conceptualized in terms of levels of maturity. These levels are sequential in nature, occur as a hierarchical progression that is not easily reversed, and involve a broad range of organizational activities and structures. In the case of crime mapping, levels of maturity represent the extent to which geographic information systems are innovating law enforcement.

In this section, we present a maturity model for geographic information systems applications consisting of eight maturity levels as illustrated in Figure 1.2. Gottschalk and Tolloczko (2007) define the following maturity levels:

I.   **Visualization of internal data.** An electronic map is used to visualize geographic areas using police data. A typical example is the mapping of hot spots. Hot spots are areas of concentrated crime (National Institute of Justice, 2005, 2006). Crime analysts look for concentrations of individual events that might indicate a series of related crimes. Computerized crime mapping is central to the development of a hot spots approach to policing (Weisburd & Lum, 2005).

II. **Visualization of external data.** An electronic map is used to visualize both police data and external data. For example, the Vancouver Police Department obtained data from the LandScan Global Population Database for spatial analysis of criminal activity. The LandScan Global Population Database has been adopted by many US and international government agencies, as well as the United Nations, for estimating populations at risk from criminal activity.

III.   **Internal communication.** The electronic map is shared with officers at different locations. For example, COSMOS (COmmunity Safety Mapping On-line System) in Birmingham is an Internet GIS-based community safety tool, designed as a central point of contact for crime and disorder reduction. It provides access to multi-agency data through interactive mapping and data query tools, and through interactive tabular and graphical profiles.

IV.   **External communication.** The electronic map is shared with other public agencies and private organizations that join the problem-solving task. For example, CADDIE (Crime and Disorder Data Information Exchange) in Sussex is an Internet-based solution designed to ensure that all 13 CDRPs (Crime and Disorder Reduction Partnerships) and partners in the county have access to relevant, accurate and timely information about crime and disorder.

V.   **Simulation of alternative patterns.** Registered hot spots and other items on the map are statistically correlated with each other, so that different crime patterns will emerge from computer simulations. A typical example is prospective hot spotting, where future locations of crime are predicted. For example, Bowers, Johnson and Pease (2004) used a moving window technique to generate prospective risk surfaces.

VI.   **Optimization among alternative actions.** Based on targets and other inputs, the system suggests an optimal solution to the problem. For example, the Devon and Cornwall Constabulary apply geo-demographics for resource allocation in policing. According to Ashby and Longley (2005), geo-demographic profiles of characteristics of individuals and small areas are important in tactical and strategic resource management in many areas of business and are becoming similarly central to efficient and effective deployment of resources by public services.

VII.   **Organization of partnership to solve problem.** The police agency is reorganized to work according to problem-oriented policing. For example, the Project Dragon provides timely daily exchange of information between Probation, the Prison Service and the Police to monitor prison releases and supports partnerships prevention responses to re-offending.

VIII.   **Strategizing for organizational performance.** The police agency makes its policing strategy based on GIS results. To be successful, Ratcliffe (2004) argues that there are fundamental training needs for managers to enable a greater understanding of the analyses presented to them, and how to use mapping to further crime prevention and reduction. At this level, executive training of police chiefs is more important than increasing the technical ability of crime analysts. According to Ratcliffe (2004), the challenge for the future of crime reduction practice in law enforcement is less to worry about the training of analysts, and more to address the inability of law enforcement management to understand and act on the crime analysis they are given. An emerging example of this maturity level is GMAC (Greater Manchester Against Crime), which operates through a business process model that is changing organizational structures and strategies. GMAC is a structure and process framework for delivering partnership working, utilizing a strategic analytical capability across Manchester.

The Norwegian Police Directorate set out a new strategy for crime prevention and community safety to be implemented by all Norwegian police districts in 2002. It was called problem-oriented policing and was initiated because of the Parliamentary White Paper no. 22 - Police Reform 2000. The police directorate defines problem-oriented policing as a work philosophy. The intention of this philosophy is to make the police more efficient in crime prevention and crime reduction (Policing,

Figure 1.2. The maturity model for GIS applications

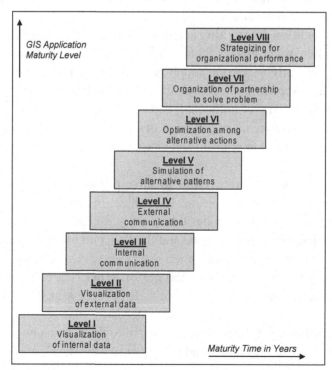

2005). Problem-oriented policing has since been taught and implemented on several maturity levels in police agencies. There are 27 police districts in Norway, each headed by a chief of police. The chief of police has full responsibility for policing within his or her district. Oslo police district is the largest with more than 2,300 employees. The Norwegian Police Directorate is managing all police districts and reporting to the Department of Justice. Since 2002, the directorate has arranged seminars and workshops for top-level police management in the theory and practice of problem-oriented policing.

An important practical implication of problem-oriented policing is electronic mapping of crime. An example of crime mapping is pocket thefts in Oslo as illustrated in Figure 1.3. Based on visualization of both internal (level I) and external (level II) data as well as internal communication (level III) and external communication (level IV) with city authorities, simulations were performed (level V), actions were discussed (level VI) and partnerships (level VII) were initiated. Restaurants were important partners since the GIS-based analysis showed that pocket theft was found near and in restaurants. The problem of pocket thefts was solved by restaurants opening wardrobes and installing hangers under guest tables. We find that the Oslo Police District has reached maturity level VII. Other police districts

Figure 1.3. Pocket thefts in Oslo

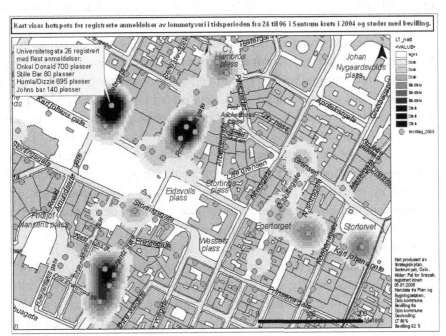

in Norway are found at lower levels. One reason for the variation in maturity is the variation in population density. Oslo being the capital and the largest city in Norway with a population of 550,000 inhabitants will typically have more geographically concentrated crimes than other police districts.

The diffusion of computerized crime mapping is based on widely available technologies. Technology is an important factor in explaining the rapid adoption of geographical information systems in mapping crime. However, the availability of a new technology is not enough to explain its widespread adoption. Weisburd and Lum (2005) found three more explanations. First, diffusion of a new technology generally begins with the wide recognition of a need for change. Second, the identification of a need, through some type of crisis or reassessment, is followed by a period of research and development. Finally, research and development concluded that law enforcement should be more focused on crime hot spots. Computerized crime mapping became central to the creation of crime hot spots by identifying clusters of addresses, which evidenced high rates of recorded crime.

After adoption of computerized crime mapping, police organizations develop in terms of crime mapping maturity as suggested by our maturity model. In an evaluation of geographical profiling software, Rich and Shively (2004) found limitations in all compared software applications. For example, only CrimeStat is able to export results to other mapping software, while only Rigel Analyst has the ability to generate reports. Both Dragnet and Rigel Analyst have the ability to manually add crime data. Based on this evaluation of software applications, mature police organizations will have to struggle to find software applications, which support levels VII and VIII in the maturity model.

The use of geographic information systems (GIS) and spatial data analysis techniques have become prominent tools for analyzing criminal behavior and the impacts of the criminal justice system on society. According to National Institute of Justice (2006), classical and spatial statistics have been merged to form more comprehensive approaches in understanding social problems from research and practical standpoints. These methods allow for the measurement of proximity effects on places by neighboring areas that lead to a multi-dimensional and less static understanding of factors that contribute to or repel crime across space. As stressed by researchers such as Ashby and Longley (2005) and Clarke (2001), it is important that law enforcement keep pace with new developments in effective crime prevention and crime investigation.

In the maturity model by Gottschalk and Tolloczko (2007), interoperability challenges occur at all levels. In particular, level VII for organization of partnership to solve problem requires electronic information from a variety of sources, such as customs, municipalities, hospitals, agricultural authorities, and schools. For example in the struggle of tracing the origins of foot and mouth disease in the UK, geographic information systems have become indispensable to effective knowledge transfer within both the public and private sector.

CONCLUSION

In this chapter we have learned that the concept of E-Government is not commonly defined. Although this, the underlying assumption of E-Government is that the use of Internet technologies should improve the ways government serve its citizens and the ways in which citizen interact with governments. Making citizen-centric efficient operations and services, governments must challenge the traditional way of cooperation, and improve technical, Semantic and organizational interoperability. When the degree of systems interoperability is high between to cooperating agencies, then transaction costs are low.

Most governments around the world started their E-Government initiatives with a focus on providing information and services to the citizens while service delivery platforms remained separate and parallel across various government agencies. In this model, service delivery was built around individual agency functions, structures, information, systems and capabilities. With the private sector leading the way, advances in accessibility and a greater use of technology have allowed an expansion of innovative information technology solutions. Now citizens and businesses around the world are increasingly demanding that their governments follow suit. Citizen groups have come to expect a 24/7 convenient user interface with ease of use, in a language the user understands and which is tailored to individual needs (United Nations, 2008).

REFERENCES

Anderson, S. W., Glenn, D., & Sedatole, K. L. (2000). Sourcing parts of complex products: evidence on transactions costs, high-powered incentives and ex-post opportunism. *Accounting, Organizations and Society, 25*(5), 723-749.

Archmann, S., & Kudlacek, I. (2008). Interoperability and the exchange of good practice cases. *European Journal of ePractice, 2*(February), 3-12.

Artz, K. W., & Brush, T. H. (2000). Asset specificity, uncertainty and relational norms: an examination of coordination costs in collaborative strategic alliances. *Journal of Economic Behavior & Organization, 41*(4), 337-362.

Ashby, D. I., & Longley, P. A. (2005). Geocomputation, geodemographics and resource allocation for local policing. *Transactions in GIS, 9*(1), 53-72.

Bekkers, V. (2007). The government of back-office integration. Organizing co-operation between information domains. *Public Management Review, 9*(3), 377-300.

Bowers, K. J., Johnson, S. D., & Pease, K. (2004). Prospective Hot-Spotting: The Future of Crime Mapping? *British Journal of Criminology, 44*(5), 641-658.

Cabinet Office. (2005a). *E-government interoperability framework version 6.1* (ISBN No. 0 7115 0468 7). London: UK Cabinet Office, E-Government Unit.

Cabinet Office. (2005b). *Geographic information: An analysis of interoperability and information sharing in the United Kingdom.* London: UK Cabinet Office, E-Government Unit.

Center for Problem-oriented Policing (2005). *The SARA model.* Retrieved December 9th, 2005, from http://www.popcenter.org/default.htm

Chainey, S., & Smith, C. (2006). *Review of GIS-based information sharing systems* (Home Office Online Report No. 02/06): The Jill Dando Institute of Crime Science, University College London.

Clarke, R. V. (2001). Effective crime prevention: Keeping pace with new developments. *Forum on Crime and Society, 1*(1), 17-33.

Clarkson, G., Jacobsen, T. E., & Batcheller, A. L. (2007). Information asymmetri and information sharing. *Government Information Quarterly, 24*(4), 827-839.

Coase, R. H. (1937). The nature of the firm. *Economica, 4*(16), 386-405.

Cui, L., Zhang, C., Zhang, C., & Huang, L. (2006). Exploring e-government impact on Shanghai firms' information process. *Electronic Markets, 16*(4), 312-328.

Doumeingts, G., Müller, J., Morel, G., & Vallespir, B. (2007). Preface. In G. Doumeingts, J. Müller, G. Morel & B. Vallespir (Eds.), *Enterprise interoperability: New xhallenges and Approaches.* London: Springer Verlag.

Drejer, A., Christensen, K. S., & Ulhoi, J. P. (2004). Understanding intrapreneurship by means of state-of-the-art knowledge management and organizational learning theory. *International Journal of Management and Enterprise Development, 1*(2), 102-119.

Eckman, B. A., Bennet, C. A., Kaufman, J. H., & Tenner, J. W. (2007). Varieties of interoperability in the transformation of the health-care information infrastructure. *IBM Systems Journal, 46*(1), 19-41.

Eisenhardt, K. M., & Martin, J. A. (2000). Dynamic capabilities: What are they? *Strategic Management Journal, 21*(10-11), 1105-1121.

Esteves, J., & Joseph, R. C. (2008). A comprehensive framework for the assessment of eGovernment projects. *Government Information Quarterly, 25*(1), 404-437.

Fedorowicz, J., Gogan, J. L., & Williams, C. B. (2007). A collaborative network for first responders: Lessons from CapWIN case. *Government Information Quarterly, 24*(4), 785-807.

Gogan, J. L., Williams, C. B., & Fedorowicz, J. (2007). RFID and interorganizational collaboration: Political and administrative challenges. *Electronic Government, an International Journal, 4*(4), 423-435.

Gottschalk, P., & Tolloczko, P. (2007). Maturity model for mapping crime in law enforcement. *Electronic Government, an International Journal, 4*(1), 59-67.

Gouscos, D., Kalikakis, M., Legal, M., & Papadopoulou, S. (2007). A general model of performance and quality for one-stop e-government service offerings. *Government Information Quarterly, 24*(4), 860-885.

Grefen, P., Ludwig, H., & Angelov, S. (2003). A three-level framework for process and data management of complex e-services. *International Journal of Cooperative Information Systems, 12*(4), 487-531.

Hancox, M., & Hackney, R. (2000). IT outsourcing: frameworks for conceptualizing practice and perception. *Information Systems Journal, 10*(3), 217-237.

Henisz, W. J., & Williamson, O. E. (1999). Comparative economic organization - Within and between countries. *Business and Politics, 1*(3), 261-277.

Home Office Research. (2000). *Not rocket science? Problem-solving and crime reduction* (Crime Reduction Research Series Paper No. 6). London: UK Development and Statistics Directorate.

Hough, M., & Tilley, N. (1998). *Getting the grease to squeak. Research lessons for crime prevention* (Crime Detection and Prevention Series Paper No. 85): Home Office Policing & Reducing Crime Unit.

Jap, S. D. (2001). Perspectives on joint competitive advantages in buyer-supplier relationships. *International Journal of Research in Marketing, 18*(1-2), 19-35.

Khalifa, M., & Liu, V. (2008). Semantic network representation of computer-mediated discussions: Conceptual facilitation form and knowledge acquisition. *Omega, 36*(2), 252-266.

Legner, C., & Lebreton, B. (2007). Business interoperability research: Present achievements and upcoming challenges. *Electronic Markets, 17*(3), 176-186.

Luna-Reyes, L. F., Gil-Garcia, J. R., & Cruz, C. B. (2007). Collaborative digital government in Mexico: Some lessons from federal Web-based interorganizational information integration initiatives. *Government Information Quarterly, 24*(4), 808-826.

National Institute of Justice. (2005). *Mapping crime: Understanding hot spots.* Washington, DC: Office of Justice Programs.

National Institute of Justice. (2006). *Mapping and analysis for public safety (MAPS).* Washington, DC: US Department of Justice.

Office of the Government Chief Information Officer. (2007). *The HKSARG interoperability framework.* Government of the Hong Kong Special Administrative Region.

Otjacques, B., Hitzelberger, P., & Feltz, F. (2007). Interoperability of e-government information systems: Issues of identification and data sharing. *Journal of Management Information Systems, 23*(4), 29-51.

Papazoglou, T. A., & Ribbers, P. M. A. (2006). *E-business: Organizational and technical foundations.* West Sussex, UK: John Wiley & Sons.

Pardo, T. A., & Tayi, G. K. (2007). Interorganizational information integration: A key enabler for digital government. *Government Information Quarterly, 24*(4), 691-715.

Pedersen, M. K., Fountain, J., & Loukis, E. (2006). Preface to the focus theme section: 'Electronic markets and e-government'. *Electronic Markets, The International Journal, 16*(4), 263-273.

Poppo, L., & Zenger, T. (2002). Do formal contracts and relational governance function as substitutes or compliments? *Strategic Management Journal, 23*(8), 707-725.

Ranerup, A. (2006). Electronic markets connecting citizens to pension reform. *Electronic Markets, The International Journal, 16*(4), 282-291.

Ratcliffe, J. H. (2004). Crime mapping and the training needs of law enforcement. *European Journal of Criminal Policy and research, 10*(1), 65-83.

Rich, B. H., & Shively, M. (2004). *A methodology for evaluating geographic profiling software.* Cambridge, MA: Abt Associates Inc.

Salleh, N. A. M., Rohde, F., & Green, P. (2006). The effect of enacted capabilities on adoption of a government electronic procurement system by Malaysian SMEs. *Electronic Markets, The International Journal, 16*(4), 292-311.

Santos, E. M. D., & Reinhard, N. (2007). Setting interoperability standards for e-government: an exploratory case study. *Electronic Government, an International Journal, 4*(4), 889-920.

Scholl, H. J., & Klischewski, R. (2007). E-government integration and interoperability: Framing the research agenda. *International Journal of Public Administration, 30*(8), 889-920.

Schooley, B. L., & Horan, T. A. (2007). Towards end-to-end government performance management: Case study of interorganizational information integration in emergency medical services (EMS). *Government Information Quarterly, 24*(4), 755-784.

State Services Commission. (2007). *New Zealand e-government interoperability framework.*

Saarinen, T., & Vepsäläinen, A. P. J. (1994). Procurement strategies for information systems. *Journal of Management Information Systems, 11*(2), 187-208.

Teece, D. J., Pisano, G., & Shuen, A. (1997). Dynamic capabilities and strategic management. *Strategic Management Journal, 18*(7), 509-533.

United Nations. (2008). *UN e-government survey. From e-government to connected governance* (No. ST/ESA/PAD/SER.E/112). New York: Department of Economics and Social Affairs, Divison for Public Administration and Development Management.

Vragov, R., & Kumar, N. (2006). Electronic markets for the allocation, financing and distribution of public goods. *Electronic Markets, The International Journal, 16*(4), 274-281.

Wang, H., Song, Y., Hamilton, A., & Curwell, S. (2007). Urban information integration for advanced e-planning in Europe. *Government Information Quarterly, 24*(4), 736-754.

Weisburd, D., & Lum, C. (2005). The diffusion of computerized crime mapping in Policing: Linking Research and Practice. *Police Practice and Research, 6*(5), 419-434.

Williamson, O. E. (1979). Transaction-cost economics: The governance of contractual relations. *The Journal of Law and Economics, 22*(2), 233-261.

Williamson, O. E. (1999). Strategy research: governance and competence perspectives. *Strategic Management Journal, 20*, 1087-1108.

Williamson, O. E. (2000). The new institutional economics: Taking stock, looking ahead. *Journal of Economic Literature, 38*(3), 595-613.

Wilson, F., van Engers, T., & Peters, R. (2007). Training eGovernment actors: Experience and future needs. *European Journal of ePractice, 1*(November), 36-47.

Chapter II
Value Configurations of Organizations

1.   VALUE CONFIGURATIONS OF ORGANIZATIONS

To comprehend the value that information technology provides to organizations, we must first understand the way a particular organization conducts business and how information systems affect the performance of various component activities within the organization. Understanding how organizations differ is a central challenge for both theory and practice of management. For a long time, Porter's (1985) value chain was the only value configuration known to managers. Stabell and Fjeldstad (1998) have identified two alternative value configurations. A value shop schedules activities and applies resources in a fashion that is dimensioned and appropriate to the needs of the client's problem, while a value chain performs a fixed set of activities that enables it to produce a standard product in large numbers. Examples of value shops are professional service organizations, as found in medicine, law, architecture and engineering. A value network links clients or customers who are or wish to be interdependent. Examples of value networks are telephone companies, logistic and postal services, retail banks and insurance companies.

This chapter presents the three value configurations – the value chain, the value shop, and the value network. Then, the three different value configurations are compared according to some key characteristics, for example use of information systems. Nine design parameters are presented as building blocks of organizational structure. Finally, this chapter shows how organizational culture might influence organizations.

1.1 The Organization as Value Chain

The best-known value configuration is the value chain. In the value chain, value is created through efficient production of goods and services based on a variety of resources. The organization is perceived as a series or chain of activities. Primary activities in the value chain include inbound logistics, production, outbound logistics, marketing and sales, and service. Support activities include infrastructure, human resources, technology development and procurement. Attention is on performing these activities in the chain in efficient and effective ways. In Figure 2.1, examples of information systems are assigned to primary and support activities. This figure can be used to describe the current IT situation in the organization as it illustrates the extent of coverage of IT for each activity. Examples of government value chains are road construction and maintenance, water supply, one-stop e-government service provision, and joint military operations.

Water supply as a value chain requires water quality management. Research illustrates the need for integration of data supporting water quality management as an example of how such integration can enable higher levels of e-government (Chen, Gangopadhyay, Holden, Karabatis, & McGuire, 2007). It presents a prototype system that allows users to integrate water-monitoring data across many federal, state, and local government organizations and provides techniques for information discovery, thus improving information quality and availability for decision making.

Figure 2.1. Examples of IT-based information systems in the value chain

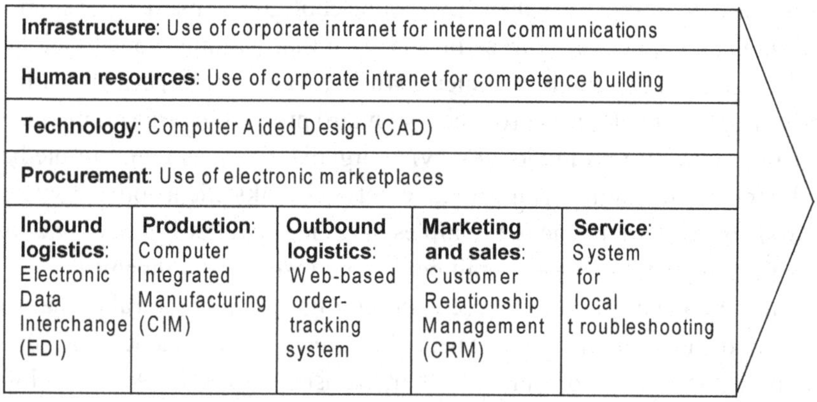

Infrastructure: Use of corporate intranet for internal communications				
Human resources: Use of corporate intranet for competence building				
Technology: Computer Aided Design (CAD)				
Procurement: Use of electronic marketplaces				
Inbound logistics: Electronic Data Interchange (EDI)	**Production**: Computer Integrated Manufacturing (CIM)	**Outbound logistics**: Web-based order-tracking system	**Marketing and sales**: Customer Relationship Management (CRM)	**Service**: System for local troubleshooting

One-stop e-government service provision is a value chain, as it handles the logistics and production of government services. It is an integrated customer-oriented administrative service offering. One-stop e-government has emerged worldwide as a trend to offer electronically administrative service packages that meet the needs of citizens' life events and business transactions, with a promise to enhance service accessibility and alleviate service delivery delays and costs (Gouscos, Kalikakis, Legal, & Papadopoulou, 2007).

Value represents the worth, utility, or importance of an entity. The classic model for value determination is Porter's (1985) value chain. The value chain identifies both primary and secondary activities in the organization and uses an economic view to explain value creation. A business organization can create value and a strategic advantage if it can differentiate itself from its competitors. Value results from either an increase in revenue or a decrease in costs. Governments can create value by reducing cost. Governments usually attempt to limit deficit and operate within a particular budget to provide goods and services for citizens (Esteves & Joseph, 2008).

Value is created in the value chain with the use of information technology. Often, technological innovation is the driving force for value creation. An innovation is an idea, a practice, or object, which is perceived as new by an individual or other unit of adoption. E-government, by definition, is an innovation because it redefines and improves transaction processing via an IT platform (Esteves & Joseph, 2008).

1.2   The Organization as Value Shop

Value cannot only be created in value chains. Value can also be created in two alternative value configurations: value shop and value network (Stabell & Fjeldstad, 1998). In the value shop, activities are scheduled and resources are applied in a fashion that is dimensioned and appropriate to the needs of the client's problem, while a value chain performs a fixed set of activities that enables it to produce a standard product in large numbers. The value shop is an organization that creates value by solving unique problems for customers and clients. Knowledge is the most important resource, and reputation is critical to organizational success.

While typical examples of value chains are manufacturing industries such as paper and car production, typical examples of value shops are law firms and medical hospitals. Often, such companies are called professional service organizations or knowledge-intensive service firms. Like the medical hospital as a way to practice medicine, the law firm provides a standard format for delivering complex legal services. Many features of its style – specialization, teamwork, continuous monitoring on behalf of clients (patients), and representation in many forums – have been emulated in other vehicles for delivering professional services (Galanter & Palay, 1991).

Joint military operations can also be regarded as value shop, in which complementary and special forces are meant to work together in joint operations to solve military, political, or humanitarian problems (e.g., operation Desert Storm in Kuwait, operation Uphold Democracy in Haiti, and operation Restore Hope in Somalia). Such operations are inherently complex in planning, coordinating logistics, maneuver, and timing of joint forces. Joint military operations such as NATO operations in Afghanistan require interoperability between national systems from participating nations. The supply chain typically involves several national information systems. The multilateral interoperability program by NATO allies has the aim to achieve interoperability of command and control information systems at all levels from corps to battalion or the lowest appropriate level, in order to support combined and joint operations, and pursue the advancement of digitization in the international arena (Multilateral Interoperability Programme, 2003).

Knowledge-intensive service organizations are typical value shops. Sheehan (2002) defines knowledge-intensive service firms as entities that sell problem-solving services, where the solution chosen by the expert is based on real-time feedback from the client. Clients retain knowledge intensive service firms to reduce their uncertainty. Clients hire knowledge-intensive service firms precisely because the client believes the firm knows something that the client does not and believes it is necessary to solve their problems. While expertise plays a role in all firms, its role is distinctive in knowledge-intensive service firms. Expert, often professional, knowledge is at the core of the service provided by the type of firm.

Knowledge-intensive service firms not only sell a problem-solving service, but equally a problem-finding, problem-defining, solution-execution, and monitoring service. Problem finding is often a key for acquiring new clients. Once the client is acquired and their problem is defined, not all problems will be solved by the firm. Rather the firm may only clarify that there is no problem (i.e. the patient does not have a heart condition) or that the problem should be referred to another specialist (i.e. the patient needs a heart specialist). If a problem is treated within the firm, then the firm needs to follow up the implementation to assure that the problem in fact has been solved (i.e. is the patient's heart now working properly?). This follows from the fact that there is often uncertainty in both problem diagnosis and problem resolution.

Sheehan (2002) has created a typology of knowledge-intensive service firms consisting of the following three types. First, knowledge-intensive service firms search for opportunities. The amount of value they create depends on the size of the finding or discovery, where size is measured by quality rather than quantity. Examples of search firms include petroleum and mineral exploration, drug discovery in the pharmaceutical industry, and research in the biotechnology industry. Second, knowledge-intensive diagnosis firms create value by clarifying problems. Once the

Figure 2.2. Examples of IT-based information systems in the value shop

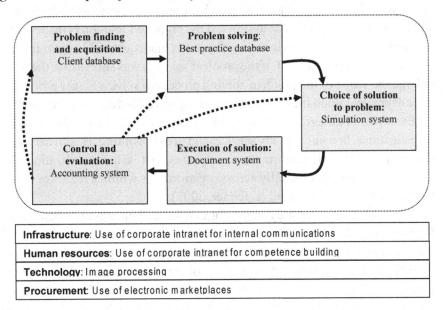

problem has been identified, the suggested remedy usually follows directly. Examples of diagnosis firms include doctors, surgeons, psychotherapists, veterinarians, lawyers, auditors and tax accountants, and software support. Finally, knowledge-intensive design firms create value by conceiving new ways of constructing material or immaterial artifacts. Examples of design firms include architecture, advertising, research and development, engineering design, and strategy consulting.

Knowledge-intensive service firms create value through problem acquisition and definition, alternative generation and selection, implementation of an alternative, and follow up to see if the solution selected resolves the problem. To reflect this process, Stabell and Fjeldstad (1998) have outlined the value configuration of a value shop as illustrated in Figure 2.2.

A value shop is characterized by five primary activities: problem finding and acquisition, problem solving, choice, execution, and control and evaluation, as illustrated in Figure 2.2. Problem finding and acquisition involves working with the customer to determine the exact nature of the problem or need. It involves deciding on the overall plan of approaching the problem. Problem solving is the actual generation of ideas and action (or treatment) plans. Choice represents the decision of choosing between alternatives. While the least important primary activity of the value shop in terms of time and effort, it is also the most important in terms of customer value. Execution represents communicating, organizing, and implementing the decision, or performing the treatment. Control and evaluation activities involve monitoring and measurement of how well the solution solved the original problem or met the original need. This may feed back into the first activity, problem finding and acquisition, for two reasons. First, if the proposed solution is inadequate or did not work, it feeds back into learning why it was inadequate and begins the problem-solving phase anew. Second, if the problem solution was successful, the firm might enlarge the scope of the problem-solving process to solve a bigger problem related to or dependent upon the first problem being solved (Afuah & Tucci, 2003).

Examples of government value shops are fire service, medical hospitals, police investigations, housing subsidy service, and urban planning. Health care, as a value shop requires effective information exchanges, that is, the mobilization of health-care information electronically across organizations within a region or community (Eckman, Bennet, Kaufman, & Tenner, 2007).

Police investigations are carried out in a value shop. An investigation is an effective search for material to bring an offender to justice. Knowledge and skills are required to conduct an effective investigation. Investigative knowledge enables investigators to determine if a given set of circumstances amounts to a criminal offence, to identify the types of material that may have been generated during the commission of an offence and where this material may be found. It also ensures that investigations are carried out in a manner, which complies with the rules of evidence, thereby increasing the likelihood that the material gathered will be admitted as evidence. Investigations are information-intensive. They often involve both public and private sector material (Kennedy, 2007).

Housing subsidy service is a value shop solving problems for poor families while living in the tension between economic and political rationality. When the ministry is confronted with major cutbacks, it affects the tasks and positions of housing corporations and municipalities (political rationality). A reduction in the amount of subsidies to be spent also affects low-income people (social and economic rationality). The activities in the housing subsidy service as value shop is concerned with balancing and solving such situations (Bekkers, 2007).

Urban planning is carried out in value shops. Urban planning is a complex task requiring multidimensional urban information. Urban planning decision-making involves many stakeholders. There are various stakeholders including urban planners, property developers, politicians, architects, engineers, transport and utility service providers, and individual citizens. The required information in planning is related to the different dimensions of the city. For example, deciding on the right location for a primary school requires geospatial, infrastructure, environmental, housing and population data (Wang, Song, Hamilton, & Curwell, 2007).

1.3   The Organization as Value Network

The third and final value configuration is the value network. A value network is a company that creates value by connecting clients and customers that are, or want to be, dependent on each other. These companies distribute information, money, products and services. While activities in both value chains and value shops are done sequentially, activities in value networks occur in parallel. The number and combination of customers and access points in the network are important value drivers in the value network. More customers and more connections create higher value to customers.

Stabell and Fjeldstad (1998) suggest that managing a value network can be compared to managing a club. The mediating firm admits members that complement each other, and in some cases exclude those that don't. The firm establishes, monitors, and terminates direct or indirect relationships among members. Supplier-customer relationships may exist between the members of the club, but to the mediating firm they are all customers. Examples of value networks include telecommunication companies, logistic and postal services, financial institutions such as banks and insurance companies, and stockbrokers.

Value networks perform three activities (see Figure 2.3):

- Development of customer network through marketing and recruiting of new customers, to enable increased value for both existing customers and new customers.
- Development of new services and improvement in existing services.
- Development of infrastructure so that customer services can be provided more efficiently and effectively.

The current IS/IT situation in a value network will mainly be described through the infrastructure that typically will consist of information technology. In addition, many of the new services may be information systems that will be used by customers in their communication and business transactions with other customers. The knowledge component will mainly be found in the services of a value network, as information systems are made available to customers to exchange relevant information.

Examples of government value networks are public safety networks, emergency medical services, shared services organizations and electronic markets. A public safety network is a value network linking departments of transportation, police, fire and other first responders in an area. A public safety network requires an or-

Figure 2.3. Examples of IT-based information systems in the value network

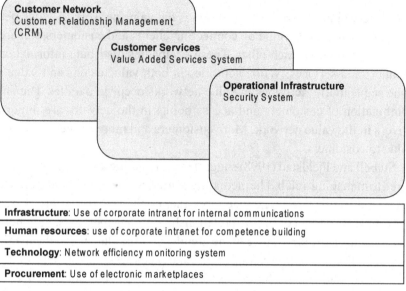

| Infrastructure: Use of corporate intranet for internal communications |
| Human resources: use of corporate intranet for competence building |
| Technology: Network efficiency monitoring system |
| Procurement: Use of electronic marketplaces |

ganizational structure, goals, and governance processes (Fedorowicz, Gogan, & Williams, 2007).

Similarly, emergency medical services as value networks represent unique and challenging dynamics and complexities to multi-organizational information sharing, including the time-critical nature of emergency services and the need for timely information in a form that can be trusted and used by emergency responders. Effective and timely service depends upon all participating organizations working cooperatively and utilizing information technology effectively (Schooley & Horan, 2007).

A shared services organization is a value network linking supply and demand for services across the entire organization. Governments are increasingly turning towards shared services organizations to consolidate and deliver services to their customers. In deciding who will offer which services, there are operational and legislative concerns. Accountability is important, as service failures or violations in information protection, privacy, and official languages complaint or other issues might create serious problems in a shared services organization (Grant, McKnight, Uruthirapathy, & Brown, 2007).

An electronic market is a value network linking supply and demand for goods and services electronically. The market paradigm implies that consumers of information and producers of information are equal on the market place. This means that producers are dependent on consumers to deliver information, and consumers are dependent on producers to receive information (Legner & Lebreton, 2007).

1.4   Comparison of Value Configurations

Value chain, value shop and value network are alternative value configurations that impact the use of information technology in the company as illustrated in Table 2.1. While the role of IT is to make production more efficient in a value chain, IT creates added value in the value shop, while IT in the form of infrastructure is the main value in the value network. Some companies have more than one value configuration, but most companies have one dominating configuration.

In the long term, business organizations can choose to change their value configurations. A bank, for example can be a value shop when it focuses on converting inputs to outputs. The value resides in the output and once you have the output, you can remove the production organization. This removal does not impact on the value of the output. The value shop is a solution provider. It's somebody that solves problems. The input is a problem. The output is a solution to the problem.

A bank that does this would view itself as a financial service operator, a financial advisor that also has the ability to provide the money. But what it would do is identify client problems, it would address those problems, it would select a solution together with the client and help to implement it. It would have stringent quality controls. As part of it's offering, it would probably supply the client with some cash as a loan or accept some of the client's cash for investment (Chatzkel, 2002). Or, the bank can be a value network, which is basically the logic of the marketplace. The bank would define its role as a conduit between people that do not have money and those people that do have money. What the bank does is to arrange the flow of cash between them. The bank will attract people with money to make deposits and investments. The bank will also attract people without money to make loans.

Table 2.1. Characteristics of value configurations

	Value Chain	**Value Shop**	**Value Network**
Value creation	Transformation of input to output	Solving clients and customers problems	Connecting clients and customers to each other
Work form	Sequential production	Integrated and cyclical problem solving	Monitored and simultaneous connections
Information systems	Making production more efficient	Adding value to the knowledge work	Main value by use of IT infrastructure
Example	Paper factory	Law firm	Telecom company

As a value network, the bank will connect people with opposite financial needs. The network consists of people with different financial needs. Over time, persons in the network may change status from money needier to money provider and vice versa (Chatzkel, 2002).

Both as a value shop and as a value network, the business organization can be identified as a bank. But it would have completely different consequences for what it will focus on doing well, what it will focus on doing itself, versus what it would not want to do itself. This provides a kind of strategic systems logic. It asks, "Which strategic system in terms of value configuration are we going to operate in?" Choosing an appropriate value configuration is a long-term decision with long-term consequences.

1.5 Organizational Structures

Organizational structure is found to influence performance and absorptive capacity for interoperability and information resource integration. It has long been argued that organizational structure is the result of organizational choices. This idea was developed by Mintzberg (1979) and applied by scholars such as Donk and Molloy (2008). According to this idea, the structure of organizations is the result of choices based on nine design parameters. Design parameters are used by organizations to divide and coordinate their work to establish desired patterns of behavior. The choices about each of the design parameters represent the building blocks of the organizational structure as illustrated in Figure 2.4. The nine design parameters are as follows (Mintzberg, 1979; Donk & Molloy, 2008):

1. **Design of positions in terms of job specialization**: The amount of tasks to be executed and the amount of control over that work. Jobs can be specialized in two dimensions. Job specialization in the horizontal dimension represents division of labor. At one extreme, the police officer is a jack-of-all-trades, forever jumping from one broad task to another. At the other extreme, he focuses his efforts on the same highly specialized task, repeated day-in and day-out even minute-in and minute out. Job specialization in the vertical dimension represents separation of work from administration. At one extreme, the police officer merely does the work without any thought as to how or why. At the other extreme, he controls every aspect of the work in addition to doing it. In the first dimension we find narrowness by horizontal job specialization (in that it deals with parallel activities) and breath by horizontal job enlargement. In the second dimension we find depth by vertical job specialization and closeness by vertical job enlargement.

2. **Design of positions in terms of behavioral formalization:** Regulating the behavior of individuals by formalization of job, workflow or rules. No matter what the means of formalization (job, workflow or rules), the effect on the person doing the job is the same: his behavior is regulated. Power over how that work is to be done passes from the police officer to that person who designs the specification, often a manager in the police district or in the national police directorate. Organizations formalize behavior to reduce its variability, ultimately to predict and control it. One prime motive for doing so is to coordinate activities. The fully formalized organization, as far as possible, is the completely controllable precise and predictable organization. There should be no confusion in the organization. Everyone knows exactly what to do. The alternative is a completely informal organization, where neither jobs nor workflows or rules are specified.

3. **Design of positions in terms of training and indoctrination:** Training is the process by which job related skills and knowledge are taught, while indoctrination is the process by which organizational norms are acquired. Professionals are trained over long periods of time, before they ever assume their positions. Often, this training takes place outside the organization, often in a police university college. The training itself usually requires a particular and extensive expertise, beyond the capacity of the organization to provide. Indoctrination is the way an organization formally socializes its members for its own benefits. Indoctrination is the process by which organizational norms are acquired.

4. **Design of superstructure in terms of unit grouping:** Establishing the formal lines of authority by combining people into units and departments. Grouping establishes a system of common supervision among positions and units. Grouping requires positions in the same group to share common tasks and resources. Grouping creates common measures of performance. When positions are to be allocated to groups, several criteria are applied, such as knowledge and skill, work process and function. Positions may be grouped according to specialized knowledge and skills that police officers bring to the job. Alternatively, positions may be grouped according to functions. When grouped according to knowledge, the same kind of experts is organized in the same group. When grouped according to function, different kinds of personnel are organized in the same group to completely carry out all tasks in that function.

5. **Design of superstructure in terms of unit size:** The span of control (distinguishing between a narrow and a wide span). This design of superstructure concerns how large each unit or work group should be. This is a question of span of control. While a tall organizational structure will be the result of small

groups, a flat structure will be the result of large groups. A linkage focusing on planning involves future thinking. A linkage focusing on control involves correcting actions as they occur.

6. **Design of lateral linkages in terms of planning and control systems:** The specification of the desired output and the assessment if the desired outputs or standards have been achieved. The purpose of a plan is to specify a desired output in the future. The purpose of performance control is to regulate the overall results of a given unit.

7. **Design of lateral linkages in terms of liaison devices:** Positions bypassing normal vertical channels to establish contacts between two units to coordinate the work of these units. Examples of liaison positions are task forces and standing committees. The standing committee is a more permanent interdepartmental grouping. It meets regularly to discuss issues of common interest. Another example of lateral linkage is the matrix structure. A weak liaison device would be a coordinator who attempts to make different parts of the organization aware of other parts' needs. A strong liaison device would be a board with power to make decisions influencing several parts of the organization.

8. **Design of decision-making systems in terms of vertical decentralization:** The power to make decisions down the chain of authority. When all power for decision-making rests at a single point in an organization with a single individual, the structure is completely centralized. When the power is dispersed among many individuals, the structure is decentralized. Centralization is the tightest means of coordinating decision-making in an organization. Vertical decentralization is concerned with the delegation of decision-power down the chain of authority.

9. **Design of decision-making systems in terms of horizontal decentralization:** Refers in general to the extent to which non-managers control decision processes. Decentralization implies transfer of power out of the line structure. Power is transformed into informal power, for example control over knowledge resources and information gathering and advice.

In addition to these nine design parameters, the shape of the organizational structure is influenced by contingency factors. Examples of contingency factors are age and size of the organization, regulation in the environment, stability in the environment, and power in terms of external control and internal control (Donk & Molloy, 2008).

A slightly different approach to organizational structure is organizational configuration. Organizational configuration is defined as a multidimensional constellation of conceptually distinct characteristics that commonly occur together. In this

Figure 2.4. Organizational structure parameters for organizations

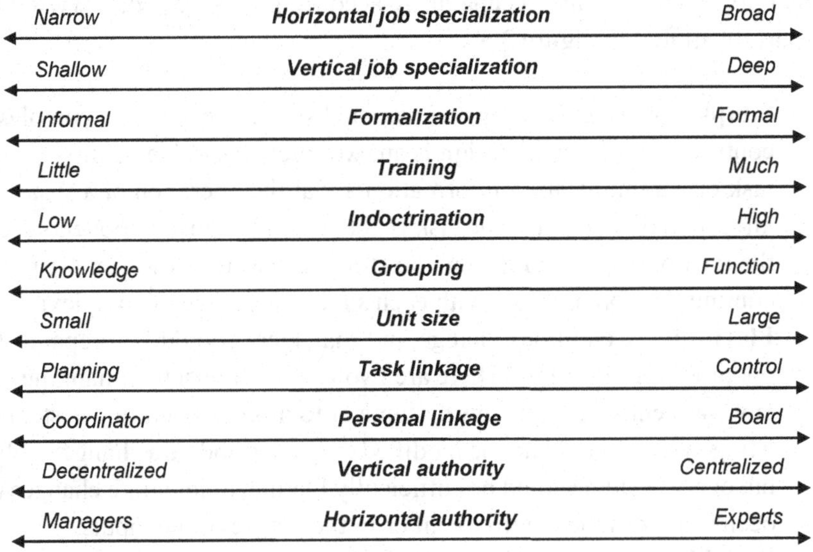

Narrow	**Horizontal job specialization**	Broad
Shallow	**Vertical job specialization**	Deep
Informal	**Formalization**	Formal
Little	**Training**	Much
Low	**Indoctrination**	High
Knowledge	**Grouping**	Function
Small	**Unit size**	Large
Planning	**Task linkage**	Control
Coordinator	**Personal linkage**	Board
Decentralized	**Vertical authority**	Centralized
Managers	**Horizontal authority**	Experts

perspective, organizations are understood as clusters of interconnected structures and practices. It represents a systemic and holistic view of organizations, where patterns or profiles rather than design parameters are related to an outcome such as performance (Fiss, 2007). Ketchen et al (1997) that an organization's performance is partially explained by its configuration.

Yet, another slightly different approach to organizational structure is organizational architecture (Ethiraj & Levinthal, 2004; Moussavou, 2006; Auteri & Wagner, 2007). The issue of structuring organizational effort became popular in the 1990s with the promotion of the concept organizational architecture (Frame, 1995). An organizational architecture provides the framework through which an organization aims to realize its core qualities as defined in executive vision and ambition. It is the framework into which business processes are deployed. It is supposed to ensure that an organization's core qualities are explored and exploited across all business processes deployed within the organization.

Organizational architecture is a metaphor of an image, and like traditional physical architecture it shapes the organizational space where life will take place. It also represents a systemic concept, which implies interdependencies between the organizational structure and other systems inside the organization in order to create a unique synergistic environment which will be more than just the sum of its parts. Some systems are competitive, effective and efficient, whereas others are not. Successful systems may be attributable to knowledge applied in designing the system or to the quality of management practiced during operations, or both.

Successful systems seem to have characteristics such as their simplicity, flexibility, reliability, economy, and acceptability according to Wikipedia (www.wikipedia. org) as illustrated in Figure 2.5:

- **Simplicity.** An effective organizational system need not be complex. On the contrary, simplicity in design is an extremely desirable quality. Consider the task of communicating information about the operation of a system and the allocation of its inputs. The task is not difficult when components are few and the relationships among them are straightforward. However, the problems of communication multiply with each successive stage of complexity.
- **Flexibility.** Conditions change and managers should be prepared to adjust operations accordingly. There are two ways to adjust to a changing operating environment: to design new systems or to modify operating systems. An existing system should not be modified to accommodate a change in objectives, but every system should be sufficiently flexible to integrate changes that may occur either in the environment or in the nature of the inputs.
- **Reliability.** System reliability is an important factor in organizations. Reliability is the consistency with which operations are maintained, and may vary from zero output (a complete breakdown or work stoppage) to a constant or predictable output. The typical system operates somewhere between these two extremes. The characteristics of reliability can be designed into the system by carefully selecting and arranging the operating components; the system is no more reliable than its weakest segment.
- **Economy.** An effective system is not necessarily an economical (efficient) system. It is often dysfunctional and expensive to develop much greater capacity for one segment of a system than for some other part. Building in redundancy or providing for every contingency usually neutralizes the operating efficiency of the system. When a system's objectives include achieving a particular task at the lowest possible cost, there must be some degree of trade-off between

Figure 2.5. Organizational architecture parameters for organizations

Simple	**Organizational system**	Complex
Rigid	**Adjustment**	Flexible
Low	**Reliability**	High
Inefficient	**Economy**	Efficient
Low	**Acceptability**	High

effectiveness and efficiency. When a system's objective is to perform a certain mission regardless of cost, there can be no trade-off.

- **Acceptability.** Any system, no matter how well designed, will not function properly unless it is accepted by the people who operate it. If the participants do not believe it will benefit them, are opposed to it, are pressured into using it, or think it is not a good system, it will not work properly. If a system is not accepted, two things can happen: (1) the system will be modified gradually by the people who are using it, or (2) the system will be used ineffectively and ultimately fail. Unplanned alterations in an elaborate system can nullify advantages associated with using the system.

Organizations are constructed, like any other kind of social system. An organization is observable through the actions and interactions of its members, both between themselves and wit people in the organization's environment. To be observable, an organization must have a domain for its activity, and it must have a set of objectives and goals. The basic elements in organization structuring include division of labor, structuring of work, and coordination as first suggested by Mintzberg (1979). Groth (1999) developed the idea of preconditions for organizing and suggested six areas where we quickly run into limits restricting organization building:

- **Capacity for work:** Both the need for organizations and their nature are strongly dependent on the nature and amount of work that has to be carried out.
- **Memory performance:** The brain has limitations in terms of storage capacity and retrieval capabilities.
- **Information processing:** The brain has limitations in terms of reasoning, problem solving and decision-making.
- **Communication:** The amount of information a person can absorb is limited by communication bandwidth.
- **Interaction:** How fast a person can interact with other persons is limited.
- **Emotion:** Ambition, likes and dislikes, instincts and preferences represent limitations.

According to Groth (1999), it is difficult to ascertain which of these abilities or properties are most important, but they all represent limitations for organizational design. Since organizational design is about developing and implementing strategy (Bryan & Joyce, 2007), it is important to be aware of human limitations. Organizations can be designed to gain from strengths and compensate for weaknesses, and to avoid threats and to prosper from opportunities. For example, hierarchy is efficient for setting aspirations, making decisions, assigning tasks, allocating resources, managing people who cannot direct themselves, and holding people accountable. Even in new times, hierarchy is needed to put boundaries around individuals and teams (Bryan & Joyce, 2007). All organizations are hierarchical, as compliance with authority is a universal feature of organizations. An authority structure is essential to decision-making and its implementation (Andersen, 2002).

Furthermore, interdependencies among elements of organizational design might represent both barriers and enablers of strategy development and implementation. Since organizations are complex entities composed of tightly interdependent and mutually supportive elements, performance is determined by the degree of alignment among the major elements. The marginal costs and benefits associated with any design element depend on the configuration of others (Rivkin & Siggelkow, 2003).

1.6   Organizational Cultures

Organizational culture is found to influence performance and absorptive capacity for interoperability and information resource integration. An organizational culture is a set of shared norms, values and perceptions, which develop when the members of an organization interact with each other and the surroundings. It is holistic, historically determined, socially constructed and difficult to change (Hofstede, Neuijen, Ohayv, & Sanders, 1990). Organizational culture might determine how the organization thinks, feels, and acts.

An occupational culture is a reduced, selective, and task-based version of culture that is shaped by the socially relevant worlds of the occupation (Christensen & Crank, 2001). Embedded in traditions and a history, occupational cultures contain accepted practices, rules, and principles of conduct that are applied to a variety of situations, and generalized rationales and beliefs (Bailey, 1995). For example, when one thinks about the investigation of a crime as a process of assembling knowledge in law enforcement, one begins to recognize that police officers are knowledge workers. The basic sets of raw material that police work with are information and interactions with people. How the police deal with these materials within their occupational culture is determined by a variety of factors, such as the skills and education police have (Fraser, 2004).

Occupational culture plays an important role in organizational performance and change. Barton (2004) identified occupational culture and its perpetuation as key barriers that have substantially impeded the success of reform agendas. Similarly, Kiely and Peek (2002) studied the culture of the British police. Interviewed inspectors and sergeants felt that most members of the organization shared the established values of the police service. In another study, Glomseth, Gottschalk and Solli-Sæther

(2007) found that occupational culture is a determinant of knowledge sharing and performance in police investigations.

To some extent, occupational culture contains what is taken for granted by members, invisible yet powerful constraints, and thus it connects cognition and action, environment and organization, in an entangling and interwoven tapestry. They act as socially validated sources one for the other (Bailey, 1995). Occupational culture arises from a set of tasks that are repeated and encapsulated into routines in various degrees, and a technology that is various and indirect in its effects (it is mediated by the organizational structure), producing a set of attitudes and an explanatory structure of belief (ideology). The tasks of policing are uncertain; they are various, unusual, and unpredictable in appearance, duration, content, and consequence. They are fraught with disorderly potential. The police officer is dependent on other officers for assistance, advice, training, working knowledge, protection in the case of threats from internal or external sources, and insulation against the public and periodic danger. The occupation emphasizes autonomy, both with respect to individual decision-making or what lawyers term 'discretion'; the public it serves and controls (officers with routinely experience adversarial relations with the public); and the rigid authority symbolized by the paramilitary structure of the organization. Finally, the occupational culture makes salient displaying, creating, and maintaining authority. The sources of the authority theme are multiple insofar as they draw on the state's authority, the public morality of the dominant classes, and the law (Bailey, 1995).

Organizational culture represents basic assumptions that are beliefs, values, ethical and moral codes, and ideologies that have become so ingrained that they tend to have dropped out of consciousness. These assumptions are unquestioned perceptions of truth, reality, ways of thinking and thinking about, and feeling that develop through repeated successes in solving problems over extended periods of time. Important basic assumptions are passed on to new members, often unconsciously.

Beliefs and values are consciously held cognitive and affective patterns. They provide explicit directions and justifications for patterns of organizational behavior, as well as the energy to enact them. Beliefs and values are also the birthplaces of basic assumptions. Police culture can be described as a confluence of themes (Christensen & Crank, 2001). Themes are areas of activity and sentiments associated with these activities, linked to each other by a dynamic affirmation. By dynamic affirmation is the idea that activities and dispositions are not easily separable ideas but reciprocally causal. Activities confirm predispositions, and predispositions lead to the selection of activities. Themes are developed around particular contours of the day-to-day working environment of the police.

CONCLUSION

A value configuration describes how value is created in a company (or government organization) for its customers. A value configuration shows how the most important business processes function to create value for customers. A value configuration represents the way a particular organization conducts business. In terms of value configurations, governments share similarities with business organizations.

REFERENCES

Afuah, A., & Tucci, C. L. (2003). *Internet business models and strategies* (2nd ed.). New York: McGraw-Hill.

Andersen, J. A. (2002). Organizational design: Two lessons to learn before reorganizing. *International Journal of Organization Theory and Behavior, 5*(3&4), 343-358.

Auteri, M., & Wagner, R. (2007). The organizational architecture of nonprofit governance: Economic calculation within an ecology of enterprises. *Public Organization Review, 7*(1), 57-68.

Bailey, W. G. (1995). *The encyclopedia of police science* (Second ed.). New York: Garland Publishing.

Barton, H. (2004). Cultural reformation: A case for intervention within the police service. *International Journal of Human Resources Development and Management, 4*(2), 191-199.

Bekkers, V. (2007). The government of back-office integration. Organizing co-operation between information domains. *Public Management Review, 9*(3), 377-300.

Bryan, L. L., & Joyce, C. I. (2007). Better strategy through organizational design. *McKinsey Quarterly*(2), 20-29.

Chatzkel, J. (2002). A conversation with Göran Roos. *Journal of Intellectual Capital, 3*(2), 96-117.

Chen, Z., Gangopadhyay, A., Holden, S. H., Karabatis, G., & McGuire, P. (2007). Semantic integration of government data for water quality management. *Government Information Quarterly, 24*(4), 716-735.

Christensen, W., & Crank, J. P. (2001). Police work and culture in a nonurban setting: An ethnographical analysis. *Police Quarterly, 4*(1), 69-98.

Donk, D. P. v., & Molloy, E. (2008). From organising as projects to projects as organisations. *International Journal of Project Management, 26*(2), 129-137.

Eckman, B. A., Bennet, C. A., Kaufman, J. H., & Tenner, J. W. (2007). Varieties of interoperability in the transformation of the health-care information infrastructure. *IBM Systems Journal, 46*(1), 19-41.

Esteves, J., & Joseph, R. C. (2008). A comprehensive framework for the assessment of eGovernment projects. *Government Information Quarterly, 25*(1), 404-437.

Ethiraj, S. K., & Levinthal, D. (2004). Bounded rationality and the search for organizational architecture: An evolutionary perspective on the design of organizations and their evolvability. *Administrative Science Quarterly, 49*(3), 404-437.

Fedorowicz, J., Gogan, J. L., & Williams, C. B. (2007). A collaborative network for first responders: Lessons from CapWIN case. *Government Information Quarterly, 24*(4), 785-807.

Fiss, P. C. (2007). A set-theoretical approach to organizational configurations. *Academy of Management Review, 32*(4), 1180-1198.

Frame, P. (1995). *Managing Projects in Organizations*. San Francisco: Jossey-Bass Publishers.

Fraser, C. (2004). Strategic information systems for policing. On *Police Executive Research Forum*. Washington, DC.

Galanter, M., & Palay, T. (1991). *Tournament of lawyers. The transformation of the big law firms*. Chicago: The University of Chicago Press.

Glomseth, R., Gottschalk, P., & Solli-Sæther, H. (2007). Occupational culture as determinant of knowledge sharing and performance in police investigations. *International Journal of the Sociology of Law, 35*(2), 96-107.

Gouscos, D., Kalikakis, M., Legal, M., & Papadopoulou, S. (2007). A general model of performance and quality for one-stop e-government service offerings. *Government Information Quarterly, 24*(4), 860-885.

Grant, G., McKnight, S., Uruthirapathy, A., & Brown, A. (2007). Designing governance for shared services organizations in the public service. *Government Information Quarterly, 24*(3), 533-538.

Groth, L. (1999). *Future Organizational Design*. Chichester, UK: John Wiley & Sons.

Hofstede, G., Neuijen, B., Ohayv, D. D., & Sanders, G. (1990). Measuring organizational cultures: A qualitative and quantitative study across twenty cases. *Administrative Science Quarterly, 35*(2), 286-316.

Kennedy, A. (2007). Winning the information wars. Collecting, sharing and analysing information in asset recovery investigations. *Journal of Financial Crime, 14*(4), 372-404.

Ketchen, D. J., Combs, J. G., Russel, C. J., Shook, C., Dean, M. A., Runge, J., et al. (1997). Organizational configurations and performance: A meta-analysis. *Academy of Management Journal, 40*(1), 223-240.

Kiely, J. A., & Peek, G. S. (2002). The Culture of the British police: Views of police officers. *The Service Industries Journal, 22*(1), 167-183.

Legner, C., & Lebreton, B. (2007). Business interoperability research: Present achievements and upcoming challenges. *Electronic Markets, 17*(3), 176-186.

Mintzberg, H. (1979). *The structuring of organizations.* Englewood Cliffs, NJ: Prentice-Hall.

Moussavou, J. (2006). Organizational architecture and decision-making. *The Journal of Portfolio Management, Fall*, 103-111.

Multilateral Interoperability Programme. (2003). Achieving international interoperability of command and control information systems (C2IS) at all levels. Retrieved July 2008, from www.mip-site.org

Porter, M. E. (1985). *Competitive advantage: Creating and sustaining competitive performance.* The Free Press.

Rivkin, J. W., & Siggelkow, N. (2003). Balancing search and stability: Interdependencies among elements of organizational design. *Management Science, 49*(3), 290-311.

Schooley, B. L., & Horan, T. A. (2007). Towards end-to-end government performance management: Case study of interorganizational information integration in emergency medical services (EMS). *Government Information Quarterly, 24*(4), 755-784.

Sheehan, N. T. (2002). *Reputation as a driver in knowledge-intensive service firms.* Unpublished doctoral thesis. Norwegian School of Management, Sandvika.

Stabell, C. B., & Fjeldstad, Ø. D. (1998). Configuring value for competitive advantage: On chains, shops and networks. *Strategic Management Journal, 19*(5), 413-437.

Wang, H., Song, Y., Hamilton, A., & Curwell, S. (2007). Urban information integration for advanced e-planning in Europe. *Government Information Quarterly, 24*(4), 736-754.

Chapter III
Resource Theory of Organizations

1.   RESOURCE THEORY OF ORGANIZATIONS

The resource theory of organizations is an influential theoretical framework for understanding how efficiency and effectiveness within organizations are achieved and how advantage might be sustained over time. This perspective focuses on the internal availability of resources in organizations. The theory assumes that organizations can be conceptualized as bundles of resources that those resources are heterogeneously distributed across organizations, and that resource differences persist over time (Eisenhardt & Martin, 2000).

First, this chapter describes the characteristics of organizational resources, strategic resources, IT resources, and slack resources. This chapter argues the importance of aligning IT resources to the organization's strategy, and a model for the effect of IT resources on organizational performance is presented. Finally, this chapter presents resource strategy as an approach which suggests that organizations should position themselves strategically based on their unique, valuable, and inimitable resources and capabilities.

1.1   Characteristics of Resources

Resources are at the heart of the resource theory. They are those specific assets that can be used to implement value-creating strategies. They include the local abilities or competencies that are fundamental to the strength of an organization such as skills in banking in money laundering investigations or in accounting in corporate tax authorities. As such, resources form the basis of unique value-creating strategies and their related activity systems that address specific functions in distinctive ways (Eisenhardt & Martin, 2000).

When one government agency wants information from another agency, then this information represents a resource for the asking agency. Wanted information is needed for the agency to perform required tasks. By obtaining information from the other agency, this agency is enabled to work properly. Obtained information represents a resource for the asking organization.

Generally, the central tenet in resource theory is that unique organizational resources of both tangible and intangible nature are the real source of competitive advantage. With resource theory, organizations are viewed as a collection of resources that are heterogeneously distributed within and across industries. Accordingly, what makes the performance of an organization distinctive is the unique bland of the resources it possesses. An organization's resources include not only its physical assets such as plant and location but also its competencies. The ability to leverage distinctive internal and external competencies relative to environmental situations ultimately affects the performance of the business.

Exploring competencies in the context of the management of information technology is a relatively recent development in the evolution of the information systems discipline. The importance of developing competencies that allow organizations to successfully take advantage of information in their specific context has been noted. The concept of competence in the information systems literature is predominantly focused upon individual competence in the form of IT skill sets rather than treated as an organizational construct. The focus has been on the technology supply side and individuals' skills, emphasizing the requirement for IT professionals to have not just technical skills but also business and interpersonal skills. More recently, change agentry as a skill for IT professionals has been proposed. The implication of this literature stream is that the solution to the problem of lacking benefits from IT can be solved by equipping IT specialists with additional skills. The inference is that the inability to deliver value from information arises from shortcomings in the IT function and among IT professionals (Peppard, Lambert, & Edwards, 2000).

Interoperability gives a client organization access to resources in the vendor organization as the vendor handles information and information technology functions for the client. Vendor resources can produce innovation, which is essential for long-term survival of the client. Quinn (2000) argues that the time is right for outsourcing innovation. Four powerful forces are currently driving the innovation revolution. First, demand is growing fast in the global economy, creating a host of new specialist markets sufficiently large to attract innovation. Second, the supply of scientists, technologists and knowledge workers has skyrocketed, as have knowledge bases and the access to them. Third, interaction capabilities have grown. Fourth, new incentives have emerged.

The essence of the resource theory of the organization lies in its emphasis on the internal resources available to the organization, rather than on the external opportunities and threats dictated by industry conditions. Organizations are considered to be highly heterogeneous, and the bundles of resources available to each organization are different. This is both because organizations have different initial resource endowments and because managerial decisions affect resource accumulation and the direction of organization growth as well as resource utilization (Løwendahl, 2000).

The resource theory of the organization holds that, in order to generate sustainable competitive advantage, a resource must provide economic value and must be presently scarce, difficult to imitate, non-substitutable, and not readily obtainable in factor markets. This theory rests on two key points. First, that resources are the determinants of organization performance and second, that resources must be rare, valuable, difficult to imitate and non-substitutable by other rare resources. When the latter occurs, a competitive advantage has been created. Resources can simultaneously be characterized as valuable, rare, non-substitutable, and inimitable. To the extent that an organization's physical assets, infrastructure, and workforce satisfy these criteria, they qualify as resources. A organization's performance depends fundamentally on its ability to have a distinctive, sustainable competitive advantage, which derives from the possession of organization-specific resources (Priem & Butler, 2001).

The resource theory is a useful perspective in strategic management. Research on the competitive implications of such organization resources as knowledge, learning, culture, teamwork, and human capital, was given a significant boost by resource theory – a theory that indicated it was these kinds of resources that were most likely to be sources of sustainable competitive advantage for organizations (Barney, 2001).

Organizations' resource endowments, particularly intangible resources, are difficult to change except over the long term. For example, although human resources may be mobile to some extent, capabilities may not be valuable for all organizations or even for their competitors. Some capabilities are based on organization-specific knowledge, and others are valuable when integrated with additional individual capabilities and specific organization resources. Therefore, intangible resources are more likely than tangible resources to produce a competitive advantage. In particular, intangible organization-specific resources such as knowledge allow organizations to add value to incoming factors of production (Hitt, Bierman, Shumizu, & Kochhar, 2001). Resource theory attributes advantage in an industry to an organization's control over bundles of unique material, human, organizational and locational resources and skills that enable unique value-creating strategies. An organization's resources are said to be a source of competitive advantage to the degree that they are scarce, specialized, appropriable, valuable, rare, and difficult to imitate or substitute.

A fundamental idea in resource theory is that an organization must continually enhance its resources and capabilities to take advantage of changing conditions. Optimal growth involves a balance between the exploitation of existing resource positions and the development of new resource positions. Thus, an organization would be expected to develop new resources after its existing resource base has been fully utilized. Building new resource positions is important if the organization is to achieve sustained growth. When unused productive resources are coupled with changing managerial knowledge, unique opportunities for growth are created (Pettus, 2001).

The term resource is derived from Latin, "resurgere", which means, "to rise" and implies an aid or expedient for reaching an end. A resource implies a potential means to achieve an end, or as something that can be used to create value. The first strategy textbooks outlining a holistic perspective focused on how resources needed to be allocated or deployed to earn benefits. The interest in the term was for a long time linked to the efficiency of resource allocation, but this focus has later been expanded to issues such as resource accumulation, resource stocks and resource flows (Haanes, 1997).

The resource theory prescribes that organization resources are the main driver of organization performance. The resources to conceive choose, and implement strategies are likely to be heterogeneously distributed across organizations, which in turn are posited to account for the differences in organization performance. This theory posits that organization resources are rent yielding, when they are valuable, rare, imperfectly imitable, and non-substitutable. Moreover, resources tend to survive competitive imitation because of isolating mechanisms such as causal ambiguity, time-compression diseconomies, embeddedness, and path dependencies (Ravichandran & Lertwongsatien, 2005).

Organizations develop organization-specific resources and then renew these to respond to shifts in the business environment. Organizations develop dynamic capabilities to adapt to changing environments. According to Pettus (2001), the term dynamic refers to the capacity to renew resource positions to achieve congruence with changing environmental conditions. A capability refers to the key role of strategic management in appropriately adapting, integrating, and reconfiguring internal and external organizational skills, resources, and functional capabilities to match the requirements of a changing environment.

If organizations are to develop dynamic capabilities, learning is crucial. Change is costly; therefore, the ability of organizations to make necessary adjustments depends upon their ability to scan the environment to evaluate markets and competitors and to quickly accomplish reconfiguration and transformation ahead of competition. However, history matters. Thus, opportunities for growth will involve dynamic capabilities closely related to existing capabilities. As such, opportunities will be most effective when they are close to previous resource use (Pettus, 2001).

According to Johnson and Scholes (2002), successful strategies are dependent on the organization having the strategic capability to perform at the level that is required for success. So the first reason why an understanding of strategic capability is important is concerned with whether an organization's strategies continue to fit the environment in which the organization is operating and the opportunities and threats that exist. Many of the issues of strategy development are concerned with changing a strategic capability better to fit a changing environment. Understanding strategic capability is also important from another perspective. The organization's capability may be the leading edge of strategic developments, in the sense that new opportunities may be created by stretching and exploiting the organization's capability either in ways which competitors find difficult to match or in genuinely new directions, or both. This requires organizations to be innovative in the way they develop and exploit their capability.

In this perspective, strategic capability is about providing products or services to customers that are valued - or might be valued in the future. An understanding of what customers' value is the starting point. The discussion then moves to whether an organization has the resources to provide products and services that meet these customer requirements.

A resource is meant to be anything that could be thought of as a human or non-human strength of a given organization. More formally, an organization's resources at a given time can be defined as those (tangible and intangible) assets that are tied to the organization over a substantial period of time. Examples of resources are brand names, in-house knowledge of technology, employment of skilled personnel, trade contracts, machinery, efficient procedures, capital etc. According to the economic school, resources include human capital, structural capital, relational capital and financial capital.

Priem and Butler (2001) find it problematic that virtually anything associated with a organization can be a resource, because this notion suggests that guidelines for dealing in certain ways with certain categories of resources might be operationally valid, whereas other categories of resources might be inherently difficult for practitioners to measure and manipulate. One example of a resource that might be difficult to measure and manipulate is tacit knowledge. Some have argued for tacit knowledge – that understanding gained from experience but that sometimes cannot be expressed to another person and is unknown to oneself – as a source of competitive advantage. Tacit knowledge in this sense is unknown to its owner until it emerges in a situation of knowledge application.

Another example is the 'CEO resources'. Recommendations have been made to top managers of poorly performing organizations that they are the cause of the problem and should think about voluntarily exiting the organization. This is a case where viewing CEOs as a resources would have more prescriptive implications for boards of directors than for the CEOs themselves. Similarly, viewing boards of directors, resources would have more prescriptive implications for the CEOs who appoint boards or the governments that regulate them than the boards themselves. Thus, some resources may be of less interest to strategy than others, depending in part on whether the resource can be manipulated and in part on the group - frequently CEOs - for whom recommendations are desired. Identifying specific resources that may be particularly effective for certain actors in certain contexts might be a helpful first step in establishing boundaries for (and contributions of) the resource view in strategic management (Priem & Butler, 2001).

Heijden (2001) measured IT core capabilities for electronic commerce. Capabilities include organization-specific routines, processes, skills, and resources. They need to be built through learning processes and cannot be readily bought. Heijden (2001) listed a total of nine core capabilities for the IS function: IS/IT governance, business systems thinking, relationship building, designing technical architecture, making technology work, informed buying, contract facilitation, contract monitoring, and vendor development.

1.2   Characteristics of Strategic Resources

Barney (2002) discusses how value, rarity, non-duplication, and organization can be brought together into a single framework to understand the return potential associated with exploiting any of a organization's resources and capabilities. The framework consists of the following five steps (Barney, 2002):

1.   If a resource or capability controlled by an organization is *not valuable*, that resource will not enable an organization to choose or implement strategies that exploit environmental opportunities or neutralize environmental threats. Organizing to exploit this resource will increase an organization's costs or decrease its revenues. These types of resources are weaknesses. Organizations will either have to fix these weaknesses or avoid using them when choosing and

implementing strategies. If organizations do exploit these kinds of resources and capabilities, they can expect to put themselves at a competitive disadvantage compared to organizations that either do not possess these non-valuable resources or do not use them in conceiving and implementing strategies. Organizations at a competitive disadvantage are likely to earn below-normal economic profits.

2. If a resource or capability is *valuable but not rare*, exploiting this resource in conceiving and implementing strategies will generate competitive parity and normal economic performance. Exploiting these valuable-but-not-rare resources will generally not create above-normal economic performance for an organization, but failure to exploit them can put an organization at a competitive disadvantage. In this sense, valuable-but-not-rare resources can be thought of as organizational strengths.

3. If a resource or capability is *valuable and rare but not costly to imitate*, exploiting this resource will generate a temporary competitive advantage for an organization and above-normal economic profits. An organization that exploits this kind of resource is, in an important sense, gaining a first-mover advantage, because it is the first organization that is able to exploit a particular resource. However, once competing organizations observe this competitive advantage, they will be able to acquire or develop the resources needed to implement this strategy through direct duplication or substitution at no cost disadvantage compared to the first-moving organization. Over time, any competitive advantage that the first mover obtained would be competed away as other organizations imitate the resources needed to compete. However, between the time a organization gains a competitive advantage by exploiting a valuable and rare but imitable resource or capability, and the time that competitive advantage is competed away through imitation, the first-moving organization can earn above-normal economic performance. Consequently, this type of resource or capability can be thought of as an organizational strength and distinctive competence.

4. If a resource is *valuable, rare, and costly to imitate*, exploiting this resource will generate a sustained competitive advantage and above-normal economic profits. In this case, competing organizations face a significant cost disadvantage in imitating a successful organization's resources and capabilities, and thus cannot imitate this organization's strategies. This advantage may reflect the unique history of the successful organization, causal ambiguity about which resources to imitate, or the socially complex nature of these resources and capabilities. In any case, attempts to compete away the advantages of organizations that exploit these resources will not generate above-normal or even normal performance for imitating organizations. Even if these organizations were able to acquire or develop the resources and capabilities in question,

the very high costs of doing so would put them at a competitive disadvantage compared to the organization that already possessed the valuable, rare, and costly to imitate resources. These kinds of resources and capabilities are organizational strengths and sustainable distinctive competencies.

5.   The question of organization operates as an adjustment factor in the framework. If an organization with a resource that is *valuable, rare, and costly to imitate, is disorganized,* some of its potential above-normal return could be lost. If the organization completely fails to organize itself to take advantage of this resource, it could actually lead the organization that has the potential for above-normal performance to earn normal or even below-normal performance.

In our e-government perspective, one organization achieves higher benefits from interoperability when the resource provided from another organization is strategic, i.e., has attributes as listed above.

Barney (2001) discusses how value and rarity of resources can be determined. *Value* is a question of conditions under which resources will and will not be valuable. Models of the competitive environment within which an organization competes can determine value. Such models fall into two large categories: (1) efforts to use structure-conduct-performance-based models to specify conditions under which different organization resources will be valuable and (2) efforts to determine the value of organization resources that apply other models derived from industrial organization models of perfect and imperfect competition.

As an example of resource value determination, Barney (2001) discusses the ability of a cost leadership strategy to generate sustained competitive advantage. Several organization attributes may be associated with cost leadership, such as volume-derived economies of scale, cumulative volume-derived learning curve economies and policy choices. These organization attributes can be shown to generate economic value in at least some market settings. The logic used to demonstrate the value of these attributes is a market structure logic that is consistent with traditional microeconomics. After identifying the conditions under which cost leadership can generate economic value, it is possible to turn to the conditions under which cost leadership can be a source of competitive advantage (i.e. rare) and sustained competitive advantage (i.e. rare and costly to imitate).

The resource theory postulates that some resources will have a higher value for one organization than for other organizations. The reasons why the value of resources may be organization-specific are multiple and include (Haanes, 1997): the experience of working together as a team, the organization possessing superior knowledge about its resources, the bundling of the resources, and the existence of co-specialized or complementary assets.

The value of a given resource may change over time as the market conditions change, e.g., in terms of technology, customer preferences or industry structure. Thus, it is often argued that organizations need to maintain a dynamic, as opposed to static, evaluation of the value of different resources.

Rarity is a question of how many competing organizations possess a particular valuable resource. If only one competing organization possesses a particular valuable resource, then that organization can gain a competitive advantage, i.e. it can improve its efficiency and effectiveness in ways that competing organizations cannot. One example of this form of testable assertion is mentioned by Barney (2001). The example is concerned with organizational culture as a source of competitive advantage. If only one competing organization possesses a valuable organizational culture (where the value of that culture is determined in ways that are exogenous to the organization), then that organization can gain a competitive advantage, i.e. it can improve its efficiency and effectiveness in ways that competing organizations cannot. Both these assertions are testable. If an organization uniquely possesses a valuable resource and cannot improve its efficiency and effectiveness in ways that generate competitive advantages, then these assertions are contradicted. One could test these assertions by measuring the extent to which a organization uniquely possesses valuable resources, e.g. valuable organizational culture, measuring the activities that different organizations engage in to improve their efficiency and effectiveness, and then seeing if there are some activities a organization with the unique culture engages in to improve its effectiveness and efficiency – activities not engaged in by other competing organizations.

Efficient organizations can sustain their competitive advantage only if their resources can neither be extended freely nor imitated by other organizations. Hence, in order for resources to have the potential to generate rents, they must be rare. Valuable, but common, resources cannot by themselves represent sources of competitive advantage because competitors can access them. Nobody needs to pay extra for obtaining a resource that is not held in limited supply.

In addition to value and rarity, inimitability has to be determined. *Inimitability* can be determined through barriers to imitation and replication. The extent of barriers and impediments against direct and indirect imitation determine the extent of inimitability. One effective barrier to imitation is that competitors fail to understand the organization's sources of advantage. The lack of understanding can be caused by tacitness, complexity and specificity that form bases for competitive advantage (Haanes, 1997).

Several authors have categorized resources. A common categorization is tangibles versus intangibles. Tangibles are relatively clearly defined and easy to identify. Tangible resources include plants, technology, land, and geographical location, access to raw materials, capital, equipment and legal resources. Tangible resources tend to be property-based and may also include databases, licenses, patents, registered designs and trademarks, as well as other property rights that are easily bought and sold.

Intangibles are more difficult to define and also to study empirically. Intangible resources encompass skills, knowledge, organizational capital, relationships, capabilities and human capital, as well as brands, company and product reputation, networks, competences, perceptions of quality and the ability to manage change. Intangible resources are generally less easy to transfer than tangible resources, as the value of an intangible resource is difficult to measure (Haanes, 1997).

Based on this discussion, we might add to the framework by Barney (2002) four more steps:

6.   If our organization with a resource that is *valuable, rare, costly to imitate, and organized is easy to substitute*, some of its potential above-normal return could be lost. If a competing organization is able to do the same task as our organization by applying a different resource, which can substitute our resource for the same task, it could actually lead our organization that has the potential for above-normal performance to earn normal or even below-normal performance.

7.   If our organization with a resource that is *valuable, rare, costly to imitate, organized and difficult to substitute is easy to move*, then again we might be in trouble in terms of not gaining sustained competitive advantage. In this case, a resource might leave the organization and join a competing organization.

8.   If our organization with a resource that is *valuable, rare, costly to imitate, organized, difficult to substitute and difficult to move, is difficult to combine*, then some potential benefits from the resource is lost. This is because many resources are of little value except when they are combined with other resources.

9.   If our organization with a resource that is *valuable, rare, costly to imitate, organized, difficult to substitute, difficult to move and easy to combine is difficult to transfer*, then we might have difficulty in transferring to clients the value that they are paying for. Here we make a distinction between moving (not desired action) and transferring (desired action).

1.3   Strategic IT Resources

The resource view started to appear in IT research one decade ago. Now IT resources can be compared to one another and, perhaps more importantly, can be compared with non-IT resources. Thus, the resource view promotes cross-functional studies through comparisons with other organization resources. In the beginning of resource studies of IT resources, IT was divided into three assets, which together with processes contribute to business value. These three IT assets were labeled human assets (e.g., technical skills, business understanding, and problem-solving orientation), technology assets (e.g., physical IT assets, technical platforms, databases, architectures, standards) and relationship assets (e.g., partnerships with other divisions, client relationships, top management sponsorship, shared risk and responsibility). IT processes were defined as planning ability, cost effective operations and support, and fast delivery. This categorization was later modified to include IT infrastructure, human IT resources, and IT-enabled intangibles.

Wade and Hulland (2004) presented a typology of IT resources, where the IT resources held by an organization can be sorted into three types of processes: inside-out, outside-in, and spanning. Inside-out resources are deployed from inside the organization in response to market requirements and opportunities, and tend to be internally focused. In contrast, outside-in resources are externally oriented, placing an emphasis on anticipated market requirements, creating durable customer relationships, and understanding competitors. Finally, spanning resources, which involve both internal and external analysis, are needed to integrate the organization's inside-out and outside-in resources.

Inside-out resources include IS infrastructure, IS technical skills, IS development, and cost effective IS operations (Wade & Hulland, 2004):

- **IT infrastructure.** Many components of the IT infrastructure (such as off-the-shelf computer hardware and software) convey no particular strategic benefit due to lack of rarity, ease of imitation, transferability and ready mobility. Thus, the types of IT infrastructure of importance are either proprietary or inimitable and complex. Despite research attempts to focus on the non-imitable and non-transferable aspects of IT infrastructure, the IT infrastructure resource has generally not been found to be a source of sustained relative advantage for government organizations.

- **IT technical skills.** IT technical skills are a result of the appropriate, updated and relevant technology skills, relating to systems hardware, operations procedure and software that are held by the IS/IT employees of an organization. Such skills do not include only current technical and technological knowledge, but also the ability and initiative to deploy, use, and manage that knowledge. Thus, this resource is focused on required technical skills that are advanced, complex, and, therefore, difficult to imitate. Although the relative mobility of IS/IT personnel tends to be high within and among organizations, some IS skills cannot be easily transferred, such as corporate-level business knowledge assets and technology integration skills, and, thus, these resources can become a source of sustained relative advantage for a government agency.

- **IT development** refers to the capability to develop or acquire new technologies, as well as a general level of alertness to and interest in emerging technologies and trends that allow an organization to quickly take advantage of new advances in technology. Thus, IT development includes capabilities associated with managing a systems development life-cycle that is capable of supporting continuous improvements in government service provision, and should therefore lead to superior organizational performance.

- **Cost effective IT operations.** This resource encompasses the ability to provide efficient and cost-effective IT operations on a predictable ongoing basis. Organizations with greater efficiency can develop a long-term efficiency and productivity advantage by using this capability to reduce costs and develop a cost leadership position in the public sector. In the context of IS operations, the ability to avoid large, persistent cost overruns, unnecessary downtime, and system failure are likely to be important success factors for superior government performance. Furthermore, the ability to develop and manage IT systems of appropriate quality that function effectively can be expected to have a significant and positive impact on performance.

Outside-in resources include external relationship management and responsiveness to market (Wade & Hulland, 2004):

- **External relationship management.** This resource represents the organization's ability to manage linkages between the IT function and personal as well as organizational stakeholders outside the organization. It can manifest itself as skills and competence to work with external suppliers to develop relevant and efficient systems and infrastructure requirements for the organization, to manage transactional relationships with outsourcing partners, or to manage social as well as contractual customer relationships by providing solutions, support, and/or customer service. Many large IT departments in the public sector rely on external partners for a significant portion of their development and operational work. The ability to cooperate with partners and manage these relationships is an important organizational resource potentially leading to superior organizational performance.

- **Public responsiveness.** Market responsiveness is based on the collection of information from external sources such as customers, vendors and media. In addition, an agency's user intelligence across departments is determining the organization's response to that learning. Public responsiveness includes the ability to initiate and manage new projects rapidly and to react quickly to changes in the population and the user community. A key aspect of public responsiveness is strategic flexibility, which allows the management to undertake strategic change when necessary.

Spanning resources include IS-business partnerships and IS planning and change management (Wade & Hulland, 2004):

- **IS-business partnerships.** This capability represents the processes of integration and alignment between the IS function and other functional areas or departments of the organization as well as top management. The importance of IS alignment, particularly with business strategy as well as user requirements, has been well documented. This resource has variously been referred to as synergy, assimilation, exploration, exploitation and partnerships. All of these studies recognize the importance of building relationships and alliances internally within the organization between the IS function and other areas or departments. Such relationships help to span the traditional gaps and reduce mutual skepticism that tends to exist between functions and departments, resulting in superior government position and organization performance. An element of this resource is the support for inter-organizational collaboration within the public sector.

- **IS planning and change management.** The capabilities to plan, implement, manage, and use appropriate technology architectures and standards also helps to span these gaps. Key aspects of this resource include the ability to anticipate future changes and growth, to understand technology trends, to choose platforms (including hardware, network, and software standards) that can accommodate this change, and to effectively manage the resulting technology change and growth. This resource has been defined variously in previous research as "understanding the business case", "problem solving orientation", "strategic instinct" and "capacity to manage IT change". It includes the ability of IS managers to understand how technologies can and should be used to the best of business processes and strategies, as well as how to motivate and manage IS personnel through the change process.

From a resource perspective, Ravichandran and Lertwongsatien (2005) argue that IS resources that are inimitable and valuable can be rent yielding. Technology assets such as networks and databases are unlikely to be rent yielding, since they could be easily procured in factor markets. However, combining hardware and software assets to create a flexible and sophisticated IT infrastructure can be non-imitable, because creating such an infrastructure requires carefully melding technology components to fit organization needs and priorities. In addition to sophisticated IT infrastructure, skilled human resources, relationships between the IS department and user departments, and IS managerial knowledge are valuable resources that are posited to be rent yielding.

In order to explore the usefulness of the resource theory for IT resources, it is necessary to explicitly recognize the characteristics and attributes of resources that lead them to become strategically important. Although organizations possess many resources, only a few of these have the potential to lead the organization to a position of sustained competitive advantage. What is it, then, that separates regular resources from those that confer a sustainable strategic benefit?

According to Wade and Hulland (2004), resource theorists have approached this question by identifying sets of resource attributes that might conceptually influence a organization's competitive position. Under this view, only resources exhibiting all of these attributes can lead to a sustained competitive advantage for the organization. We have already mentioned Barney's (2001) attributes of value, rareness, inimitability, non-substitutability, combination and exploration.

In addition, an important seventh attribute is immobile. Once an organization establishes a competitive advantage through the strategic use of resources, competitors will likely attempt to amass comparable resources in order to share in the advantage. A primary source of resources is factor markets. If organizations are able to acquire the resources necessary to imitate a rival's advantage, the rival's advantage will be short-lived. Thus, a requirement for sustained competitive advantage is that resources be imperfectly mobile or non-tradable.

To govern IT resources in an efficiently and effectively, it is necessary to understand the strategic attributes of each resource. In Table 3.1, an example illustrates of how strategic IT resources can be identified. The scale from 1 (little extent) to 5 (great extent) is applied. In this example, we see that IT infrastructure is the IT resource with the greatest potential to lead to sustained competitive advantage, which would contradict that the IT infrastructure resource has generally not been found to be a source of sustained competitive advantage for organizations. On the other hand, cost-effective IT operations have the least potential.

Wade and Hulland (2004) suggest that some of the resources create competitive advantage, while others sustain that advantage. A distinction is made between resources that help the organization attain a competitive advantage and those that help the organization to sustain the advantage. These two types of resource attributes can be thought of as, respectively, ex ante and ex post limits to competition. Ex ante limits to competition suggest that prior to any organizations establishing a superior resource position, there must be limited competition for that position. If any organization wishing to do so can acquire and deploy resources to achieve the position, it cannot by definition be superior. Attributes in this category include value, rarity, and appropriateness. Ex post limits to competition mean that subsequent to an organization's gaining a superior position and earning rents, there must be forces that limit competition for those rents. Attributes in this category include replicate ability, substitutability, and mobility.

Table 3.1. IT resources in terms of strategic importance based on attributes

Attributes Resources	Valuable	Rare	Exploitable	Inimitable	Non-substitutable	Combinable	Immobile	Total
IT infrastructure	4	2	5	5	2	5	4	27
IT technical skills	4	2	3	3	4	4	3	23
IT development	4	3	3	3	4	3	2	22
Cost-effective IT operations	4	2	3	2	4	3	1	19

Damianides (2005) applied a different approach to identify resources. He defined the following naturally grouped processes of IT resources: plan and organize, acquire and implement, deliver and support, and monitor and evaluate. He also developed an IT governance checklist, listing questions to ask to uncover IT issues, questions to ask to find out how management addresses the IT issues, and questions to self-assess IT governance practices.

Melville, Kraemer and Gurbaxani (2004) developed an integrative model of IT business value to link information technology and organizational performance. In a resource perspective, they found that IT is a valuable resource, but the extent and dimensions are dependent upon internal and external factors, including complementary organizational resources of the organization and its trading partners, as well as the competitive and macro environment.

Similarly, Santhanam and Hartono (2003) applied resource theory to link information technology capability to organization performance. Their results indicate that organizations with superior IT capability indeed exhibit superior current and sustained organization performance when compared to average industry performance, even after adjusting for effects of prior organization performance.

1.4   Slack Resources

Ang (1993) studied the etiology of IT outsourcing, and this section references her work. She argues that any analysis of outsourcing will typically incorporate the effects of managerial discretionary power on substantive administrative choices. Inclusion of managerial-behavioral factors to understanding outsourcing is consistent with the view of managerial choices to be the primary link between an organization and its environment. The importance of managerial discretion in the operations of the organization has been widely acknowledged in organization theory. In general, the separation of ownership from control of the organization gives rise to problems of controlling managerial behavior. It can be emphasized that when ownership is thinly spread over a large number of shareholders in an organization, control lies in the hands of the managers who themselves own only a tiny fraction of the organization's equity. These circumstances permit managers a greater discretion and decision latitude over substantive domains such as resource allocation, administrative choices, and product market selection.

Organizations with abundant slack tend to induce greater managerial discretion. Slack is defined as the difference between total resources and total necessary payments. It refers to the excess that remains once an organization has paid its various internal and external constituencies to maintain their cooperation. Slack can further be defined as a cushion of excess resources available in an organization that will either solve many organization problems or facilitate the pursuit of goals outside the realm of those dictated by optimization principles. An organization's slack reflects its ability to adapt to unknown or uncertain future changes in its environment. Accordingly, uncommitted or transferable slack resources would expand the array of options available to management. Instead of distributing slack resources back to shareholders, managers tend to retain and invest slack resources in new employees, new equipment, and other assets to promote asset capitalization. One primary reason for retaining earnings within the organization is that increased asset capitalization, the primary indicator of organization size, enhances the social prominence, public prestige, and political power of senior executives.

Investments in IT represent a major approach to asset capitalization in organizations. IT may symbolize organization growth, advancement, and progress. Because investments in IT can promote social prominence and public prestige, managers are induced to utilize slack resources to internalize IS services. Inducements toward investments in in-house IS services are further reinforced by well-publicized case studies that demonstrate the competitive advantage and new business opportunities afforded by IT. The above reasoning suggests that managers may exhibit a penchant for building up internal IT resources such as IS employees, equipment, and computer capacity when organizations possess slack resources. In contrast, when slack resources are low, managers tend to conserve resources in response to the anxiety provoked by loss of financial resources. Anxiety is provoked because the loss of financial resources is often attributed to managerial incompetence and organizational ineffectiveness. As a result, leaders are more likely to be blamed and replaced when financial performance is poor. In response to the anxiety provoked by loss of financial resources, decision makers have been observed to reduce costs through downsizing the company by selling off physical assets and laying off workers.

Companies may even sell IT assets at inflated rates to external service providers to generate short-term financial slack. The companies then reimburse the service provider by paying higher annual fees for a long-term outsourcing contract lasting eight to ten years. In other words, long term facilities management contracts can be drawn where the service providers agree to purchase corporate assets, such as computer equipment, at prices substantially higher than the market value and to provide capital to the company by purchasing stock from the company. Arrangements such as these permit companies to maintain capital, defer losses on the disposition of assets, and at the same time, show an increase in financial value on the balance sheet. But, because these arrangements also involve companies paying higher fees over the life of the contract, company financial statements are thus artificially inflated and do not reflect the true financial picture of the institution.

According to Ang (1993), when slack resources are low, we would expect organizations to downsize internal IS services by selling off IT assets, and reducing IS personnel and occupancy expenses; in effect, outsourcing IS services. Thus, we would expect that organizations are less likely to outsource when slack resources are high and more likely to outsource when slack resources are low.

Besides managerial discretion over slack resources, top management's perception of the criticality of IT may differ. According to the dependence-avoidance perspective of the organization, organizations will avoid comprising their autonomy, particularly when the resource is vital for the organization's survival. The strength of an organization's aversion to loss of autonomy is thus a function of the criticality of the resource. The organization will proactively struggle to avoid external dependency, which is, outsourcing, regardless of efficiency considerations as long as it depends on IT for survival. The value of IT for competitive advantage intensifies the pressure on organizations to internalize sophisticated IS services to avoid leakage of competitive information.

Although it is generally accepted that IT is critical for information-intensive organizations, not all members of top management teams attach the same degree of criticality to IT. Perceptions of the CIOs and CEOs of IT importance tend to be misaligned. While CIOs recognize IT as vital to an organization's strategy, CEOs with little background in IT tend to regard IS services as back-room operations, an expense to be controlled rather than a strategic investment to be capitalized. Generally, CEOs' perceptions of IT criticality are as important as, if not more important than, those of the CIOs' with respect to IS sourcing decisions because IS investments represent a significant financial outlay for corporations. Sometimes management policies and direction of IT use are dictated by the CEOs' psychological involvement and participation in IS. Thus, we would expect that the greater the perceived criticality of IT to the organization, the less likely the organization will outsource its IS services (Ang, 1993).

1.5   Aligning IT Resources to the Organization's Strategy

Strategic alignment includes enterprise wide strategic planning, practical strategic planning, and the importance of the CIO's involvement as a full participant in the strategic planning process and strategic resource management. Once the executive team agrees on the strategic plan, it is the CIO's responsibility to see that the IT resources are aligned with those strategies. The CIO works to align resources to strategy on two levels: within the IT organization and its strategies, and those of the IT organization within the company as a whole. Once the strategic plan for the IT organization is in alignment with the overall company's strategic plan, the CIO aligns the IT resources to the IT organization's strategic plan and validates that alignment with the strategic plans of the peers and partners. Real alignment means that all local strategic plans support the achievement of company strategy. As an enabler of local and global strategy, the CIO and the IT organization figure as one of the company's primary strategic resources (Schubert, 2004).

Alignment is the capacity to demonstrate a positive relationship between information technologies and accepted measures of performance. The means by which alignment takes place is the allocation of resources. Understanding which and how many resources are needed and how much time is required to accomplish goals and meet commitments is key to a CIO's success and to the success of the IT organization (Schubert, 2004).

When information technology human capital is a strategic resource, its effective management represents a significant organizational capability. Ferratt, Agarwal, Brown and Moore (2005) applied configuration theory to examine organizational practices related to the management of IT human capital. Organizations manage human capital by instituting a variety of human resource and work practices. Such practices typically include activities associated with recruiting workers with desired competencies, providing training and development opportunities, designing jobs and performance appraisal processes, developing compensation systems, and the like. Collectively, this set of practices for managing workers is an organization's configuration of human resource management (HRM) practices and is a proximal determinant of significant outcomes, such as employee turnover, job performance, job satisfaction, and organization performance.

Ferratt et al. (2005) ask the question: Given the potentially bewildering variety in practices that organizations can implement, how do CIOs make strategic choices about IT HRM practices? There are at least three choices here. One theoretical perspective, the universalistic approach, argues that there is a set of HRM practices that is effective across multiple organizational contexts regardless of situational contingencies. This best practice or high performance work system approach exhorts all organizations to implement specific practices for managing workers, e.g., extensive training and incentive pay, to realize desired outcomes. A second perspective, the contingency approach, suggests that the effects of HRM practices on outcomes are moderated by a variety of contingency variables such as organization strategy. Finally, the configuration perspective focuses attention on patterns of HRM practices that exhibit nonlinear, synergistic effects on outcomes. Configuration theories therefore focus on the identification of sets of practices, recognizing that the benefit of adopting one practice may increase with the adoption of other complementary practices.

Building on the theoretical foundation of configuration analysis and previous research in management of human capital, Ferratt et al. (2005) empirically investigated predictions about the relationship between different bundles of human resource practices and IT staff turnover rates. They developed two hypotheses regarding the relationship of IT HRM configurations to turnover. They tested these hypotheses based on a field survey of more than 100 IT organizations. The first hypothesis suggested that organizations with a human capital focused configuration for managing IT professionals will have significantly lower IT staff turnover rates than organizations with a task focused configuration for managing IT professionals. This hypothesis was confirmed in the empirical study. The second hypothesis suggested that organizations with intermediate IT HRM configurations will have IT staff turnover rates higher than those organizations with a human capital focused configuration and lower than those organizations with a task focused configuration. Intermediate configurations represent strategies for IT professionals between the extremes of short-term and long-term investment strategies. This hypothesis was not confirmed in the empirical study.

1.6   Effect of IT Resources on Organizational Performance

Ravichandran and Lertwongsatien (2005) drew on resource theory to examine how information systems resources and capabilities affect organization performance. This section references their work. A basic premise in their work was that an organization's performance could be explained by how effective the organization is in using information technology to support and enhance its core competencies. It was assumed that it is the targeted use of IS assets that is likely to be rent yielding.

Ravichandran and Lertwongsatien (2005) developed the theoretical underpinnings of this premise and proposed a model that interrelates IS resources, IS capabilities, IT support for core competencies, and organization performance. The model was empirically tested using data collected from 129 organizations in the United States. The results provide strong support for the research model and suggest that variation in organization performance could be explained by the extent to which IT is used to support and enhance an organization's core competencies. The results also support the proposition that an organization's ability to use IT to support its core competencies is dependent on IS functional capabilities, which, in turn, are dependent on the nature of human, technology, and relationship resources of the IS department.

Core competencies are the basis for organizations to compete in the market. Core competencies can be categorized into market-access, integrity-related, and functionality-related competencies. Market-access competencies include all those that allow an organization to be in close proximity to its customers, identify their needs effectively, and respond in a timely manner to shifts in customer needs and tastes. Capabilities to segment and target markets precisely and tailor offerings to match the demands of customers are examples of market-access competency. Integrity-related competencies include those that allow an organization to offer reliable products and services at competitive prices and deliver them with minimal inconvenience. Efficient manufacturing operations, streamlined supply chains, and integrated business processes are some indicators of integrity-related competencies. Finally, functionality-related competencies are those that enable an organization to offer unique products and services with distinctive customer benefits. This competency reflects strengths in product development and the innovation potential of an organization (Ravichandran & Lertwongsatien, 2005).

Organization competencies are developed over a period of time and reflect choices made by the organization about resource acquisition and deployment. All organizations have limited IT resources and have to make choices about how these resources are deployed. Choices that result in embedding IT within areas of critical importance to the organization are likely to yield resource bundles that are dissimilar to those of the competitors, which in turn, can be rent yielding. Embedding IT within areas of core competence makes the IS assets inimitable by making it difficult for competitors to create similar bundles of complementary IS and organizational assets as well as understand the contributions of IS assets to organization performance. Thus, other things being equal, organizations that target IS initiatives toward core competencies are likely to realize greater value from their IS assets than those that are less focused in their IT deployment (Ravichandran & Lertwongsatien, 2005).

Using IT to improve activities that are integral to an organization's core competencies results in resource bundles that are unlikely to be easily imitated by competitors because of isolating mechanisms such as causal ambiguity and resource connectedness. For example, Wal-Mart's ability to perform better than most of its competitors in the retail industry is partly due to the complementarities between its business practices and its use of IT. Despite attempts by other retailers to copy Wal-Mart's IT systems, they fail to replicate its success in reaping returns from IT investment because of difficulties in understanding how IT and business capabilities interact to affect Wal-Mart's performance (Ravichandran & Lertwongsatien, 2005).

Ravichandran and Lertwongsatien's (2005) findings about causal relationship between IS capabilities and IT support for core competencies and those between IS resources and IS functional capabilities highlight the path and time dependencies involved in using IT in pursuit of organization strategies. Organizations that have successfully used IT to gain competitive advantage have been able to do so because of a history of choices about the acquisition and deployment of IS resources. Their research model is illustrated in Figure 3.1. This model can serve as a basis for IS performance evaluation. By providing empirical evidence that IT support for core competencies has a positive effect on organization performance, their study highlights that CIOs have to do more than invest in the latest technologies or develop a strong IT department. The results indicate that CIOs have to clearly understand

Figure 3.1. Model for effect of information systems resources on organization performance

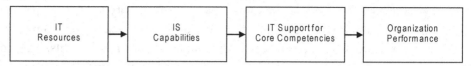

the strategic thrust of the organization and institute mechanisms to ensure that IS capabilities are channeled toward areas of importance to the organization. Among other things, this requires close interactions with business managers and the CEO to play an active role in IT deployment decisions.

1.4   Resource Strategy

Strategic management models traditionally have defined the organization's strategy in terms of its product/market positioning – the products it makes and the markets its serves. The resource approach suggests, however, that organizations should position themselves strategically based on their unique, valuable, and inimitable resources and capabilities rather than the products and services derived from those capabilities. Resources and capabilities can be thought of as a platform from which the organization derives various products for various markets. Leveraging resources and capabilities across many markets and products, rather than targeting specific products for specific markets, becomes the strategic driver. While products and markets may come and go, resources and capabilities are more enduring.

According to Hitt et al. (2001), scholars argue that resources not only enable an organization in doing what it has to do, but also form the basis of organizational strategies and are critical in the implementation of those strategies as well. Therefore, organization resources and organization strategy seem to interact to produce positive returns in terms of efficiency and effectiveness. Organizations employ both basic tangible resources (such as buildings and financial resources) and critical intangible resources (like human capital and reputation) in the development and implementation of strategy. Outside of natural resource monopolies such as government run oil companies, intangible resources such as land regulation expertise are more likely to produce an advantage because they are often rare and socially complex, thereby making them difficult to imitate. When a rich citizen has well-paid lawyers to fight for building a new home on a public beach by privatizing the beach, the municipality has an advantage if government officials possess land regulation knowledge that is non-imitable, non-replaceable, combinable and exploitable.

According to Barney (2001), resource theory includes a very simple view about how resources are connected to the strategies an organization pursues. It is almost as though once an organization becomes aware of the valuable, rare, costly to imitate, and non-substitutable resources it controls, the actions the organization should take to exploit these resources will be self-evident. That may be true some of the time. For example, if an organization possesses valuable, rare, costly to imitate, and non-substitutable economies of scale, learning curve economies, access to low-cost factors of production, and technological resources, it seems clear that the organization should pursue a cost leadership strategy.

However, it will often be the case that the link between resources and the strategy of an organization is not being so obvious. Resource strategy has to determine when, where and how resources may be useful. Such strategy is not obvious, since an organization's resources may be consistent with several different strategies, all with the ability to create the same level of competitive advantage. In this situation, how should an organization decide which of these several different strategies it should pursue? According to Barney (2001) this and other questions presented by Priem and Butler (2001) concerning the resource theory of the organization indicate that the theory is still a theory in many respects, and that more conceptual and empirical research has to be conducted to make the theory more useful to business executives who develop resource strategies for their organizations.

Resource strategy is concerned with the mobilization of resources. Since perceived resources merely represent potential sources of value-creation, they need to be mobilized to create value. Conversely, for a specific resource to have value it has to increase or otherwise facilitate value-creation. The activity whereby tangible and intangible resources are recognized, combined and turned into activities with the aim of creating value is the process here called resource mobilization. The term *resource mobilization* is appropriate, as it incorporates the activity-creation based on both individual and organizational resources, as well as tangibles and intangibles. According to Haanes (1997), alternative terms such as resource allocation, resource leveraging or resource deployment are appropriate when describing the value-creation based on tangible resources, but less so for intangibles. For example, a competence cannot be allocated, as the person controlling it has full discretion over it. Moreover, the competence can be used in different ways. An engineer can choose to work for a different organization and to work with varying enthusiasm. Also, the same engineer can choose not to utilize his or her competence at all. The term resource mobilization is, thus, meant to cover the value-creation based on all types of resources, and it recognizes that all activity creation has a human aspect.

In strategic management and organization theory, the importance for the organization of reducing uncertainty and its dependence on key resources that it cannot fully control has received much attention. If a large part of the resource accumulation takes place in terms of increased competences that key professionals could easily use for the benefit of other employers, the organization needs to set priorities in terms of linking these individually controlled resources to the organization. Loewendahl (2000) suggests three alternative strategies. The simplest strategy, which may be acceptable to some organizations, involves minimizing the dependence on individual professionals and their personal competence. In this sense, the organization chooses to avoid the dependence on individual tangibles. A second strategy is that of linking the professionals more tightly to the organization and reducing the probability of losing them. The third alternative strategy involves increasing the organizationally controlled competence resources without reducing the individually controlled resources. Such a strategy leads to a reduction in the relative impact of individual professionals on total performance, without reducing the absolute value of their contributions. Organizations that have been able to develop a high degree of organizationally controlled resources, including relational resources that are linked to the organization rather than to individual employees, are likely to be less concerned about the exit and entry of individual professionals and more concerned about the development and maintenance of their organizational resource base.

According to Maister (1993), there is a natural, but regrettable, tendency for professional organizations, in their strategy development process, to focus on new things: What new markets does the organization want to enter? What new clients does the organization want to target? What new services does the organization want to offer? This focus on new services and new markets is too often a cop-out. A new specialty (or a new office location) may or may not make sense for the organization, but it rarely does much (if anything) to affect the profitability or competitiveness of the vast bulk of the organization's existing practices.

On the other hand, an improvement in competitiveness in the organization's core businesses will have a much higher return on investment since the organization can capitalize on it by applying it to a larger volume of business. Enhancing the competitiveness of the existing practice will require changes in the behavior of employees. It implies new methods of operating, new skill development, and new accountabilities. Possible strategies for being more valuable to clients can be found in answers to the following questions (Maister, 1993):

- Can we develop an innovative approach to *hiring* so that we can be more valuable to clients by achieving a higher caliber of staff than the competition?
- Can we *train* our people better than the competition in a variety of technical and counseling skills so that they will be more valuable on the marketplace than their counterparts at other organizations?
- Can we develop innovative *methodologies* for handling our matters (or engagements, transactions or projects) so that our delivery of services becomes more thorough and efficient?

- Can we develop systematic ways of helping, encouraging, and ensuring that our people are skilled at client *counseling* in addition to being top suppliers?
- Can we become better than our competition at accumulating, disseminating, and building our organization-wide expertise and experience, so that each professional becomes more valuable in the marketplace by being *empowered* with a greater breadth and depth of experience?
- Can we organize and *specialize* our people in innovative ways, so that they become particularly skilled and valuable to the market because of their focus on a particular market segment's needs?
- Can we become more valuable to our clients by being more systematic and diligent about *listening* to the market: collecting, analyzing, and absorbing the details of their business than does our competition?
- Can we become more valuable to our clients by investing in research and *development* on issues of particular interest to them?

In resource strategy, there has to be consistency between resources and business. The logic behind this requirement is that the resources should create a competitive advantage in the business in which the organization competes. To meet this requirement, corporate resources can be evaluated against key success factors in each business. When doing so, it is important to keep in mind that in order to justify retaining a business, or entering a business, the resources should convey a substantial advantage. Merely having pedestrian resources that could be applied in an industry is seldom sufficient to justify entry or maintain presence in an attractive industry (Collis & Montgomery, 1997).

Moreover, managers must remember that, regardless of the advantage of a particular corporate resource appears to yield, the organization must also compete on all the other resources that are required to produce and deliver the product or service in each business. One great resource does not ensure a successful competitive position, particularly if an organization is disadvantaged on other resource dimensions (Collis & Montgomery, 1997).

CONCLUSION

According to the resource theory of the organization, performance differences across organizations can be attributed to the variance in the organizations' resources and capabilities. Resources that are valuable, unique, and difficult to imitate can provide the basis for organizations' competitive advantages. In turn, these competitive advantages produce positive returns. According to Hitt et al. (2001), most of the few empirical tests of the resource theory that have been conducted have supported positive, direct effects of resources. In our e-government perspective, interoperability gives an organization access to IS/IT resources in another organization. When the resource provided is strategic, i.e., has attributes as listed above, the organization achieve higher benefits from interoperability.

REFERENCES

Ang, S. (1993). *The etiology of information systems outsourcing.* Unpublished doctor of philosophy thesis. University of Minnesota, USA.

Barney, J. B. (2001). Is the resourced-based "view" a useful perspective for strategic management research? Yes. *Academy of Management Review, 26*(1), 41-56.

Barney, J. B. (2002). *Gaining and sustaining competitive advantage.* Upper Saddle River, NJ: Prentice Hall.

Collis, D. J., & Montgomery, C. A. (1997). *Corporate strategy - Resources and the scope of the firm.* Chicago: McGraw-Hill.

Damianides, M. (2005). Sarbanse-Oxley and IT governance: New guidance on IT control and compliance. *Information Systems Management, 22*(1), 77-85.

Eisenhardt, K. M., & Martin, J. A. (2000). Dynamic capabilities: What are they? *Strategic Management Journal, 21*(10-11), 1105-1121.

Ferratt, T. W., Agarwal, R., Brown, C. V., & Moore, J. E. (2005). IT human resource management configurations and IT Turnover: Theoretical synthesis and empirical analysis. *Information Systems Research, 16*(3), 237-255.

Heijden, H. V. D. (2001). Measuring IT core capabilities for electronic commerce. *Journal of Information Technology, 16*(1), 13-22.

Hitt, M. A., Bierman, L., Shumizu, K., & Kochhar, R. (2001). Direct and moderating effects of human capital on strategy and performance in professional service firms: a resourced-based perspective. *Academy of Management Journal, 44*(1), 13-28.

Haanes, K. B. (1997). *Managing resource mobilization: Case studies of Dynal, Fiat Auto Poland and Alcatel Telecom Norway.* Unpublished doctoral thesis. Copenhagen Business School, Denmark.

Johnson, G., & Scholes, K. (2002). *Exploring corporate strategy.* Harlow, UK: Pearson Education, Prentice Hall.

Løwendahl, B. R. (2000). *Strategic management of professional service firms* (2nd ed.). Denmark: Copenhagen Business School Press.

Maister, D. H. (1993). *Managing the professional service firm*. New York: Free Press.

Melville, N., Kraemer, K., & Gurbaxani, V. (2004). Information technology and organizational performance: An integrative model of IT business value. *MIS Quarterly, 28*(82), 283-322.

Peppard, J., Lambert, R., & Edwards, C. (2000). Whose job is it anyway? Organizational information competencies for value creation. *Information Systems Journal, 10*(4), 291-322.

Pettus, M. L. (2001). The resourced-based view as a development growth process: evidence from the deregulated trucking industry. *Academy of Management Journal, 44*(4), 878-896.

Priem, R. L., & Butler, J. E. (2001). Is the resourced-based view a useful perspective for strategic management research? *Academy of Management Review, 26*(1), 22-40.

Quinn, J. B. (2000). Outsourcing innovation: The new engine of growth. *Sloan Management Review, 41*(4), 13-28.

Ravichandran, T., & Lertwongsatien, C. (2005). Effect of information systems resources and capabilities on organization performance: A resource-based perspective. *Journal of Management Information Systems, 21*(4), 237-276.

Santhanam, R., & Hartono, E. (2003). Issues in linking information technology capability to organization performance. *MIS Quarterly, 27*(19), 125-153.

Schubert, K. D. (2004). *CIO survival guide: The roles and responsibilities of the chief information officer*. Hoboken, NJ: John Wiley & Sons.

Wade, M., & Hulland, J. (2004). Review: The resource-based view and information systems research: Review, extension, and suggestions for further research. *MIS Quarterly, 28*(1), 107-142.

Chapter IV
Information Resource Integration

1.   INFORMATION RESOURCE INTEGRATION

If a region or nation is to make the best use of its information assets and reduce duplication in gathering data, information sharing across the public sector is essential. For example, from tracing the origins and spread of foot and mouth disease to locating crime hot spots for law enforcement, geographic information systems have become indispensable for effective knowledge transfer within both the public and private sector. The potential importance of GIS is indicated in recent studies. For instance a recent US study showed that projects, which had adopted and implemented geospatial interoperability standards had an ROI (return on investment) of 119%, which means that for every dollar invested, there were annual cost savings of more than a dollar (Cabinet Office, 2005).

Integrating information resources governments are challenged by several important issues, such as data information quality, information asymmetry that cause imbalance, and identity management (i.e. privacy of data about natural persons and legal entities). These topics are cover in the beginning of this chapter. These issues are followed by examples of inter-organizational information integration in emergency medical services, urban planning, and a regional E-Procurement project. In this chapter we also discuss several theoretical approaches to inter-organizational integration. Managing integration projects is an important issue because many E-Government initiatives have a project orientation. At the end of the chapter two cases–the case of state funded tourism marketing and the case of national registers–are presented.

1.1 Semantic Integration of Government Data

Many normative models of E-Government typically assert that horizontal and vertical integration of data flows and business processes represent the most sophisticated form of E-Government, delivering the greatest payoff for both governments and users. With this sophistication, might come great complexity of design and implementation that spans the domains of information systems, information policy and public administration.

Research has illustrated how the integration of data supporting water quality management addresses this complexity in setting and implementing water quality policy (Chen, Gangopadhyay, Holden, Karabatis, & McGuire, 2007). Data integration problems arise from water quality sources such as states, territories and agencies. Data integration creates unique data needs and problems, such as how to interpret information derived from multiple sources, of variable quality, using different formats, and collected according to different protocols and procedures.

Existing tools for managing these data are not integrated nor do they provide any sort of data analysis capability to allow water resource managers to make informed decisions. The combination of both organizational and data complexity creates fundamental challenges to developing policies, based upon a robust information stream, which are responsive to a wide range of stakeholder interests. Such a problem setting represents the kind of challenge that sophisticated E-Government systems are supposed to address (Chen et al., 2007).

In the case of water quality data described by Chen et al. (2007), numerous organizations and individuals (e.g., volunteers) collect water quality data. Ideally one should integrate all possible data into a uniform format, but in practice this is difficult to accomplish because data sources do not agree on a universal format. Therefore, a hybrid approach was developed, that integrates the metadata (including information on how to access data sources, when and where the data are collected, which parameters are monitored, etc.) of all data sources. The approach only fully integrates data from key sources, such as data from the Environmental Protection Agency (EPA) and the U.S. Geological Survey. Thus, this approach enables water quality managers and policy makers to search the integrated metadata, to locate any source of interest, and to manually download data from that source; or access the fully integrated data as if the data were from a single source.

An important issue in Semantic integration of government data is information quality. Klischewski and Scholl (2008) argue that a core challenge of E-Government integration and interoperation is the computer-supported sharing of information, where little attention has been paid to information quality. They argue that information quality is central to government agencies' willingness to share or use shared information. They demonstrate in their research how information quality serves as an indispensable capstone and common ground in cross-agency information sharing and interoperation projects. They distinguished between desired, negotiated and emergent information quality, and how these are linked to the choice of organizational arrangements and relevant standards.

1.2   Information Asymmetry and Information Sharing

Although much digital divide research focuses on access to technology, another cause of the divide is the lack of information awareness that Clarkson, Jacobsen and Batcheller (2007) call information asymmetry. Information asymmetry often stems from inadequate information sharing and can result in negative consequences for both the information poor and the information rich. Information asymmetry exists when a party or parties possess greater informational awareness pertinent to effective participation in a given situation relative to other participating parties. In the context of electronic government, we may find information rich and information poor agencies in public sector.

To illustrate the negative consequences of information asymmetry and the potential benefits of information sharing, Clarkson et al. (2007) developed a typology to classify information asymmetry into two categories, horizontal and vertical, and identified those information-sharing practices that cause the imbalance. They studied modern American Indian tribes and found both horizontal and vertical asymmetry. First, Indian tribes face horizontal information asymmetry when they attempt to access the capital markets, and second, they face vertical information asymmetry in terms of law enforcement data sharing.

As efforts succeed in removing the impediment of access to information systems through technical and Semantic interoperability, they may only uncover forms of information asymmetry that continue due to ingrained practices of information sharing. As shown in the tribal context by Clarkson et al. (2007), increased information sharing could help resolve information asymmetries impeding economic development and the prosecution of crimes.

At the same time, poor information awareness by some agencies makes it difficult for them to demonstrate the cause and severity of their condition and coordinate responses. By selecting an information sharing response to a specific instance of information asymmetry based on whether that asymmetry is horizontal or vertical, agencies can maximize the likelihood of alleviating the information asymmetry.

1.3   Identity Management in Information Resources

In government organizations, information systems often handle sensitive data about individuals and other organizations, using various kinds of identifiers. The growing cooperation of organizations results in the need to share and exchange such data. This collection and sharing, however, is affected by privacy concerns.

In a study by Otjacques, Hitzelberger and Feltz (2007), results from exploratory research in the government sector are described, focusing on the way public organizations manage identity-related data and the sharing of such data, either with other public agencies or with private organizations. Despite significant progress in harmonizing the legal and administrative provisions and technical standards in the European Union, the study shows that there are still considerable cross-country differences regarding this subject. These differences—together with the growing mobility of goods, persons, and related data within, for example, the European Union—cause particular challenges for information systems in digital government in such regions.

Information systems involve data about entities. An entity is a phenomenon, which can be distinctly identified, e.g. natural persons and legal entities. Thus, identity can be defined as a synonym for an individual particular human being or a particular enterprise. Similarly, identification can be defined as the association of data and attributes with a particular human being or a particular enterprise. There are numerous candidate attributes that allow for making such an association. Privacy of data becomes an issue whenever data is processed that can or must be related to people. This is why identification and data protection and sharing are related issues. Therefore, transfer, sharing, interconnection, and exchange of personal data between public agencies in a country as well as between countries are problematic. For example, in some countries there is a standard single identifier for each person, while Germany and Hungary are explicitly against the installation of such numbers because of data protection concerns (Otjacques et al., 2007).

1.4   Inter-Organizational Information Integration

Information integration is a critical component in the design and implementation of several advanced information technologies, such as data mining and visualization. Organizations must establish and maintain collaborative relationships in which knowledge sharing is critical to resolving numerous issues related to data definitions and structures, diverse database designs, highly variable data quality, and incompatible network infrastructure (Pardo & Tayi, 2007).

These integration processes often involve new work processes and significant organizational change. They are also embedded in larger political and institutional environments that shape their goals and circumscribe their choices. Integrating and sharing information across traditional government boundaries involves complex interactions among and with technical and organizational processes. From a technical perspective, system designers and developers must regularly overcome problems related to the existence of multiple platforms, diverse database designs and data structures, highly variable data quality, and incompatible network infrastructure (Pardo & Tayi, 2007).

Schooley and Horan (2007) presented a case study of inter-organizational information integration in emergency medical services. The conceptual framework is called the time-critical information services framework. This framework aids in the study of time-critical information services that is, public services that are highly time and information dependent. It is a heuristic that allows for a multidimensional view of end-to-end system performance and information sharing therein for time information critical services such as emergency medical services.

The case study findings indicate that information systems are used to manage the performance of individual organizations and their respective separate segments of an emergency incident. Information systems are also used in a partial manner to capture and analyze time stamp data across multiple organizations, which in this case includes primarily the pre-hospital organizations. An information system to integrate and manage end-to-end data, including data from the hospitals and trauma centers, is an important goal (Schooley & Horan, 2007).

1.5   The Case of Urban Information Integration

Urban planning is a complex task requiring multidimensional urban information (spatial, social, criminal, economic, etc.). The need for assistance in performing urban planning tasks has led to the rapid development of urban information systems. To succeed, there is a need for information resource integration. It is important to allow information from the various sources to be shared and integrated.

Research by Wang, Song, Hamilton and Curwell (2007) focuses on technical approaches for multidimensional information integration, especially spatial information integration. They explored a centralized database approach, accepting various data sources and data formats through a series of converters. This design reflects the idea of information sharing and integration. On the one hand, stakeholders are able to contribute information in different formats to the database through converters.

On the other hand, stakeholders can access the database through a standard and universal database interface.

Wang et al. (2007) find the idea of distributed data but uniform and standard interface very useful. It is always difficult to collect and manage all the data sets in a physically centralized database. In particular, when converting object data types into a relational database, the data model will be complicated. The approach of a standard interface is a solution because there will be fewer requirements to convert data from one format to another and store it. Instead the data stays where it is, in its native format. The standard interfaces and the converters will act as an "on demand wrapper" of the various data formats and give standard access to all users.

1.6   The Case of E-Procurement

The system Procure is an e-service aimed at more than 2,000 public local entities in the region of Burgundy (France) with three key objectives: a) bringing together all public entities for their purchases, b) giving companies, especially small ones, a single entry to all tenders and the capability to respond electronically to them, and c) to be the pilot E-Government regional project in France (Fléri, Moutet, & Cimander, 2007).

According to Fléri et al. (2007), Procure is the first regional e-service with the objective of fostering industry competition, improving the quality of the public purchaser's job and reducing costs. During the first two years, more than 14,000 tenders were published on the platform leading to 121,000 downloads of RFPs (request for proposals). After two years, the existing service was used by 7,500 companies, among which a large majority of small and medium sized enterprises.

The system platform is managed by a governance structure, in which the regional legal entities are stakeholders. The system provides its services to all legal entities autonomous in terms of procurement, such as universities, high schools and chambers of commerce. The organizational model employed is a combination of centralization of functions and services fulfillment, and decentralization and autonomy for service provisions (Fléri et al., 2007).

1.7   Theoretical Approaches to Inter-Organizational Integration

To understand the behavior of different government agencies at the level of organizational interoperability, some theories might help. In the following, we present a selection of theories, which might be applied to study organizational interoperability.

Agency theory has broadened the risk-sharing literature to include the agency problem that occurs when cooperating parties have different goals and division of labor. The cooperating parties are engaged in an agency relationship defined as a contract under which one or more persons (the principal(s)) engage another person (agent) to perform some service on their behalf which involves delegating some decision making authority to the agent (Jensen & Meckling, 1976). Agency theory describes the relationship between the two parties using the metaphor of a contract. According to Eisenhardt (1985), agency theory is concerned with resolving two problems that can occur in agency relationships. The first is the agency problem that arises when the desires or goals of the principal and agent conflict and it is difficult or expensive for the principal to verify what the agent is actually doing. The second is the problem of risk sharing that arises when the principal and agent have different risk preferences. The first agency problem arises when the two parties do not share productivity gains. The risk-sharing problem might be the result of different attitudes towards the use of new technologies. Because the unit of analysis is the contract governing the relationship between the two parties, the focus of the theory is on determining the most efficient contract governing the principal-agent relationship given assumptions about people (e.g., self-interest, bounded rationality, risk aversion), organizations (e.g., goal conflict of members), and information (e.g., information is a commodity which can be purchased).

Alliance theory is concerned with partnership, often referred to as alliance. Das and Teng (2002b) studied how alliance conditions change over the different stages of alliance development to understand the development processes. They defined the following stages in the alliance development process:

- **Formation Stage.** Partner firms approach each other and negotiate the alliance. Partner firms then carry out the agreement and set up the alliance by committing various types of resources. The alliance is initiated and put into operation. Alliances will be formed only under certain conditions. These conditions include a relatively high level of collective strengths, a low level of inter-partner conflicts, and a high level of interdependencies.
- **Operation Stage.** Not only is the formation stage directly influenced by alliance conditions, the transition from the formation stage to the operation stage are also dictated by the same alliance conditions variables. During the operation stage, partner firms collaborate and implement all agreements of the alliance. The alliance will likely grow rapidly in size during this stage, somewhat akin to the growth stage of organizational life cycles. Other than the growth route, an alliance may also be reformed and/or terminated at this stage.

- **Outcome Stage.** During this stage, alliance performance becomes tangible and can, thus, be evaluated with some certainty. There are four possible outcomes for an alliance at this stage – stabilization, reformation, decline, and termination. A combination of outcomes is also possible, such as a termination after reformation. Alliance reformation and alliance termination do not necessarily signal alliance failure. Reformation and termination may be the best option under certain circumstances, such as the achievement of pre-set alliance objectives. Alliance condition variables continue to play a decisive role in the outcome stage. The particular alliance outcome will depend on the condition of the alliance.

Das and Teng (2003) discussed partner analysis and alliance performance. An important stream of research in the alliance literature is about partner selection. It emphasizes the desirability of a match between the partners, mainly in terms of their resource profiles. The approach is consistent with the resource-based theory of the firm, which suggests that competitors are defined by their resources profiles.

According to *network theory* (Afuah & Tucci, 2003), a network exhibits network externalities. An organization exhibits network externalities when it becomes more valuable to members as more people take advantage of it. A classic example from technology is the telephone, where the value for each subscriber increases exponentially with the number of network subscribers, to whom you can talk and get services from.

Contractual theory is concerned with the role of contracts in social systems. Luo (2002) examined how contract, cooperation, and performance are associated with one another. He argues that contract and cooperation are not substitutes but complements in relation to performance. A contract alone is insufficient to guide evolution and performance. Since organized crime often involves both intra-organizational as well as inter-organizational exchanges that become socially embedded over time, cooperation is an important safeguard mechanism mitigating external and internal hazards and overcoming adaptive limits of contracts. The simultaneous use of both contractual and cooperative mechanisms is particularly critical to organized crime in an uncertain environment. Relational contract theory was created by Macneil (2000), who has been doing relational contracts since the mid-1960s, and who by contract means relations among people who have exchanged, are exchanging, or expect to be exchanging in the future – in other words, exchange relations. He finds that experience has shown that the very idea of contract as relations in which exchange occurs – rather than as specific transactions, specific agreements, specific promises, specific exchanges, and the like – is extremely difficult for many people to grasp. Either that or they simply refuse to accept that contract can be defined as relations among people in an exchange. Macneil (2000) searched for roots to summarize contract in a useful manner. He tried to distill what he found into a manageable number of basic behavioral categories growing out of those roots. Since repeated human behavior invariably creates norms, these behavioral categories are also normative categories. He identified the following ten common contract behavioral patterns and norms: (1) Role integrity – requiring consistency, involving internal conflict, and being inherently complex, (2) Reciprocity – the principle of getting something back for something given, (3) Implementation of planning, (4) Effectuation of consent, (5) Flexibility, (6) Contractual solidarity, (7) The restitution, reliance, and expectation interests (the linking norms), (8) Creation and restraint of power (the power norm), (9) Proprietary of means, and (10) Harmonization with the social matrix, that is, with supra-contract norms. Relational contract theory postulates that where the ten common contract norms are inadequately served, exchange relations of whatever kind will fall apart.

Theory of core competencies is a popular theory in most public and private organizations. According to Prahalad and Hamel (1990), core competencies are the collective learning in the organization, especially how to coordinate diverse production skills and integrate multiple streams of technologies. Since core competence is about harmonizing streams of technology, it is also about the organization of work and the delivery of value.

Relational exchange theory is based on relational norms. Contracts are often extremely imperfect tools for controlling opportunism. While relational contracts may mitigate some opportunistic behavior, significant residual opportunism may remain. It is possible that transactors using relational contracts may incur significant ex-post bargaining costs as they periodically negotiate contract adjustments (Artz & Brush, 2000).

Stakeholder theory implies that the identification of stakeholders and their needs is important for decision-making in organizations. A stakeholder is any group or individual who can affect, or is affected by, the achievement of a corporation's purpose. Stakeholder theory is distinct because it addresses morals and values explicitly as a central feature of managing organizations. The ends of cooperative activity and the means of achieving these ends are critically examined in stakeholder theory in a way that they are not in many theories of strategic management (Phillips, Freeman, & Wicks, 2003). According to Archmann and Kudlacek (2008), interoperability is not an end itself, but a tool to solve the problems of different stakeholders.

Theory of organizational boundaries claims that the resource-based view, transaction costs, and options perspectives each explain only a portion of managerial motivation for decisions on organization boundaries. The rationale supporting the choices organizations make regarding member sourcing is multidimensional; firms are not only seeking potential sources of competitive advantage, but are also seeking to avoid opportunism and to preserve or create flexibility. There has been renewed debate on the determinants of firm boundaries and their implications for performance. According to Schilling and Steensma (2002), the widely accepted framework of transaction cost economics has come under scrutiny as a comprehensive theory for firm scale and scope. At the heart of this debate is whether the underlying mechanism determining firm boundaries is a fear of opportunism (as posited by transaction cost economics), a quest for sustainable advantage (as posed by resource-based view theorists and others), a desire for risk-reducing flexibility (as has recently gained increased attention in work on options), or a combination of factors. Although perspectives on firm boundaries such as transaction costs or the resource-based view are based on fundamentally different motivations for pursuing hierarchical control over market contracts, they rely on common resource or context attributes as antecedents.

Social exchange theory was initially developed to examine interpersonal exchanges that are not purely economic. Several sociologists are responsible for the early development of this theory. These theorists view people's social behavior in terms of exchanges of resources. The need for social exchange is created by the scarcity of resources, prompting actors to engage one another to obtain valuable inputs. Social exchange can be defined as voluntary actions of individuals that are motivated by return they are expected to bring and typically in fact bring from others. Social exchange can be viewed as an ongoing reciprocal process in which actions are contingent on rewarding reactions from others. There are important differences between social exchanges and economic exchanges. Social exchanges may or may not involve extrinsic benefits with objective economic value. In contrast to economic exchanges, the benefits from social exchanges often are not contracted explicitly, and it is voluntary to provide benefits. As a result, exchange partners are uncertain whether they will receive benefits. Thus social exchange theory focuses on the social relations among the actors that shape the exchange of resources and benefits. While its origins are at the individual level, social exchange theory has been extended to organizational and inter-organizational levels (Das & Teng, 2002a).

1.8   Managing Integration Projects

There is a growing demand for project management skills as a consequence of the project orientation of many E-Government initiatives. Interoperability initiatives adopt the project approach to handle special tasks more efficiently and effectively. Project management is being viewed as a flexible form of general management, which enables organizations to integrate, plan, and control schedule-intensive and one-of-a-kind endeavors in order to improve performance and reach organizational goals.

Table 4.1. Comparison of general management and project management (Maylor, 2005)

General management	Project management
Responsible for managing the status quo	Responsible for overseeing change
Authority defined by management structure	Lines of authority 'fuzzy'
Consistent set of tasks	Ever-changing set of tasks
Responsibility limited to their own function	Responsibility for cross-functional activities
Works in 'permanent' organizational structures	Operates within structures which exist for the life of the project
Tasks described as 'maintenance'	Predominantly concerned with innovation
Main task is optimization	Main task is the resolution of conflict
Success determined by achievement	Success determined by achievement of stated end-goals
Limited set of variables	Contains intrinsic uncertainties

The job of the project manager is demanding, complex and varied, requiring the ability to handle many loose ends in critical situations. Communication between team members and the entire network is vital to support a shared understanding of the project and its goals. Managing projects therefore requires a combination of skills including interpersonal ability, technical competencies, creativity, solution orientation, and effectiveness, along with the capability to understand the situation and people and then dynamically integrate appropriate leadership behavior (Pant & Baroudi, 2008). A comparison of general management versus project management is illustrated in Table 4.1. Life cycle of a project is illustrated in Figure 4.1.

What is a project? Frame (1995) defined projects by their characteristics:

- Goal orientation. Projects are directed at achieving specific results – that is, they are goal oriented. It is these goals that drive the project and all planning and implementation efforts are undertaken so as to achieve them.
- Coordinated undertaking of interrelated activities. Projects are inherently complex. They entail carrying out multiple activities that are related to each other in both obvious and subtle ways.
- Limited duration. Projects are undertaken in a finite period of time. They are temporary. They have defined beginnings and ends.
- Uniqueness. Projects are, to a degree, non-recurring, one-of-a-kind undertakings. However, the extent of uniqueness varies considerably from project to project.

Figure 4.1. Integration project life cycle phases

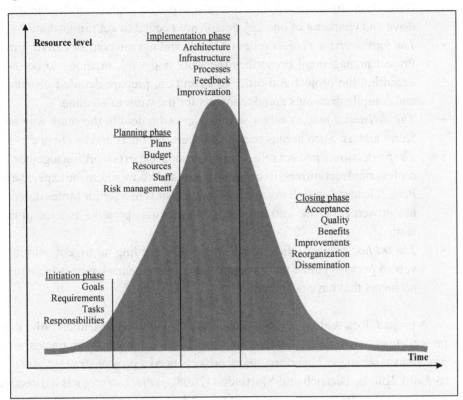

Similarly, in order to speak of a project, the following criteria need to be met (Frame, 1995):

- Any non-repetitive activity
- A low volume, high-variety activity
- A temporary endeavor undertaken to create a unique product or service
- Any activity with a start and a finish
- A unique set of coordinated activities, with definite starting and finishing points, undertaken by an individual or organization to meet specific performance objectives within defined schedule, cost and performance parameters.

Projects can be organized in different ways. Donk and Molloy (2008) classify projects into the following five categories:

- *The simple project* relies on the agency and vision of the project leader. It is typically an initiative of an entrepreneurial project leader. Here the enthusiasm, drive and charisma of one key person are needed to get things done.
- *The bureaucratic project* relies on stable and not too complex environments. Project management prescribes the work and work methods to be used in executing the project and order of execution, prepare detailed instructions, and compile drawings and documents for the work to be done.
- *The divisional project* relies on managers who deal in the same way on different arenas. Such arenas may be markets, products and/or clients.
- *The professional project* relies on professional experts working together. Each professional recognizes his or her own part and know where the expertise ends. Project leadership will normally be in the hands of a senior professional, who has proven expertise and knowledge in previous projects as a member of a team.
- *The ad hoc project* relies on an urgent task needing an urgent solution. Involved persons adjust their attention and make themselves available to solve problems that have occurred.

A project does seldom serve a single base or parent organization only. Rather, projects tend to live their own lives in complex environments with unclear overall governance schemes. Therefore, many projects need a project strategy. According to Artto, Kujala, Dietrich and Martinduo (2008), *project strategy* is a direction in a project that contributes to success of the project in its environment:

- *Project direction* might be goals, plans, guidelines, means, methods or governance systems including reward and penalty schemes. These elements include a capability to directly or indirectly affect the project's course. Project direction and its elements may change even on a frequent basis, which suggests that project and its strategy are dynamic.
- *Contribution* is the assumed effect of the direction. Since the direction matters and makes a difference, it will contribute an effect.
- *Success* refers to how well the project is able to accomplish its goals. Each project stakeholder may have different and conflicting criteria for evaluating projects' degree of success. However, a project can be successful by meeting its self-established goals that may be against the interest of even major stakeholders.
- *Environment* refers to the world outside the project's boundaries with which the project as an open system must continuously interact.

Project strategy is related to survival of an organized crime. From a project's point of view, criteria for measuring survival and success and respective managerial actions may be quite different depending on the kind of crime to be carried out in the project. When implementing the project strategy, tasks such as time planning, critical chain project management, cost and quality planning, plan analysis and risk management, project structure and team(s), and management and leadership become important.

Becker, Algermissen and Niehaves (2006) developed a procedure model for process oriented E-Government projects. They argue that there is a lack of process orientation in public administration. The procedure model includes characteristics such as transferring from one employee to another, many offices participating, and frequent media breaks.

1.9   The Case of State Funded Tourism Marketing

Marketing of tourist attractions and tourism destinations often require an integrated approach, where several attractions and destinations merge to form a destination image attractive to potential tourists. Often, local governments initiate and fund integration approaches to stimulate the local tourist industry. As government funding becomes available, tourist hotels, museums and sceneries often choose to improve their interoperability (Choi, Lehto, & Morrison, 2007; Shields, 2006).

If we look at Norway, the main reason for visiting this country seems to be the scenery: fjords, mountains and waterfalls are linked together by spectacular travel routes. The scenery can be viewed and admired and provides a basis for recreational activities and experiences. Visitor centers are located close to glaciers, wild countryside and wildlife. Both nationally and internationally, Norway's scenery has been marketed and established as the country's trademark, with similarities to Canadian mountain holidays marketing (Hudson & Miller, 2005). Considerably less attention is paid to Norway's cultural attractions. According to statistics from Innovation Norway for 2008, however, some four million people visited the ten most popular cultural attractions in Norway during the summer of 2007. This is despite the fact that no consolidated and strategic marketing effort with respect to the cultural attractions appears to exist, be it on an individual basis or in cooperation with others.

Attractions do not comprise one homogenous group; they have different conditions and requirements in terms of their relationship with the market. Their organizational culture will therefore most likely influence marketing and market communication strategies. To what degree cultural institutions consider themselves as having a role to play as tourist attractions often depends on the current regime and administration. However, we worked on the assumption that those that appear on Innovation Norway's list of attractions have a defined role as an attraction, even though this entails debate as to how the institutions' resources should be prioritized. Do attractions use sufficient and appropriate resources for communicating with the market in order to meet their visitor targets? This question is linked to the attractions' market communication in an international market. Is this done based on an integrated communications strategy that conveys what the attractions have to offer and is adapted to the target groups' evaluation criteria? Can theories for developing attractions in combination with an integrated theory of market communication provide Norwegian tourism with strategic competitive advantages?

The increasing importance of cultural attractions and the significance of tourism for Norwegian art and culture make it vital to understand which aspects of these are relevant to tourism, and what tourists actually visit and like to visit. While tourists' expectations of an experience may well coincide with the expectations and needs of local communities, they may also differ. Attractions have many themes, resources and forms of presentation. A central issue is therefore whether this imposes a differentiation in themes with respect to the different markets.

E-Government initiatives are concerned with the Internet as an integrated channel for market communication of tourism destinations. Destination image representation on the Web is important, as the Internet has become an image formation agent. The Internet has drastically transformed the distribution and marketing of tourism products (Choi et al., 2007).

Governments would like to see an integrated communication approach, where attractions, actors and regions are integrated. Evolution of integration can be defined in terms of stages of growth for integrated market communication as illustrated in Figure 4.2:

- **Stage 1**. In the *integrated media approach*, different media for market communication are applied independent of each other. The only integration that occurs is related to each single media. For example, different information elements about one single tourist attraction are integrated on a Web site for this attraction, and advertising in i.e. magazines, newspapers, brochures and catalogs. Hu and Wall (2005) define tourist attraction as a permanent resource, either natural or human-made, which is developed and managed for the primary purpose of attracting visitors. Cultural tourist attractions are the content of cultural tourism, which exists because tourists want either to experience living places and cultures other than their own, or to gain access to foreign cultures, different in time and space. Therefore, cultural tourism is defined as tourism constructed, proffered and consumed explicitly or implicitly as cultural appreciation, either as experiences or through schematic knowledge gaining (Kantanen & Tikkanen, 2006).

- **Stage 2**. In the *integrated attraction approach*, one actor with one attraction integrates media communication in several channels, with use of both mass communication and individual communication, and with both personal and non-personal media. At this stage, we can see a consistent communication about the market offering, based on the target groups whishes end needs. It is assumed that different target groups are reached through different channels, where each tourist decision-making process is influenced (Bargeman & Poel, 2006).

- **Stage 3**. In the *integrated industry approach*, one industry integrates several similar attractions from many actors, as we can see in arts, museums and some festivals. The market offering is consistent, and communicated on the target groups premises. And the actors are developing a coherent marketing communication strategy, integrating public relations, advertising, sales promotion, personal selling, database management, information center and Internet. While attractions do not comprise one homogeneous group, marketing synergy might be achieved by displaying the varieties as well as the similarities of cultural attractions. This combination of variety of similarity might be successfully presented on the Internet (Wu, Wei, & Chen, 2008).

- **Stage 4**. In the *integrated region approach*, several attractions from several actors in several tourist industries integrate their market communication. Also

Figure 4.2. Stage model for integrated market communication

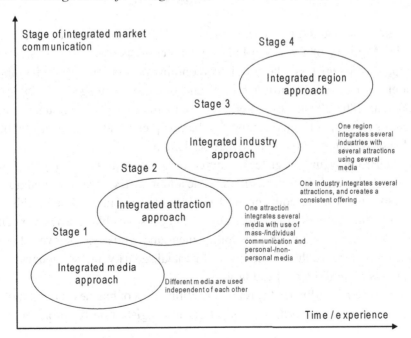

here we see an integrated and coherent marketing communication strategy, developed on a competitive market offering and other sub-strategies as the business areas and the organizational basis. An example might the approach attempted by Canadian mountain holidays (Hudson & Miller, 2005). If Norway is defined as a region, a consolidated and strategic marketing effort with respect to the cultural attractions, much more than four million people might be expected to visit the ten most popular cultural attractions in the country during a summer season. Even more importantly, an integrated market communication approach would create many more visits to less known cultural attractions. The core might be national art institutions that are for the most part state-funded (Shields, 2006).

These stages represent levels of interoperability in terms of integration between media, attraction, actor and region. Interoperability is referring to a property of diverse systems and organizations enabling them to work together. Interoperability is the ability of all involved parties to share information and integrate information and businesses processes by use of common standards for mutual benefits (Scholl & Klischewski, 2007). For example, a Web site is to be integrated with other media, covering all attractions by all actors in a region to be classified as a stage 4 Web site, while at the same time reach target segments and exploit existing resources in the best possible way.

1.10 The Case of National Registers

The Brønnøysund Register Center in Norway is a government body under the Norwegian Ministry of Trade and Industry, and consists of several different national computerized registers. These registers contain information and key data about such matters as (www.brreg.no): liabilities and titles in mortgaged movable property, more than 280 000 business enterprises, more than 1 300 000 annual accounts and auditor's reports of limited companies, bankruptcies and compulsory liquidations, and approximately 200 000 marriage settlements.

The Brønnøysund Register Center contributes towards creating improved and more orderly conditions in business, trade and industry. Openness and traceability serve to counter white-collar crime. Reliable, impartial information yields financial security. The center is an administrative agency responsible for a number of national control and registration schemes for business and industry. The overall aim of the center is to improve the conditions for financial security and efficiency of business and industry, and the public at large.

The center coordinates the reporting obligations of business organizations. The aim is to prevent superfluous collection and registration of information, which will especially alleviate the workload for small and medium-sized businesses. The register classifies and catalogues information in the various databases. If the register discovers that two or more public authorities or agencies ask the same kind of questions of the same type of companies, these bodies must cooperate so that their questions are asked only once. The Act relating to the Register of Reporting Obligations stipulates that the public authorities and agencies must cooperate.

The Brønnøysund Register Center is one of Norway's largest electronic database centers, and thus a useful source of information for many people. Most Norwegians have at one point or another been in contact with the center. Whether as a business manager, lender, used car buyer, journalist or individual person, both Norwegians and foreigners have access to much of the information stored at the center. Each day the center answers thousands of electronic inquiries by providing online services. New technology will make it even simpler in the future to provide information to the center as well as retrieve information from the center. To improve the service by application of new technology, the center participates in a number of national and international projects.

One of the projects is named SERES (Semantics register for electronic collaboration – Semantikkregisteret for elektronisk samhandling). This project includes development of system support tools, method system, guidelines and administrative routines. SERES is both an IT system and an information model repository for promotion of Semantic interoperability in the public sector. It is based on the idea of establishing a coherent information model described in an easily comprehensible and commonly accepted and used modeling language (UML). The system is implemented as an Internet based, multi user, multi layer Java application (J2EE). Users from any public institution may have access to SERES (Bergstrøm, 2007). The UML class diagram is used in SERES, where the data types are called Semantic types and are organized as a taxonomy starting with the set of Core Data from UN/CEFACT. The information model is composed of a set of domain models that may have different levels of harmonization with other domain models and varying adherence to an agreed set of modeling guidelines. These guidelines require that information classes are directly or indirectly related to a harmonized core information model and that all data types are Semantic types (Bergstrøm, 2007).

CONCLUSION

In this chapter we have discussed the complexity of information resource integration. Although governments have succeeded in removing the impediments of access to information systems through technical and Semantic interoperability, there are still challenges. One issue is lack of information awareness (often called information asymmetry), which stems from inadequate information sharing and can result in negative consequences for both information poor and information rich. Another issue, information quality, is central to government agencies' willingness to share and use shared information. Information quality serves as an indispensable capstone and common ground in cross-agency information sharing and interoperation projects, but little attention has been paid to this issue. Government information systems often handle sensitive data about individuals or organizations. Thus, transfer, sharing, interconnection, and exchange of personal data across organizational boarders, becomes an issue.

In a UK study, partners in data sharing in the public sector were central government, agencies, local authorities, emergency services, health agencies and voluntary organizations. When asked about barriers to data sharing in GIS, the most frequent response was "unaware of what information other organizations have" followed by "constrained by the Data Protection Act or other security/privacy issues" and "concerned that our data will be misrepresented by others" (Cabinet Office, 2005).

REFERENCES

Afuah, A., & Tucci, C. L. (2003). *Internet business models and strategies* (2nd ed.). New York: McGraw-Hill.

Archmann, S., & Kudlacek, I. (2008). Interoperability and the exchange of good practice cases. *European Journal of ePractice, 2*(February), 3-12.

Artto, K., Kujala, J., Dietrich, P., & Martinsuo, M. (2008). What is project strategy? *International Journal of Project Management, 26*(1), 4-12.

Artz, K. W., & Brush, T. H. (2000). Asset specificity, uncertainty and relational norms: an examination of coordination costs in collaborative strategic alliances. *Journal of Economic Behavior & Organization, 41*(4), 337-362.

Bargeman, B., & Poel, H. (2006). The role of routines in the vacation decision-making process of Dutch vacationers. *Tourism Management, 27(4), 707-720.*

Becker, J., Algermissen, L., & Niehaves, B. (2006). A procedure model for process oriented E-Government projects. *Business Process Management Journal, 12*(1), 61-75.

Bergstrøm, Y. (2007, May 21-23). *Statistical data collection adjusted to an industry specific organization.* Paper presented at the Seminars on Registers in Statistics - methodology and quality, Helsinki.

Cabinet Office. (2005). *Geographic information: An analysis of interoperability and information sharing in the United Kingdom.* London: Cabinet Office, E-Government Unit.

Chen, Z., Gangopadhyay, A., Holden, S. H., Karabatis, G., & McGuire, P. (2007). Semantic integration of government data for water quality management. *Government Information Quarterly, 24*(4), 716-735.

Choi, S., Lehto, X. Y., & Morrison, A. M. (2007). Destination image representation on the Web: Content analysis of Macau travel related Websites. *Tourism Management, 28*(1), 118-129.

Clarkson, G., Jacobsen, T. E., & Batcheller, A. L. (2007). Information asymmetri and information sharing. *Government Information Quarterly, 24*(4), 827-839.

Das, T. K., & Teng, B.-S. (2002a). Alliance constellations: A social exchange perspective. *Academy of Management Review, 27*(3), 445-456.

Das, T. K., & Teng, B.-S. (2002b). The dynamics of alliance conditions in the alliance development process. *Journal of Management Studies, 39*(5), 725-746.

Das, T. K., & Teng, B.-S. (2003). Partner analysis and alliance performance. *Scandinavian Journal of Management, 19*(3), 279-308.

Donk, D. P. v., & Molloy, E. (2008). From organising as projects to projects as organisations. *International Journal of Project Management, 26*(2), 129-137.

Eisenhardt, K. M. (1985). Control: Organizational and economic approaches. *Management Science, 31*(2), 134-149.

Fléri, L. F., Moutet, G., & Cimander, R. (2007). Regional shared eGovernment in the region of Burgundy: The case of eProcurement. *European Journal of ePractice, 1*(November), 60-72.

Frame, P. (1995). *Managing Projects in Organizations.* San Francisco: Jossey-Bass Publishers.

Hu, W., & Wall, G. (2005). Environmental management, environmental image and the competitive tourists attraction. *Journal of Sustainable Tourism, 44*(7), 1255-1277.

Hudson, S., & Miller, G. A. (2005). The responsible marketing of tourism: The case of Canadian mountain holidays. *Tourism Management, 26*(2).

Jensen, M. C., & Meckling, W. H. (1976). Theory of the firm: Managerial behavior, agency costs and ownership structures. *Journal of Financial Economics, 3*(4), 305-360.

Kantanen, T., & Tikkanen, I. (2006). Advertising in low and high involvement cultural tourism attractions: Four cases. *Tourism and Hospitality Research, 6*(2), 99-110.

Klischewski, R., & Scholl, H. J. (2008). Information quality as capstone in negotiating e-government integration, interoperation and information sharing. *Electronic Government, an International Journal, 5*(2), 203-225.

Luo, Y. (2002). Contract, cooperation, and performance in international joint ventures. *Strategic Management Journal, 23*(10), 903-919.

Macneil, I. R. (2000). Relational contract theory: Challenges and queries. *Northwestern University Law Review, 94*(3), 877-907.

Maylor, H. (2005). *Project management* (3rd ed.). Harlow, UK: Prentice Hall, Pearson Education.

Otjacques, B., Hitzelberger, P., & Feltz, F. (2007). Interoperability of e-government information systems: Issues of identification and data sharing. *Journal of Management Information Systems, 23*(4), 29-51.

Pant, I., & Baroudi, B. (2008). Project management education: The human skills imperative. *International Journal of Project Management, 26*(2), 124-128.

Pardo, T. A., & Tayi, G. K. (2007). Interorganizational information integration: A key enabler for digital government. *Government Information Quarterly, 24*(4), 691-715.

Phillips, R., Freeman, R. E., & Wicks, A. C. (2003). What stakeholder theory is not. *Business Ethics Quarterly, 13*(4), 479-502.

Prahalad, C. K., & Hamel, G. (1990). The core competence of the corporation. *Harvard Business Review, 68*(3), 79-91.

Schilling, M. A., & Steensma, H. K. (2002). Disentangling the theories of firm boundaries: A path model and empirical test. *Organization Science, 13*(4), 387-401.

Scholl, H. J., & Klischewski, R. (2007). E-government integration and interoperability: Framing the research agenda. *International Journal of Public Administration, 30*(8), 889-920.

Schooley, B. L., & Horan, T. A. (2007). Towards end-to-end government performance management: Case study of interorganizational information integration in emergency medical services (EMS). *Government Information Quarterly, 24*(4), 755-784.

Shields, P. O. (2006). State-funded tourism marketing: The effectiveness of state travel guides for the college market. *Journal of Travel & Tourism Marketing, 20*(2), 31-49.

Wang, H., Song, Y., Hamilton, A., & Curwell, S. (2007). Urban information integration for advanced e-planning in Europe. *Government Information Quarterly, 24*(4), 736-754.

Wu, S.-I., Wei, P.-L., & Chen, J.-H. (2008). Influential factors and relational structure of Internet banner advertising in the tourism industry. *Tourism Management, 29*(2), 221-236.

Chapter V
Stages of E–Government Interoperability

1.   STAGES OF E-GOVERNMENT INTEROPERABILITY

Improved interoperability between public organizations as well as between public and private organizations is of critical importance to make electronic government more successful (Pardo & Tayi, 2007; Wang, Song, Hamilton, & Curwell, 2007). The mobilization of electronic information across organizations has the potential of modernizing and transforming information exchanges. The current information exchanges are, however, often inefficient and error-prone (Eckman, Bennet, Kaufman, & Tenner, 2007). Exchanges of information and services are fragmented and complex, dominated by technical as well as organizational problems. High-ranking issues among the defining purposes of e-government are highly agile, citizen-centric, accountable, transparent, effective, and efficient government operations and services (Scholl & Klischewski, 2007). For reaching such goals, the integration of government information resources and processes, and thus the interoperation of independent information systems are essential. Yet, most integration and interoperation efforts meet serious challenges and limitations.

The purpose of this chapter is to develop a stage model and maturity levels for interoperability in digital government. By identifying development stages, scholars and practitioners have a framework within which they can diagnose the current situation and plan for future improvements in interoperability. Specifically, the objective of this conceptual and exploratory chapter is an attempt to identify issues and to develop models for interoperability based on maturity levels.

1.1 Stage Models in Organizational Studies

Stages of growth models have been used widely in both organizational research and management practice. According to King and Teo (1997), these models describe a wide variety of phenomena–the organizational life cycle, product life cycle, biological growth, change management, etc. These models assume that predictable patterns (conceptualized in terms of stages, levels or phases) exist in the growth of organizations, the sales levels of products, IT maturity, and the growth of living organisms. These stages (1) are sequential in nature, (2) occur as a hierarchical progression that is not easily reversed, (3) evolve a broad range of organizational activities and structures, and (4) are dependent on contingent actions at each stage to progress to the next stage.

Organizational stage models suggest that organizations follow certain steps into higher levels as they evolve and develop. The assumption is that organizational evolution is upward and sequential. In particular, these models suggest that the challenges and requirements for organizational success vary with different stages, and thus, organizational actions must change as the stages change (Pfarrer, Decells, Smith, & Taylor, 2008).

Benchmark variables are often used to indicate characteristics at each stage of growth. A one-dimensional continuum might be established for each benchmark variable. The measurement of benchmark variables can be carried out using simple Likert scaling or more advanced Guttman scales (Frankfort-Nachmias & Nachmias, 2002). Guttman scaling is a cumulative scaling technique based on ordering theory that suggests a cumulative relationship between the elements of a domain and the items on a test.

Various multistage models have been proposed for organizational evolution over time. For example, Nolan (1979) introduced a model consisting of six stages for information technology maturity in organizations, which later was expanded to nine stages by other researchers. Earl (2000) suggested a stages of growth model for evolving the e-business in both private and public enterprises, consisting of the following six stages: external communication, internal communication, e-commerce, e-business, e-enterprise, and transformation, while Rao and Metts (2003) presented a stage model for electronic commerce development in small and medium sized enterprises. In the area of knowledge management technology, Housel and Bell (2001) developed a five level model. In the area of knowledge management systems, Gottschalk (2007) developed a four-stage model applied to knowledge management in law firms as well law enforcement. Gottschalk and Tolloczko (2007) developed a maturity model for mapping crime in police investigations, while Gottschalk and Solli-Sæther (2006) developed a maturity model for IT outsourcing relationships for outsourcing partners. Each of these models identifies certain characteristics in terms of benchmark variables that typify organizations in different stages of growth. Among these multistage models, models with four stages seem to have been proposed and tested most frequently in the literature (King & Teo, 1997).

A recent example is a stages of growth model for corrupt organizations, where the four-stage model proposed by Pfarrer et al. (2008) is concerned with organizational actions that potentially increase the speed and likelihood that an organization will restore its legitimacy with stakeholders following a transgression. The four stages are labeled discovery, explanation, penance, and rehabilitation respectively.

The concept of stages of growth has been widely employed for many years. Already two decades ago, Kazanjian and Drazin (1989) found that a number of multistage models have been proposed, which assume that predictable patterns exist in the growth of organizations, and that these patterns unfold as discrete time periods best thought of as stages. These models have different distinguishing characteristics. Stages can be driven by the search for new growth opportunities or as a response to internal crises. Some models suggest that organizations progress through stages while others argue that there may be multiple paths through the stages.

Kazanjian (1988) applied dominant problems to stages of growth. Dominant problems imply that there is a pattern of primary concerns that organizations face for each theorized stage. In organizations, dominant problems can shift from lack of skills to lack of resources to lack of strategy associated with different stages of growth. Kazanjian and Drazin (1989) argue that either implicitly or explicitly, stages of growth models share a common underlying logic. Organizations undergo transformations in their design characteristics, which enable them to face the new tasks or problems that growth elicits. The problems, tasks or environments may differ from model to model, but almost all suggest that stages emerge in a well-defined sequence, so that the solution of one set of problems or tasks leads to the emergence of a new set of problems and tasks, that the organization must address.

Stage of maturity models of e-government illustrate that, over time, providing users with seamless information and service delivery involves a greater degree of complexity across several dimensions of e-government. These models suggest that e-government capabilities begin modestly and initially provide static, one-way information, but grow more sophisticated and add interactive and transactional capabilities. These models predict an ultimate evolution of e-government that includes horizontal and vertical integration and the development of true portals and seamlessness in inter-organizational exchanges (Chen, Gangopadhyay, Holden, Karabatis, & McGuire, 2007).

According to Chen et al. (2007), three models of e-government maturity point this out, but in somewhat different ways. One model displays, in some detail, the policy, technology, data, and organizational issues that must be resolved for organizations to progress to higher levels of e-government maturity with an attendant increase in benefits for both government organizations and end-users. Achieving more mature levels of e-government requires higher levels of both technology and organizational complexity.

Another model identified the following four stages of e-government integration: (1) catalogue with online presence, catalogue presentation, and downloadable forms, (2) transaction with services and forms online, working database, and supporting online transactions, (3) vertical integration with local systems linked to higher level systems and within similar functionalities, and (4) horizontal integration with systems integrated across different functions and real one stop shopping for citizens (Chen et al., 2007).

The third model stresses increasing levels of data integration required for true transformational e-government, but warns that such data integration raises significant privacy issues when the data involve personally identifiable information. Chen et al. (2007) comment that these models imply, but only sometimes make explicit, that the complexity of these various forms of integration have likely resulted in many organizations reaching the highest level of e-government maturity.

1.2 Stage Model for Interoperability

Based on the reviewed literature on systems interoperability and stages of growth models, we are now ready to present a potential stage model for e-government interoperability. Semantic interoperability is defined as the extent to which information systems using different terminology are able to communicate. Organizational interoperability is defined as the extent to which organizations using different work practices are able to communicate. The stages are illustrated in Figure 5.1.

- **Stage 1.** In *work process*, each employee does his or her tasks in a way that is adopted to both organization and person. By aligning work processes in inter-operating organizations, e-government interoperability increases. Alignment is possible in sub-processes as well as complete processes and sets of processes. As argued by Fahey, Srivastava, Sharon and Smith (2001), there is a need to capture, analyze, and project the transformational impact of electronic government on organizational work processes in intra- as well as inter-organizational relationships. At this stage, integration and efficiency in work processes from interoperability is important.

- **Stage 2**. In *knowledge sharing*, a flow strategy is focused on collecting and storing knowledge in interoperating organizations (Hansen, Nohria, & Tierney, 1999). While electronic work processes handle information, knowledge work is handled by employees in collaborating organizations (Bock, Zmud, & Kim, 2005; Wickramasinghe, 2006). At this stage, effectiveness and learning in inter-organizational relationships from interoperability is important. Organizations must establish and maintain collaborative relationships in which knowledge sharing is critical to resolving numerous issues related to data definitions and structures, diverse database designs, highly variable data quality, and incompatible network infrastructure (Pardo & Tayi, 2007).

- **Stage 3**. In *value creation*, inter-operating organization may have different value configurations. A distinction is often made between value chains, value shops, and value networks (Stabell & Fjeldstad, 1998). The best-known value configuration is the value chain. In the value chain, value is created through efficient production of goods and services based on a variety of resources. Primary activities in the value chain include inbound logistics, production, outbound logistics, marketing and sales, and service. In the value shop, value is created through creative problem solving for clients based on knowledge resources. Primary activities include problem identification, solutions, decisions, implementation, and evaluation (Sheehan, 2005). In the value network, value is created through efficient connections of subscribers to the network. Primary activities include services, contacts, and infrastructure. Interoperability at this stage of value creation is concerned with interactions between primary activities in different value configurations present in electronic government. While a public hospital is a problem-solving organization for patients, having value shop as the dominant value configuration, a public transportation authority is a production organization, having value chain as the dominant value configuration. At this stage, added value from interoperability is important.

- **Stage 4**. In *strategic alignment*, interoperating organizations apply two-way linked planning with reciprocal integration in strategy work. The purpose of integration is to support and influence organizational strategy (King & Teo, 1997). The role of information technology functions is to be a resource supporting and influencing organizational strategy. At this stage, synergies among interoperating organizations are important. There are no conflicting goals as often found at lower stages.

The cumulative effect of higher stages of interoperability might be measured in terms of transaction cost reduction. Legner and Lebreton (2007) argue that transaction cost theory seems to be an appropriate approach to quantify interoperability as interoperability issues are the result of the division of work and occur in

Figure 5.1. Stage model for e-government interoperability

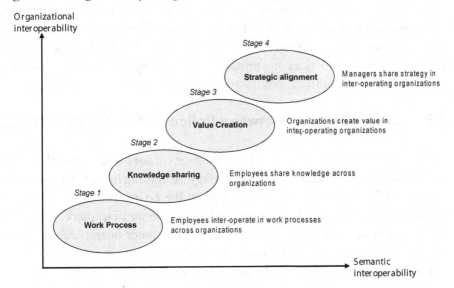

the context of exchanges between organizational actors. Transaction cost theory concurs that the transaction between interoperating organizations is the basic unit of analysis and regards governance as the means by which order is accomplished in a relation in which potential conflict threatens to undo or upset opportunities to realize mutual gains.

Five attributes of information exchange are positively associated with transaction costs: (1) necessity of investments in durable, specific assets; (2) infrequency of transacting; (3) task complexity and uncertainty; (4) difficulty in measuring task performance; and (5) interdependencies with other transactions. Overall, higher stages of interoperability will reduce impacts of these attributes on transaction costs. First, investments in hardware and software have to be carried out at Stage 1 to allow inter-organizational work processes. Second, task complexity and uncertainty is reduced by knowledge sharing at Stage 2. Third, measuring task performance is possible in value creation at Stage 3. Finally, interdependencies are strategically aligned at Stage 4. Only the attribute of infrequency of transaction is not necessarily impacted by higher interoperability stages.

The starting point for the stage model is standardization. According to Papazoglou and Ribbers (2006), interoperability requires standardization in four dimensions: technology, syntax, Semantics, and pragmatics. Technology standards concern middleware, network protocols, and security protocols. Syntax standardization means that the network e-government organization has to agree on how to integrate heterogeneous applications based on the structure or language of the messages exchanged. Normally, commonly acceptable data structures are chosen to represent well-known constructs, e.g. object descriptions. Semantic standards constitute agreements in extension to syntactic agreements on the meanings of the terms used for an organization's information systems. Pragmatic standards, finally, are agreements on practices and protocols triggered by specific messages, such as orders and delivery notifications.

1.3   Interoperability Between Police and Customs in Norway

To clearly delineate the separation between stages in our model, we study interoperability between police and customs in Norway. According to the UN e-Government Survey for 2008, Norway is ranked third on the e-Government readiness index by the United Nations. This is a rank after Sweden and Denmark, and ahead of the United States and Netherlands. As a base, computer interoperability between police and customs imply that information exchange on criminal activity in terms of trafficking and smuggling is technically feasible.

Process interoperability between police and customs is achieved when police investigations are supported by border-control information, and border-control is supported by information from police investigations. For example, passing vehicles with registration number and time is useful to police investigations, while information on suspects from law enforcement is useful to border control. At this level, we may find Web syndication. Web syndication is a form of syndication in which Web site material is made available to multiple other sites. It refers to making Web feeds available from a site in order to provide other people with a summary of the Web site's recently added contents, such as latest news or forum posts.

Knowledge interoperability occurs when police and customs share knowledge about organized crime and criminal organizations. For example, trafficking in women to Norway from Nigeria occur mostly on Oslo airport, while women from Ukraine are transported by car via Sweden. Heroin from Afghanistan travels through Kurdistan and Denmark to Norway by Albanian crime groups, while cocaine from Colombia travels via the Netherlands to Norway. Sharing knowledge on organized crime will improve knowledge development and knowledge management in both law enforcement and customs service. At this level, we may find federated identity. Federated identity implies that a person's user information in terms of assembled identity is stored across multiple distinct identity management systems. Electronic information is joined together by use of the common token, which is usually the user name.

In our example of police and customs in Norway, both organizations have several value configurations depending on public service functions. In the case of police investigations, value shop is the appropriate value configuration. Similarly, in the case of customs control at airports, harbors and land borders, customs personnel represent a value shop configuration. Hence, value interoperability is possible and feasible by combining primary activities from the two agencies.

For example, when a lorry loaded with family boats from Latvia passed the border of Norway, police had instructed customs to let the lorry pass. The reason was that Norwegian police knew there were narcotics in terms of amphetamine hidden in one of the boats. Since the lorry was part of organized crime, the police wanted to follow it to its destination. Customs, however, were desperately in need of success and stopped the lorry, invited the press and told how much narcotics they had been able to capture. Criminal police was upset. In our perspective this situation occurred because the two federal organizations have conflicting goals. While customs authority is concerned with confiscating smuggling goods, police authority is concerned with fighting organized crime (Dean, Fashing, & Gottschalk, 2006). At this final stage 4, there should be no such conflicting goals among interoperating organizations anymore.

1.4   Public Sector Entrepreneurship

An important approach to change in general and to aligned change in particular is entrepreneurship. An entrepreneur is a person who operates a new enterprise or venture and assumes some accountability for the inherent risk. The newly and modern view on entrepreneurial talent is a person who takes the risks involved to undertake a business venture. Entrepreneurship is often difficult and tricky, as many new ventures fail. In the context of the creation of for-profit enterprises, entrepreneur is often synonymous with founder. Most commonly, the term entrepreneur applies to someone who creates value by offering a product or service in order to obtain certain profit. The majority of recent theories in the business and managerial economic literature assumes that the economic performance of small and medium-sized firms depends largely on the entrepreneurs' (or team's) capacities. Even so, economists still do not fully understand the relationship between entrepreneurs and firm performance (Thomas & Mancino, 2007).

The entrepreneurial process is the result of a complex interaction between individual, social and environmental factors. Taken separately, neither the personality of the entrepreneur nor the structural characteristics of the environment can, on their own, determine an organization's performance. In order to provide an example of the relationship between entrepreneurs' subjective characteristics/traits and organizational performance, Thomas and Mancino (2007) carried out an empirical study. The study aimed to explain how the presence of entrepreneurs' specific subjective characteristics can influence an organization's strategic orientation and, as a consequence, local development.

By analyzing several subjective characteristics taken from a sample of 101 successful entrepreneurs from southern Italy, Thomas and Mancino (2007) found that certain issues emerge regarding the link between the economic performance of the ventures launched in this area and the weak level of growth. Successful entrepreneurs' behavior and decisions were heavily influenced by family support. The entrepreneurial culture of the family also tended to substitute the protective role played by public institutions. The entrepreneurial decisions of local entrepreneurs were triggered both by their need to rid themselves of poverty and their feeling that they are destined to continue the family business, the majority of them being the children of entrepreneurs. Most of the interviewees were classified as necessity rather than opportunity entrepreneurs.

An entrepreneur might be driven by a compulsive need to find new ways of allocating resources. He or she might be searching for profit-making opportunities and engineer incremental changes in products and processes. While strongly innovative entrepreneurs tend to champion radical changes in resource allocation by making new product markets and pioneering new processes, weakly innovative entrepreneurs tend to seek small changes in resource allocation to explore profit making opportunities between already established activities (Markovski & Hall, 2007).

Aligned development of systems interoperability requires entrepreneurship. Public sector organizations should develop entrepreneurial capabilities in their provision of public goods and services and their interactions with private sector providers. Extending an entrepreneurial culture into the operations of public organizations to enable co-operating digital government will take time, as changes need thorough planning and involvement.

Entrepreneurship is about exploiting opportunities, such as opportunities available to the government, businesses and citizens at higher levels of interoperability. Entrepreneurship is fundamentally important to firms and government agencies worldwide. Entrepreneurship is the core of the dynamics of development, and the entrepreneur is the driving force for change. An entrepreneur is an innovator, a leader, a creator, a discoverer, an equilibrator, and more. An entrepreneur represents human action of an individual within any organization providing essential innovative services regardless of their organizational position.

According to Kor, Mahoney and Michael (2007), entrepreneurship typically liberalizes the economy, promotes foreign investment, infuses new technology, and increases economic standards of living. Understanding better how entrepreneurship enhances the economic development of poorer nations and creates economic wealth within developed nations requires increased effort by researchers, especially within an institutional context.

Entrepreneurial employees can provide a wide range of entrepreneurial services to their organization including generating and evaluating innovative ideas related to services, technology, and administrative organization, inter-organizational information systems and guiding the direction and governance of an organization's evolution. Entrepreneurial employees are individuals who typically seek opportunities in a subjective manner. Subjective entrepreneurial discovery takes place as entrepreneurs seek to seize the opportunities afforded by political and economic frictions, such as uncertainties in inter-organizational relationships and technological conditions, which are typically not known in advance, and may only be resolved over time (Kor et al., 2007).

The entrepreneurial function for interoperability in e-government is characterized by the exercise of judgment in decision-making. Judgment is where individuals take decisions without access to any generally agreed rule that could be implemented using publicly available information known to be true. Therefore, entrepreneurs act under uncertainty. Entrepreneurs are agents of development acting with limited available information.

A government agency exists because of entrepreneurship. For some agencies, the founding entrepreneur may have been active several centuries ago. The entrepreneur(s) initiated the establishment of a new public organization. Public organizations are realizations of entrepreneurial visions. Witt (2007) argues that the essential part of an entrepreneurial service of restructuring government resources is the provision of a cognitive input in the form of a 'business conception'. A business conception consists of subjective, sometimes highly idiosyncratic imaginings in the mind of (potential) entrepreneurs of what business is to be created, and how to do it. Like a cognitive framework, a business conception is the entrepreneurs' interpretation and application of available information into restructuring of government.

Jacobides and Winter (2007) phrased the question: How do entrepreneurs choose the boundaries of their own ventures? To answer this question, they started from the premise that while entrepreneurs believe themselves to have superior ideas in one or multiple parts of value creation arenas; they are characteristically short of cash, and of the ability to convince others to provide it. This premise motivates a simple model in which the entrepreneur has a value-adding set of ideas for parts of a value creation arena (e.g., interoperability between health service and police investigation). Assuming that the entrepreneur's objective is to maximize government success, it might be observed that initial scope depends not only on available cash, but also on how much value the entrepreneur's ideas add to each participant in the digital government. Entrepreneurs will focus on the areas that provide the maximum profit and minimum risk per available cash.

Audretsch and Keilbach (2007) operationalized entrepreneurialism in terms of entrepreneurial behavior that involves the activities of individuals who are associated with creating new organizations rather than the activities of individuals who are involved with maintaining or changing the operations of on-going established organizations. Accordingly, entrepreneurial thinking and the cognitive process associated with the identification of an opportunity can be viewed in conjunction with the decision to engage in entrepreneurial action.

The entrepreneur's task is to discover and exploit opportunities, defined most simply as situations in which there are interoperability benefits to be achieved in integration activity. Opportunity discovery is about valuable information and knowledge for which there is a market. Hence, identification of valuable information and knowledge is linked to the identification of valuable markets that they serve. Opportunity discovery relates to the generation of value, where the entrepreneur determines or influences the set of resource choices required to create value (Hsieh, Nickerson, & Zenger, 2007).

Entrepreneurial leadership is characterized by judgment in decision-making. Judgment is where individuals make decisions without access to any generally agreed rule that could be implemented using publicly available information known to be true. An entrepreneur will work for interoperability based on his or her judgment, without standard decision-making rules or tools from traditional management. Judgment refers primarily to business decision-making when the range of possible future outcomes is generally unknown. Judgment is required when no obviously correct model or decision rule is available or when relevant data is unreliable or incomplete (Foss, Foss, Klein, & Klein, 2007).

Entrepreneurial judgment is ultimately judgment about the control of resources. As an innovator, a leader, a creator, a discoverer and an equilibrator, the entrepreneur exercises judgment in terms of resource acquisition and allocation to prosper from interoperability benefits. As founder and developer of the government project or enterprise, the entrepreneur must exercise judgmental decision-making under conditions of uncertainty (Foss et al., 2007).

An important task in entrepreneurial leadership is to stimulate organizational citizen behavior among public employees in the cooperating organizations. Organizational citizen behavior supports the organization and goes beyond an individual's job assignment and tasks. Examples include cooperation with others, volunteering for additional tasks, orienting new employees, offering to help others accomplish their work, and voluntarily doing more than the job requires. Organizational citizen behavior is performance that supports the social and psychological environment in which task performance takes place. This behavior exceeds the minimum role requirements of the job, it is not easily enforceable, and performing it is usually at the discretion of the individual (Bergeron, 2007). Thus, individuals who spend time on these support activities are considered 'good citizens' in the digital government.

Entrepreneurial management manifests itself in a regime in the organization. A regime is the set of rules, both formal and informal, that regulate the operation of government activities and its interaction with society. Regime change is sometimes needed to take advantage of new technological and organizational opportunities. One dimension of a regime is employment, where employment regime is dependent on the employees' major work motivation, the mode of coordinating and controlling employees, and the standard for selecting staff (Witt, 2007).

Since entrepreneurship is about personal initiative, it is about both male and female entrepreneurs. An interesting question is whether there are gender differences in entrepreneurship. In a study of female immigrant entrepreneurs, Low (2008) found that female immigrant entrepreneurs made a significant contribution to the Australian economy. The study examined the economic contributions of a group of Asian-born women entrepreneurs in Sydney. The empirical study showed that they make significant economic contributions to the creation of new businesses and jobs in addition to other non-quantifiable economic benefits to Australia.

In another gender-oriented study, Reavley and Lituchy (2008) conducted a six-country analysis of self-reported determinants of success. They studied female entrepreneurs in Canada, Ireland, Czech Republic, Poland and Japan. The women became entrepreneurs because they felt rejected – a phenomenon sometimes labeled the 'push factor'. While some women defined success in terms of profits, many used non-financial factors such as number of clients, number of employees, years in business, or because 'my peers say so'. The most important factor identified in the study was networking. Business education and training was second.

Similarly, Seet, Ahmad and Seet (2008) was interested in differences between female and male entrepreneurs in Singapore in terms of personality traits. Personality traits studied included sociable, decisive, authoritative, goal-oriented, self-confidence, anxious, risk-taking, intuitive, internal locus of control, optimism, self-confident, and leader. Their results showed that a majority of the female entrepreneurs regarded themselves as more anxious as compared to their male counterparts. Females rated themselves lower in the aspects of self-confidence and optimism. The study findings also showed that Singaporean male entrepreneurs have significantly higher internal locus of control than their female counterparts.

1.5   Public Sector Demographics

Stages of e-government are dependent on the qualifications of the inhabitants for all services used by persons in the society. If the skill level is low and the access to computers is limited, then the potential for digital government is low.

There are also many users who have various disabilities from color-blindness to being visually impaired. Although in the US, Section 508 is in existence, many government Web sites do not comply with anything but the minimal standards. This means that when the readers read the pages, the alt tags are present; however, they are not descriptive. Many contain "click here" with no description as to where that link will take the user. This makes it difficult for those who are visually impaired to make use of the e-government Web sites. Standardization and integration of e-government Web sites is crucial to ensure section 508 standards are not just minimally met.

Usability issues for older adults, those with disabilities, and color blindness, for example, do also need to be taken into account. Many older adults are users of e-government Web sites as well as the people working within e-government. Older adults aged sixty years and over face design barriers to the use of state and federal government Web sites due to aging vision.

E-government Web sites should also be standardized for Web sites in other languages. In the US, many government Web sites set up in Spanish are not accurate, still contain English words for major categories, or do not truly reflect an actual Spanish translation.

Shneiderman (2000) argued for pushing human-computer interaction research to empower every citizen. He looked for universal usability, since the goal of universal access to information and communication services is compelling.

CONCLUSION

The stage model for interoperability developed in this chapter, suggests that governments follow certain steps into higher levels as they evolve and develop. In particular, the stage model for e-government interoperability shows predictable patterns of growth from business process interoperability, to knowledge management interoperability, to value configuration interoperability and into strategy position interoperability. In particular, these models suggest that the challenges and requirements for organizational success vary with different stages, and thus, organizational actions must change as the stages change.

REFERENCES

Audretsch, D. B., & Keilbach, M. (2007). The Theory of Knowledge Spillover Entrepreneurship. *Journal of Management Studies, 44*(7), 1242-1254.

Bergeron, D. M. (2007). The potential paradox of organizational citizenship behavior: Good citizens at what costs? *Academy of Management Review, 32*(4), 1078-1095.

Bock, G.-W., Zmud, R. W., & Kim, Y.-G. (2005). Behavioral intention formation in knowledge-sharing: Examining the roles of extrinsic motivators, social-psychological forces, and organizational climate. *MIS Quarterly, 29*(1), 87-111.

Chen, Z., Gangopadhyay, A., Holden, S. H., Karabatis, G., & McGuire, P. (2007). Semantic integration of government data for water quality management. *Government Information Quarterly, 24*(4), 716-735.

Dean, G., Fashing, I. A., & Gottschalk, P. (2006). Profiling police investigate thinking: A study of police officers in Norway. *International Journal of the Sociology of Law, 34*(4), 221-228.

Earl, M. J. (2000). Evolving the e-business. *Business Strategy Review, 11*(2), 33-38.

Eckman, B. A., Bennet, C. A., Kaufman, J. H., & Tenner, J. W. (2007). Varieties of interoperability in the transformation of the health-care information infrastructure. *IBM Systems Journal, 46*(1), 19-41.

Fahey, L., Srivastava, R., Sharon, J. S., & Smith, D. E. (2001). Linking e-business and operating processes: The role of knowledge management. *IBM Systems Journal, 40*(4), 889-907.

Foss, K., Foss, N. J., Klein, P. G., & Klein, S. K. (2007). The entrepreneurial organization of heterogeneous capital. *Journal of Management Studies, 44*(7), 1165-1186.

Frankfort-Nachmias, C., & Nachmias, D. (2002). *Research methods in the social sciences* (Fifth ed.). London: Arnold.

Gottschalk, P. (2007). Information systems in police knowledge management. *Electronic Government, an International Journal, 4*(2), 191-203.

Gottschalk, P., & Solli-Sæther, H. (2006). Maturity model for IT outsourcing relationships. *Industrial Management & Data Systems, 106*(2), 200-212.

Gottschalk, P., & Tolloczko, P. (2007). Maturity model for mapping crime in law enforcement. *Electronic Government, an International Journal, 4*(1), 59-67.

Hansen, M. T., Nohria, N., & Tierney, T. (1999). What's your strategy for managing knowledge? *Harvard Business Review, 77*(2), 106-116.

Housel, T., & Bell, A. H. (2001). *Measuring and managing knowledge*. Boston: MacGraw-Hill Irwin.

Hsieh, C., Nickerson, J. A., & Zenger, T. R. (2007). Opportunity discovery, problem solving and a theory of the entrepreneurial firm. *Journal of Management Studies, 44*(7), 1255-1277.

Jacobides, M. G., & Winter, S. G. (2007). Entrepreneurship and firm boundaries: The theory of a firm. *Journal of Management Studies, 44*(7), 1213-1241.

Kazanjian, R. K. (1988). Relation of dominant problems to stages of growth in technology-based new ventures. *Academy of Management Journal, 31*(2), 257-279.

Kazanjian, R. K., & Drazin, R. (1989). An empirical test of a stage of growth progression model. *Management Science, 35*(12), 1489-1503.

King, W. R., & Teo, T. S. H. (1997). Integration between business planning and information systems planning: Validating a stage hypothesis. *Decision Science, 28*(2), 279-308.

Kor, Y. Y., Mahoney, J. T., & Michael, S. C. (2007). Resource, capabilities, and entrepreneurial perceptions. *Journal of Management Studies, 44*(7), 1187-1212.

Legner, C., & Lebreton, B. (2007). Business interoperability research: Present achievements and upcoming challenges. *Electronic Markets, 17*(3), 176-186.

Low, A. (2008). Economic outcomes of female immigrant entrepreneurship. *International Journal of Entrepreneurship and Small Business, 5*(3/4), 224-240.

Markovski, S., & Hall, P. (2007). Public sector entrepreneurialism and the production of defense. *Public Finance and Management, 7*(3), 260-294.

Nolan, R. L. (1979). Managing the crisis in data processing. *Harvard Business Review, 57*(2), 115-116.

Papazoglou, T. A., & Ribbers, P. M. A. (2006). *E-business: Organizational and technical foundations.* West Sussex, UK: John Wiley & Sons.

Pardo, T. A., & Tayi, G. K. (2007). Interorganizational information integration: A key enabler for digital government. *Government Information Quarterly, 24*(4), 691-715.

Pfarrer, M. D., Decells, K. A., Smith, K. G., & Taylor, M. S. (2008). After the fall: Reintegrating the corrupt integration. *Academy of Management Review, 33*(3), 730-749.

Rao, S. S., & Metts, G. (2003). Electronic commerce development in small and medium sized enterprises: A stage model and its implications. *Business Process Management, 9*(1), 11-32.

Reavley, M. A., & Lituchy, T. R. (2008). Successful women entrepreneurs: A six-country analysis of self-reported determinants of success - more than just dollars and cents. *International Journal of Entrepreneurship and Small Business, 5*(3/4), 272-296.

Scholl, H. J., & Klischewski, R. (2007). E-government integration and interoperability: Framing the research agenda. *International Journal of Public Administration, 30*(8), 889-920.

Seet, P. S., Ahmad, N. H., & Seet, L. C. (2008). Singapore's female entrepreneurs - are they different? *International Journal of Entrepreneurship and Small Business, 5*(3/4), 257-271.

Sheehan, N. T. (2005). Why old tools won't work in the "new" knowledge economy. *Journal of Business Strategy, 26*, 53-60.

Shneiderman, B. (2000). Universal usability. *Communications of the ACM, 43*(5), 85-91.

Stabell, C. B., & Fjeldstad, Ø. D. (1998). Configuring value for competitive advantage: On chains, shops and networks. *Strategic Management Journal, 19*(5), 413-437.

Thomas, A., & Mancino, A. (2007). The relationship between entrepreneurial characteristics, firms' positioning and local development. *Entrepreneurship and Innovation, 8*(2), 105-114.

Wang, H., Song, Y., Hamilton, A., & Curwell, S. (2007). Urban information integration for advanced e-planning in Europe. *Government Information Quarterly, 24*(4), 736-754.

Wickramasinghe, N. (2006). Expanding the exploratory power of agency theory for the knowledge economy. *International Journal of Management and Enterprise Development, 3*(5), 510-520.

Witt, U. (2007). Firms as realizations of entrepreneurial visions. *Journal of Management Studies, 44*(7), 1125-1140.

Chapter VI
Frameworks for Aligned Development

1.   FRAMEWORKS FOR ALIGNED DEVELOPMENT

Alignment is the adjustment of an object such as a system, a procedure or a process in relation with other objects so that they work better together. For example, strategic alignment refers to business structure and information technology fit in relation to business strategy and external environment. When alignment is attained, then an organization improves its relative performance as compared to other organizations.

The concept of alignment was originally based on the fit in the context of organizational psychology and became an important concept in the management literature. The construct of alignment is difficult to develop, due to the ambiguity and complexity of management and organizational alignment. There have been a number of integrated conceptual frameworks in the recent decades attempting to understand and provide insights into the business-IT alignment complexity (e.g., Chan, Huff, Barclay, & Copeland, 1997; Reich & Benbasat, 2000; Sabherwal & Chan, 2001).

In this chapter we present both theoretical-based and practical-based frameworks for aligned development. Researchers have developed for example, integration models, frameworks for modeling of cross-organizational business processes, framework for aligned development of collaborative networks, and a three-level framework for information sharing and cross-organizational process enactment. Governmental information integration initiatives are also described for example the Hong Kong framework, Web-based inter-organizational initiatives in Mexico, UN's connected governance framework, and electronic voting in Geneva. In this chapter we also take a look at Unified Enterprise Modeling Language (UEML) and Service-Oriented Architecture (SOA).

1.1 Cross-Organizational Back-Office Integration

In electronic government, a distinction can be made between the front and back offices of public service delivery organizations. The interaction between citizens and civil servants occurs in the front office, while in the back office, the assessment of inquiries as well as the supporting registration activities takes place. Back office activities normally require the exchange of information between the back offices of different agencies. However, back-office co-operation is found to be a serious problem (Bekkers, 2007).

Bekkers (2007) phrased the question: Given the political nature of back-office integration, should cross-organizational back-office integration be seen as a command and control challenge or a process of management challenge? He argues that comparative case study research has primarily shown that integration is the outcome of a process in which offices have been able to create a shared understanding about the necessity of integration and in which conflicting rationalities, with their own core values, internal logic and legitimacy, have to be weighed against each other. Integration is a goal-searching, incremental process, which should anticipate a changing political agenda in order to gain support. Bekkers (2007) found that understanding is reached through the ongoing recognition of the interdependencies among back-offices, and as a result of a focus on the content of the problem and not on jurisdictions and costs. Trust and political and legal pressure are the lubricants that facilitate this process.

The integration of back offices implies the integration of information domains. An information domain is a unique sphere of influence, ownership and control over information–its specification, format, exploitation and interpretation. Integration models are being introduced for domain integration. One integration model is integration of back offices through centralization. A super-coordinated back office–as a shared information domain– is created that uses the communication and transaction channels of other organizations in order to provide equivalent services. The other organizations are linked with a database in one central back office, which leads to a situation labeled *pooled coupling* by Bekkers (2007).

Another integration model is labeled *sequential coupling*, when back offices operate as sequential links in the same service delivery chain. Here, the exchange of information is improved within the chain through the introduction of workflow and supply chain information management. Interfaces facilitate the flow of information between links.

There is a third model mentioned by Bekkers (2007) as well. The distinction between the back offices becomes irrelevant when these offices use the same database consisting of unique information that identifies the status of a person or object. Relevant data are collected at one administrative point, in relation with one administrative procedure, and are used and re-used by several other agencies in relation to other services. This can be called *reciprocal coupling*.

1.2   Cross-Organizational Business Processes

Increasing interconnection of organizations is a global trend. Independent organizational units or entire organizations build temporary or permanent collaborations, which pool resources, capabilities, and information to achieve a common objective. New business models are emerging and existing procedures are redesigned, forming inter-organizational processes between several agencies (Greiner, Legner, Lippe, & Wende, 2007). Inter-organizational processes are labeled cross-organizational business processes (CBP) by Greiner et al. (2007). The successful implementation of CBPs requires a clear understanding of the common processes across all involved stakeholders. It also needs a structured approach to interlink internal processes of an organization into a CBP.

Greiner et al. (2007) developed a framework to support modeling of cross-organizational business processes. The framework operates at three levels: business level, technical level, and execution level. As illustrated in the figure, internal focus is present in organizational processes. Opening up for external links is occurring at all three levels. Similarly, cross-organizational processes have to be determined at all three levels as illustrated in Table 6.1.

Table 6.1. Modeling framework for cross-organizational business processes

Process Level	Organizational Process	External Link Process	Cross-Organizational Process
Business Level	*Internal positioning*	*Semi-internal positioning*	*External positioning*
Technical Level	*Internal effectiveness*	*Semi-internal effectiveness*	*External effectiveness*
Execution Level	*Internal Efficiency*	*Semi-internal efficiency*	*External efficiency*

There are two dimensions in the framework: level and process. At each intersection between the two framework dimensions, a possible process model can be identified to capture tasks and relationships of cross-organizational interactions. Thus, it should be ensured that all relevant perspectives on CBP models as well as the processes required for different user views of the processes are properly captured and modeled. To complete the modeling framework, a modeling procedure is required that describes in which order models have to be created to make best use of the framework and to ensure best possible integration of existing models. Concerning the creation of views and CBPs, Greiner et al. (2007) identified three possible alternatives:

- An inside-out approach where each organization starts with the identification of their internal processes and the creation of external links.
- An outside-in approach where the partners start identifying a common picture of the interaction in terms of a CBP model.
- A both-side approach where one partner starts with its links to both partners and internal processes.

In terms of the different levels of abstraction, the current practice in process modeling is the outside-in approach. CBPs are first defined on business level, refined on the technical level and then implemented into an executable model for each partner (Greiner et al., 2007).

1.3 Architectural Options

There are always alternatives when working on information systems generally and interoperability in particular. In a management perspective, it is always important to present alternatives. A nice example is Eckman, Bennet and Kaufman (2007), who present architectural options for health-care information exchange. They found four major software architectures, or interoperability approaches, available to implement a health-care information exchange: data federation, data warehousing, information distribution (one-to-many, sometimes referred to as publish-subscriber), and one-to-one transactional messaging (Eckman et al., 2007):

1. **Federated (decentralized) architecture**. In data federation, data is distributed among a number of independent repositories. Data may be stored in multiple locations, including, for example, at multiple health-care providers, each with a multiplicity of data repositories. The central infrastructure operated by the exchange accesses this data based on a central index. Information systems within an organization may have their own independent indexes. It is the

responsibility of the central index in the operability stack to map to the appropriate data store.

2. **Warehouse (centralized) architecture.** A data warehouse, a high-performance storage system including more than one repository for various data types, is maintained in the central infrastructure. For example, the entire history of all patients could be stored in the central repository, which would allow for the widest variety of uses for the data.

3. **Information distribution (one-to-many) architecture.** In a one-to-many messaging architecture, each system shares information that is entered into the system and processes all information that it receives. The interoperability stack does not maintain a persistent store of the information, but is merely a clearing-house for information distribution. The transaction hub in the interoperability stack is defined as the component that ensures a reliable transmission infrastructure. Each published piece of data must be maintained in the transaction hub until it is delivered to all subscribers. The interoperability stack in the one-to-many architecture model operates much like an electronic mailing list server. Each enterprise within the exchange that has data entered into its systems publishes the relevant data outward to the interoperability stack. All other agencies participating in the exchange that have subscribed to data feeds receive the data from the transaction hub. The receiver of the data is then responsible for processing the information that it receives.

4. **One-to-one transactional messaging architecture.** With the one-to-one architecture, each member of the exchange can communicate with other members. The interoperability stack for this pattern is the most lightweight and requires the least investment in platform components.

These alternatives do all have advantages and disadvantages. According to the contingent approach to management, situational factors for e-government will determine which architecture is better. Typically, there is a broad spectrum of stakeholders, each of whom plays a different role in deciding future interoperability architecture. When designing a real-world system, one should not consider the four alternatives as mutually exclusive. Rather, to satisfy all of the many stakeholders in a dynamic landscape of requirements, Eckman et al. (2007) argue that one should build into an interoperable infrastructure the ability to adapt to changing real-time requirements.

1.4   Collaborative Networks

A framework for aligned development is the concept of a collaborative network suggested by Fedorowicz, Gogan and Williams (2007). A collaborative network represents the joint organizational entity, infrastructure, business processes, re-sources, and relationships, which support a shared effort to provide some collective benefit, whether it is a program, service, or a product. An inter-organizational system provides the connecting infrastructure (computing and networking hardware, application software, and databases) to support the exchange of information across organizational boundaries on a continuing basis.

Collaborative networks are created when agencies agree to share information on an ongoing basis. The collaborative network may be governed informally, or it may have formal governance mechanisms and an explicit organizational structure. Whether governed formally or informally, the collaborative network has its own strategy, governance structure, inter-organizational systems, and other systems, processes, and resources apart from the strategies, governance structures, systems, processes, and resources of each of the participating agencies (Fedorowicz et al., 2007).

Development of collaborative networks faces many challenges. Their leaders must agree upon and manage the collaboration process as well as design and implement the inter-organizational systems that support and deliver the content and tools needed by each participant. Many factors in the external environment, the agency context, and the collaborative network itself can affect the collaboration process and systems design (Fedorowicz et al., 2007).

Fedorowicz et al. (2007) presented findings from a case study of CapWin, a collaborative network created to enable first responders to share information across jurisdictional and functional boundaries as they work together during emergencies and other critical events. The study examined how aspects of the external environment and the agency context impeded or facilitated the CapWin collaborative network and the inter-organizational system that supports it. In the study, factors affecting information sharing and collaborative processes were identified:

- **External environment**
  - *Critical events.* Elections, new administrations; crises; media, interest group, or public demands
  - *Economics.* Competitive pressures and agreements; economic conditions (employment, recession, inflation, etc.); federal, state, or local budget deficit or surplus, fiscal timing
  - *Politics.* Federal, state, and local laws and regulations; government agenda, election politics and outcome, partisan division within and/or between branches of government, separation of powers, federalism, public opinion
- **Agency context** (for each participating agency)
  - *Strategy.* Institutional charter, vision; objectives, priorities

- ○ *Governance.* Membership, roles, relationships, delineation of authority, policies or directives
- ○ *Resources.* Availability of staff, funding for research and development, experimental projects, ongoing operations
- ○ *Processes.* Operations and procedures
- ○ *IT infrastructure.* Compatibility and interoperability of networks, applications, databases
- **Collaborative network**
- **Strategy.** Collaborative agreement and/or charter, vision, objectives, priorities
- **Governance.** Membership, roles, formal or informal relationships, delineation of authority, policies or directives
- **Resources.** Funding sources; operational business model
- **Processes.** Collaborative and inter-organizational operations and procedures, which implement decisions and support activities related to strategy, governance, and resources
- **IT infrastructure.** The inter-organizational system(s)

In the case of CapWIN, aligned development started in 1999 and was completed in 2005, indicating that time was required to cope with many of the factors listed above. The September 11, 2001 terrorist attacks on the World Trade Center was an example of a critical event in the external environment that caused the CapWIN project to intensify (Fedorowicz et al., 2007).

1.5   One-Stop E-Government Service Provision

Citizens and businesses face significant obstacles during their interaction with public administrations and governments, having to cope with bureaucracy, ambiguous procedures, functional disintegration, vague, and/or overlapping authority structures and information fragmentation. One-stop e-government represents an approach and a framework for solving such difficult problems, as described by Gouscos, Kalikakis, Legal and Papadopoulou. (2007). One-stop e-government has emerged as a trend to offer electronically administrative service packages that meet the needs of citizens' life events and business transactions, with a promise to enhance service accessibility and alleviate service delivery delays and costs.

Gouscos et al. (2007) argue that traditionally, one-stop government developments have been based on approaches concerned with interoperability through standardization. Such frameworks call for some degree of technical "homogenization" of service provision schemes, based on communication and collaboration through common protocols and formats, as prerequisite to interoperability. However, one-stop government initiatives based on adoption of common standards and re-engineering of internal processes may face significant implementation risks due to a number of technical, organizational, regulatory, or political obstacles to standardization, especially in multi-national settings.

Gouscos et al. (2007) argue that an alternative to this rigid approach is the general workflow for one-stop service provision. It is based on externally operating workflows that invoke internal administrative processes as they currently are. According to the workflow alignment approach, end-users are able to (1) browse the service offerings of intermediation hubs and (2) submit requests for one-stop service transactions. Upon arrival of a user request, the intermediation hub shall (3) identify involved services, competent service providers, and additional user input requirements, and (4) request end-users for additional input as appropriate. Upon provision of requested input by end-users, the intermediation hub (5) undertakes forwarding of user input to individual service providers, (6) employing knowledge about one-stop service workflows to trigger, and (7) co-ordinate individual service transactions. Service providers, then, enact their internal processes in order to (8) serve the individual service cases forwarded by the intermediation hub, and upon completion (9) deliver results back to the latter, where final service results are (10) synthesized and (11) returned to requesting end-users. The complexity of the internal co-ordination between the intermediation hub and the individual service providers is transparent to the requesting end-users, as end users' requests may be monitored and presented.

1.6   The Hong Kong Framework

In Hong Kong, the interoperability development framework supports the government's strategy of providing client-centric joined-up services by facilitating the interoperability of technical systems between government departments, as well as between government systems and systems used by the public, including citizens and businesses (Government CIO, 2007).

The interoperability framework defines a collection of specifications aimed at facilitating the interoperability of government systems and services. By bringing together the relevant specifications under an overall framework, IT management and developers can have a single point of reference when there is a need to identify the required interoperability specifications that should be followed for a specific project. By adopting these interoperability specifications, systems designers can ensure interoperability between systems while at the same time enjoy the flexibility to select different hardware, and systems and application software to implement solutions (Government CIO, 2007).

For existing systems, the framework says that conformance to certain specifications may not be readily achieved, given the diversity of current platforms and systems. Existing systems are required to consider conformance to the interoperability framework only when there is a new requirement for government to public integration, and only in respect of the modifications that specifically relate to external interfaces. Migration to the interoperability framework must be considered when a major functional change is being performed. In either case, connection or changes to existing systems are required to conform to the framework only when it is financially and functionally prudent to introduce compliance with the interoperability framework (Government CIO, 2007).

The development of an interoperability alignment is a long-term, ongoing strategy that must continually be reviewed and updated. Given the emergence of new business requirements and the pace of technological advancement, there are likely to be frequent changes to the specifications. In Hong Kong, the technical specifications under the interoperability framework will be reviewed every 6 to 12 months (Government CIO, 2007).

Other national frameworks are similar to the Hong Kong framework. For example, the New Zealand e-government interoperability framework is a set of policies, technical standards, and guidelines. It covers ways to achieve interoperability of public sector data and information resources, information and communications technology, and electronic business processes. It enables any agency to join its information, technology or processes with those of any other agency using a predetermined framework based on open (i.e., non-proprietary) international standards (State Services Commission, 2007).

1.7   A Three-Level Framework

In electronic government, the cooperation between agencies is specified in a changing environment. The aligned development includes a specification that is tailored towards information sharing and cross-organizational process enactment. Process enactment, however, relies on intra-organizational process specifications that have to comply with the infrastructure available in an organization for process and data management. Therefore, Grefen, Ludwig and Angelov (2003) developed a three-level process and data specification framework:

1.   **Internal level.** The internal level is geared towards enactment of processes in the context of a specific organization, e.g. by means of workflow management systems. The internal level is a mapping of the conceptual level, where mapping is a combination of translation (specialization for a specific platform) and refinement. The internal process specification is used to have local parts of cross-organizational processes enacted by process support systems. Workflow

management systems are a general infrastructure for the automated support of business process enactment. Often, these systems are separate entities in an information system infrastructure, and sometimes they are embedded in other systems.

2. **Conceptual level.** The conceptual level is the centerpiece of process specification. It is independent from external use and internal implementation. It is used for conceptual reasoning about the process, e.g. for design and analysis purposes. The conceptual level is a combination of abstraction and aggregation of the internal level. The process exhibited by an organization to the outside world is usually less detailed than the implementation of the same process actually enacted by the organization. Consequently, several process aggregation levels exist. The mapping between these aggregation levels is dealt with by a process refinement hierarchy.

3. **External level.** The external level is geared towards communicating process specification between different organizations. It can be considered a projection of the conceptual level, where projections uses hiding and translation operations. Interoperability of processes is the main focus of the external level. A process specification at the external level can be a high-level abstraction of a complex process that on the conceptual level is considerably refined into separate sub-processes. Still the process specifications at the external level should not be too general as they may turn the process of information exchange into a black box process, thereby not allowing the fine-grained cooperation that is required in dynamic relationships.

Grefen et al. (2003) argue that the three-level approach to business process specification provides a clear separation of concerns in business process design, thereby increasing quality, flexibility and reusability of process specifications in cross-organizational settings. This separation of concerns is becoming increasingly important, as the complexity of automated cross-organizational processes grows through the advent of digital government.

1.8 Web-Based Inter-Organizational Initiatives

One of the most comprehensive institutional frameworks to study information technologies in government settings is the technology enactment theory, which explains the effects of organizational forms and institutional arrangements on the information technology used by government agencies. The technology enactment framework pays attention to the relationships among information technology, organizations, embeddedness, and institutions. Luna-Reyes, Gil-Garcia and Cruz (2007) argue that institutional arrangements and organizational structures shape not only the enacted technology, but also other processes and results of government IT projects. They studied collaborative digital government in Mexico in terms of federal Web-based inter-organizational information integration initiatives.

The national e-Mexico system is an "umbrella" initiative to develop government services and applications for the Mexican society. The mission of e-Mexico is to "be an agent for change in the country, integrating efforts from diverse public and private actors in the elimination of the digital divide and other socioeconomic differences among Mexicans, through a system with technical and social components to offer basic services on education, health, commercial interchange, and government services, being at the same time leader in Mexican technological development" (Luna-Reyes et al., 2007).

E-Mexico strategy is organized around three axes or lines of action, and with a value-oriented and collaboration focus. The purpose of these three axes is (1) to create infrastructure that allows citizens to connect to the Internet through digital community centers mainly in public schools and libraries; (2) to produce content in four areas: e-learning, e-health, e-economy, and e-government; and (3) to develop a technical architecture for the Mexican government (Luna-Reyes et al., 2007).

Luna-Reyes et al. (2007) argue that this strategy has been successful, as more than 19,000 Web pages in 19 contents portals were available in the e-Mexico portal in 2006. More than 3 million Web pages are displayed every month, and 17 virtual communities share information and experiences through the e-Mexico portal.

1.9 Electronic Markets

Markets have purely been the prerogative of business, not of government, which have relied upon bureaucracy as the way to administer society. The advent of e-government has created new opportunities to apply market mechanisms in government. Collaboration between agencies to solve complex issues, the citizen in focus, and public private partnerships are three examples to achieve better government using electronic markets.

The practice of markets has a long history. On a market, there is supply and demand. Electronic markets have supply and demand for information. Governments adopting electronic markets to inform citizens better as customers with a choice embark upon a line of development where information economics becomes relevant to the design of government triggered costs. Informed customers trade well than lesser informed which is why consumer policy and competition policy both support measures to ensure information quality and availability.

Embarking on digital government is more than applying information systems to government administration. It is to embark upon a trajectory of electronic markets according to the thesis of information value integration. Pedersen, Fountain and

Loukis (2006) claim that electronic markets represent a viable and fruitful conceptualization of the change from bureaucratic government to digital government, meaning government as a decision-making and allocating mechanism, wedded to periodic public elections of politicians constrained in the short run by constitutional institutions, yet having the potential power to change constitutional rules in the long run, legitimately authorized to govern and to appoint civil servants to enforce obligations and to service the needs of the public.

Electronic marketplace adoption by government is affected by several factors (Wang, Song, Hamilton, & Curwell, 2007):

- **Performance expectancy.** An agency will be positive to electronic markets because of the economic and other benefits that electronic markets offer.
- **Effort expectancy.** An agency may adopt electronic markets if they are easy to use and implement.
- **Institutional influence.** Examples of such influences are trend followers, public request, and other influences.
- **Facilitating conditions.** Examples of such conditions include system compatibility, familiarity with business practices, and special funding for interoperability projects.

1.10 Connected Governance

Connected governance is a framework for alignment that ensures integrated information flows, new transactional capacities, as well as new mechanisms for feedback, consultation and more participative forms of democracy. Underlying the concept of connected governance is a systematic approach to collection, reuse and sharing of data and information. To achieve connected governance, the following steps are required (United Nations, 2008):

1. Intra-government process re-engineering: efficient, responsive and tailored government to reflect citizen needs
2. Inter-government process re-engineering: efficient, joined-up and borderless government:
    a. Vertical cooperation/integration between levels
    b. Horizontal cooperation/integration between agencies at same level
    c. Multi-stakeholder cooperation (with private and third sectors)
3. Re-engineer legacy technology, processes, skills and mindsets.

Underlying the concept of connected governance is a systematic approach to collection, reuse and sharing of data and information. The key platform on which connected government is built upon is the concept of interoperability, which, according to UN (2008), is the ability of government organizations to share and integrate information by using common standards. Strengthening connected governance concepts within e-government is an important step towards improving the coordination processes and systems within and across government agencies and organizations and changing the way that government operates. Improving the government agencies' capability to transfer and exchange information is critical and will require the improved interoperability between agencies' information systems. In the longer term it will require agencies to adopt and implement common information policies, standards and protocols.

Governments transform themselves into a connected entity that responds to the needs of its citizens by developing an integrated back office infrastructure. This is the most sophisticated level of online e-government initiatives and is characterized by (United Nations, 2008):

- Horizontal connections (among government agencies)
- Vertical connections (central and local government agencies)
- Infrastructure connections (interoperability issues)
- Connections between governments and citizens
- Connections among stakeholders (government, private sector, academic institutions, non-government organizations and civil society).

From the perspective of more horizontal but in reality networked governance solutions that are the essence of service transformation and effective security strategies, the two fundamental questions that remain stubbornly unanswered according to the (United Nations, 2008) are:

- How to motivate public managers to share data and, more generally, to work jointly for the public good
- How to understand and influence the range of barriers, from psychological and social to structural, political and technical, that mitigate across cross-agency initiatives

In order to better illustrate such tensions, the Swedish experience of public management and their recent quest for interoperability provides a useful case study as described by the UN (2008). Although one of the most prosperous and technologically sophisticated countries in the world, the Swedish government has faced critics both internally and externally pointing out that the traditional culture of decentralized agency autonomy does not lend itself easily to achieving government-wide capacities.

Swedish government, having studied several other European country experiences, concluded that many such models being developed elsewhere would not be workable in their context. The main reason is what they term as the contractual model of public sector management underpinned by a networked administration. According to the contractual model, an administrative unit decides for itself whether external services and functions are sufficiently attractive for the unit to use them or pay for this use. According to the networked administration, government is composed of independently managed units that rely on functions and resources provided by other such units or private companies, and form part of permanent and temporary cooperative structures.

1.11 Modeling Methods for Interoperability

A number of modeling methods and approaches exist for the purpose of aligned development. An example is the unified enterprise modeling language (UEML), which is an ongoing effort to develop an intermediate language for modeling enterprises and related domains, such as information systems. The aim is to support integrated use of enterprise and information systems models expressed using different languages (Opdahl & Berio, 2007).

The UEML construct template provides a standard, integrative format for representing modeling constructs. Entries of the construct template are derived from a UEML meta model. Template entries are filled in by gradually using concepts to build a UEML ontology that is rooted in central ontological concepts. This ontology grows incrementally as more modeling constructs are added, whether centrally by some UEML management organ or locally within an enterprise that uses UEML. As a consequence, when two modeling constructs, from the same or from different languages, have both been described using the UEML-template, the exact correspondences between them can be identified in terms of the common ontology. This paves the way for comparison, consistency checking, update reflection, view synchronization and model-to-model translation. Therefore, Opdahl and Berio (2007) define UEML as a web (or family) of languages that co-exist while at the same time relate precisely to each other.

In addition to UEML, there are a number of other modeling methods. Examples are activity diagrams, XML, and OWL. The idea is to improve interoperability through model-based generation of systems. For example, Touzi, Lorré, Bénaben and Pingaud (2007) demonstrated how a collaborative information system might be interoperable through model-based generation. In their approach, a collaborative process model focuses on process interaction, data interaction, and application interaction in a collaborative information system.

1.12   Service-Oriented Architecture

Another approach to alignment is service-oriented architecture (SOA), where the technology side is aligned to the business side by making the technology optional for systems. SOA is an architectural style that attempts to support business processes by being an independent infrastructure. It is an approach defining and provisioning the IT infrastructure that is supposed to allow different applications to exchange data and participate in business processes loosely coupled from the operating systems and programming languages underlying those applications (www.wikipedia.org).

Still in 2008, many government organizations seemed to have unrealistic expectations concerning benefits of SOA. While the idea and the concept of loosely coupled infrastructure and applications has great potential, experience so far in implementing this idea has for the most part been less successful.

Service-oriented architecture is an architectural style of attempting to build software applications that promotes loose couplings between components. Increasing interconnections among businesses and agencies in need of interoperability have created a demand for services that have published contracts and interfaces. The ambition is for systems to dynamically discover interconnections when needed. SOA appears to many executives to be an appropriate technique for satisfying such needs. In addition, SOA also is assumed to provide methods to allow applications of different generation to interact with each other and coexist.

A modern SOA must meet the requirement of interoperability. Interoperability between different systems and programming languages provides the basis for integration between applications on different platforms. For technical interoperability, it is implemented through a communication protocol. One example of such communication is based on the concept of messages and messaging. Using messages across defined message channels decreases the complexity of the end application, thereby allowing the developer of an application to focus on critical application functionality instead of the intricate needs of a communication protocol (www. wikipedia.org).

To meet the requirements of Semantic interoperability, a modern SOA must apply a terminology for its data elements that are loosely coupled to various terms used in application systems. To meet the requirements of organizational interoperability, SOA seems to be short of contribution.

SOA represents a model in which functionality is decomposed into distinct units (services), which can be distributed over a network and can be combined together and reused to support business applications. These services communicate directly with each other by passing data from one service to another, or by coordinating an activity between two or more services. Therefore, the concept of service-oriented architecture is often seen as building upon the tradition of distributed computing and modular programming (www.wikipedia.org).

Service-oriented architecture is a paradigm for organizing and utilizing distributed capabilities that may be under the control of different ownership situations, which is typically the case in interoperability situations. According to the paradigm, SOA provides a uniform means to offer, discover, transfer, interact with and use capabilities to produce desired effects consistent with measurable preconditions and expectations. Architects of organizational structures believe that SOA can help organizations respond more quickly and cost-effectively to changing public and political conditions. This style of architecture promotes reuse at the macro service level rather than micro sub service level. It should also simplify interconnection to–and usage of–existing IT legacy systems and assets (www.wikipedia.org).

SOA is an architectural style whose goal is to achieve loose coupling among interacting software agents to achieve interoperability without forcing integration. A service is a unit of work done by a service program to achieve desired end results for a service consumer. Both provider in terms of service program and consumer in terms of application user are roles played by software agents on behalf of their owners (webservices.xml.com).

Implementing a service-oriented architecture means to deal with heterogeneity in an interoperability perspective. A flexible, yet standardized architecture might be required to better support the connection of various applications and the inter-organizational sharing of information. SOA is a paradigm for one such architecture. It claims to unify business processes by structuring large applications as an ad-hoc collection of smaller modules labeled services. These applications can be used by different individuals as well as groups of people both inside and outside an agency. New applications built from a mix of services from the global pool tend to exhibit greater flexibility and uniformity. Building all applications from the same pool of services makes achieving interoperability much easier, while limiting the choices of independent organizations (www.wikipedia.org).

SOAs build applications based on software services. Services are intrinsically independent units of functionality, which have no calls to each other embedded in them when first implemented. They typically implement functionalities most IT users would recognize as a service, such as filling out an online application for a building permit, reviewing tax statements, or submitting a high school priority request. Instead of services embedding calls to each other in their source code, protocols are defined which describe how one or more services can communicate with each other. The architecture then relies on a business process support link and sequence services, in a process known as orchestration, to meet a new or existing business system requirement (www.wikipedia.org).

Interoperability is an important guiding principle for service-oriented architectures. SOAs are commonly built using Web services standards that have gained broad industry acceptance. These standards (also referred to as Web service specifications) are expected to provide greater interoperability and some protection from lock-in to proprietary vendor software. Furthermore, basic profiles and basic security profiles are developed to enforce compatibility (www.wikipedia.org).

With the increasing use of software applications for the conduct of business, the need to link software applications of co-operating organizations with minimal effort and in short timeframes is becoming ever more evident. This need for interoperability has stimulated not only SOA but also a similar approach labeled service-oriented computing (SOC). SOC is emerging as a promising paradigm for enabling the flexible interconnection of autonomously developed and operated applications within and across organizational boundaries (Dijkman & Dumas, 2007). SOC is a distributed application integration paradigm in which the functionality of existing applications (the services that they provide) is described in a way that facilitates its use in the development of applications which integrate this functionality. The resulting integrated applications can themselves be exposes as services, leading to networks of interacting services known as service compositions or composite services (Dijkman & Dumas, 2007). SOC brings along a number of specific requirements over previous paradigms (such as object-oriented or component-oriented) that should be taken into account by service-oriented design (Dijkman & Dumas, 2007, p. 338):

- **Autonomy:** As services are expected to be developed by autonomous teams, service-oriented design is an inherently collaborative process involving multiple stakeholders from different organizational units. This raises the issue that certain organizational units may opt not to reveal the internal business logic of their services to others, making it difficult (yet indispensable) to ensure global consistency.
- **Coarse granularity:** Services are highly coarse-grained, at least more so than objects and components. Often, a service maps directly to a business object or activity (e.g. a purchase order or a flight booking service). It follows that the design of services (and in particular composite ones) is a complex activity. It involves reconciling disparate aspects such as the involved providers and consumers, their interfaces, interactions, and collaboration agreements, their internal business processes, data, and legacy applications.
- **Process awareness:** As services often correspond to business functionality exported by an organizational unit, they are likely to be part of long-running interactions driven by explicit process models. Hence, service-oriented design should take into account the business processes as part of which services oper-

ate and interact, and in particular, the integration (or retrofitting) of services into business processes. This effectively places service-oriented design at the crossroads between software and enterprise design.

At IBM, a top-down approach to service-oriented architecture was implemented. The IBM enterprise architecture is designed to ensure effective linkages between enterprise business and IT deliverables. It is a means to integrate business strategy, process, data, applications, and infrastructure. Enterprise architecture governance attempts to unify design approaches with a set of published principles, architecture criteria, standards, and guidelines (Walker, 2007).

1.13 Training E-Government Actors

As governments evolve into more online and interoperable governmental processes and services, the traditional civil servant must develop as the organizer and manager of processes and services that increasingly propagate towards business, education, health and other domains critical to citizens. As a consequence, there is a need to train civil servants into their new roles.

Wilson, van Engers and Peters (2007) recommend training sessions on methodology to be organized as action learning and problem based learning. In addition, a range of support tools for service design exercises might be used as well. Case studies are also useful.

1.14 The Case of Shared Services Organizations

As shared services organizations become more popular as a service management and delivery option in government, properly defining and setting up the governance structure for aligned development continues to be a key success factor. A shared services organization is essentially a business unit or organizational entity within the public service that delivers specialized, value-added services across the entire domain.

Grant, McKnight, Uruthirapathy and Brown (2007) studied governance design for shared services organizations in the public sector. The term governance structure is used to outline the hierarchy of committees, boards, bodies, or forums that execute the management of, and oversee the delivery of, the goods and/or services of the service organization. The governance structure details how many levels or layers of committees there are and outlines each of their primary roles. Their roles, accountabilities, and responsibilities assigned to the levels and committees of the organization will differ based on how some of the core processes of the organization are implemented.

Aligned development in the case of shared services will occur for both strategic and operational concerns. Grant et al. (2007) argue that strategic and operational concerns should be separated. The design of shared services is most effective when those who deliver service to clients are separate from those who ensure compliance with corporate policy and standards. While strategic processes align inter-organizational directions, operational processes align service provision from various sources.

1.15   The Case of Joint Military Operations

With few national exceptions, future military operations will be combined and joint, conducted as part of an alliance or coalition force. Such operations require units and formations of participating nations to operate subordinated to or in co-operation with each other. Key to any operation will be effective command and control across national boundaries and between multinational formations or units.

The successful execution of fast moving operations will require both an accelerated decision-action cycle, increased tempo of operations, and an ability to conduct operations simultaneously within combined/multinational formations at a higher quality of decisions. The integration of information technology into command structures and procedures will have a profound effect on the execution of command and control. Commanders require pertinent information in order to enhance their decision-making and command capabilities.

The multilateral interoperability program (Multilateral Interoperability Programme, 2003) by NATO allies is a framework for aligned development to enhance operational effectiveness at every level of command by enabling the sending, receiving, filtering, and processing of ever-increasing amounts of digital information. Battle spaces such as Afghanistan require forces to be more dispersed over a larger area of intelligence interest, with longer lines of communications, and with the requirement to provide timely and secure information in accordance with the commander's priorities. When a Norwegian soldier was wounded in Afghanistan in December 2007, a German surgeon in a British military camp treated him.

The role of the multilateral interoperability program (MIP) in this context is to produce an infrastructure service that will allow national land component systems to exchange predetermined information with systems of other nations. The framework consists of the establishment of communications and information systems connectivity and the establishment of information exchanges. As much as possible, the MIP solution will be integrated into existing operational practices, with the goal of providing seamless interoperability within a multinational force. The common interface is defined by a data model and comes from the analysis of a wide spectrum of allied information exchange requirements. Among its features the most remarkable are:

- It models the information that allied component commanders need to exchange (both vertically and horizontally)
- It serves as the common interface specification for the exchange of essential battle space information.

System developers incorporate the MIP specification and include a single interface to it. Thereafter no further interfaces are required to interoperate with any other MIP enabled system. The function, implementation and display of the host communication and control application are not the concern of MIP.

The MIP program is not a formal NATO program. It is rather a voluntary and independent activity by the participating nations. The active nations in the MIP program are: Australia, Austria, Belgium, Canada, Czech Republic, Denmark, Finland, France, Germany, Greece, Hungary, Italy, Lithuania, Netherlands, Norway, Poland, Portugal, Romania, Slovenia, Spain, Sweden, Turkey, United Kingdom, and United States.

1.16   The Case of Electronic Voting

The following presentation of electronic voting is derived from Chevallier, Warynski and Sandoz (2007). With the vote through the Internet, citizens are introduced to a new way of voting, complementary to ballot box and postal voting. The democratic principle "one person – one vote" must be respected. The first recorded vote is preserved, and possible later votes are normally discarded. The process of voting has to remain simple and explainable in electronic voting. The voter must also be able to verify that the system correctly understand his or her choice, whereas the vote must be kept secret with regard to third parties. The system must prevent the voter making a choice that can lead to the cancellation of a vote (for example choosing both YES and NO, or choosing more candidates than the number of seats available), while still leaving open the possibility to vote blank (Chevallier et al., 2007).

Globally an electronic voting system must be auditable and present a sufficient degree of transparency to satisfy controllers from all political parties and abroad. The system's execution must be logged in such a manner to reveal every tentative on fraud. The system must be available 24 hours a day, 7 days a week during the voting period. Voting must not be possible before or after the voting interval of time (Chevallier et al., 2007).

From a technological point of view, the front end must be available on the largest possible number of home platforms covering most of the electorate. Finally the system must remain under the ownership and control of the government. Therefore, licensing fees per vote or per voter in any form are problematic and should not be considered (Chevallier et al., 2007). The debate around electronic voting has mainly focused on voting on electronic machines in polling stations. (Chevallier et al., 2007) argue that online voting or remote electronic voting is inherently different:

- The centralized infrastructure in Internet voting enables the administration to thoroughly control it. Real-time sensors can activate alarms, while logs record the details of the system's functioning.
- The centralized infrastructure requires only a limited number of skilled people to operate it. It can also be supervised by the electoral commission. A separation of privilege can be implemented between the group of civil servants operating the system and between the members of the electoral commission, in order to achieve transparency and public control.

Internet voting is nevertheless a paperless ballot. This feature is one of the most controversial in the current debate about electronic voting. From (Chevallier et al., 2007) point of view, there are two aspects to consider, the proof of vote and the verifiability:

- *Proof of vote*. In manual systems, the voter receives no proof of vote. In an electronic system, the final screen may inform the citizen of the date and time of the recording of the vote.
- *Vote verifiability*. Only valid and readable vote should be stored in the system. A recount should be possible, based on mirror databases that should be created.

The basic infrastructure of an electronic voting system is composed of the network, the servers and a monitoring system. The network should be designed to protect database servers that manage the electronic ballot box. The servers should be protected by several layers of firewalls and should not be accessible directly from the Internet (Chevallier et al., 2007).

CONCLUSION

As illustrated in this chapter, there is no single framework for aligned interoperability development that will solve all interoperability problems. Rather, a combination of frameworks will be appropriate when trying to solve interoperability problems. Solutions to interoperability challenges are dependent on the situation, requiring a contingent approach to aligned development.

REFERENCES

Bekkers, V. (2007). The government of back-office integration. Organizing co-operation between information domains. *Public Management Review, 9*(3), 377-300.

Chan, Y. E., Huff, S. L., Barclay, D. W., & Copeland, D. G. (1997). Business strategic orientation, information strategic orientation, and strategic alignment. *Information Systems Research, 8*(2), 125-150.

Chevallier, M., Warynski, M., & Sandoz, A. (2007). Success factors of Geneva's e-voting system. *European Journal of ePractice, 1*(November), 47-59.

Dijkman, R., & Dumas, M. (2007). Service-oriented design: A multi-viewpoint approach. *International Journal of Cooperative Information Systems, 13*(4), 337-368.

Eckman, B. A., Bennet, C. A., Kaufman, J. H., & Tenner, J. W. (2007). Varieties of interoperability in the transformation of the health-care information infrastructure. *IBM Systems Journal, 46*(1), 19-41.

Fedorowicz, J., Gogan, J. L., & Williams, C. B. (2007). A collaborative network for first responders: Lessons from CapWIN case. *Government Information Quarterly, 24*(4), 785-807.

Gouscos, D., Kalikakis, M., Legal, M., & Papadopoulou, S. (2007). A general model of performance and quality for one-stop e-government service offerings. *Government Information Quarterly, 24*(4), 860-885.

Government CIO. (2007). *The HKSARG Interoperability Framework.* Government of the Hong Kong special administrative region: Office of the government chief information officer.

Grant, G., McKnight, S., Uruthirapathy, A., & Brown, A. (2007). Designing governance for shared services organizations in the public service. *Government Information Quarterly, 24*(3), 533-538.

Grefen, P., Ludwig, H., & Angelov, S. (2003). A three-level framework for process and data management of complex e-services. *International Journal of Cooperative Information Systems, 12*(4), 487-531.

Greiner, U., Legner, C., Lippe, S., & Wende, K. (2007). Business interoperability profiles. In R. Goncales, J. P. Müller, K. Mertins & M. Zelm (Eds.), *Enterprise interoperability II* (pp. 865-877). London: Springer Verlag.

Luna-Reyes, L. F., Gil-Garcia, J. R., & Cruz, C. B. (2007). Collaborative digital government in Mexico: Some lessons from federal Web-based interorganizational information integration initiatives. *Government Information Quarterly, 24*(4), 808-826.

Multilateral Interoperability Programme. (2003). *Achieving international interoperability of command and control information systems (C2IS) at all levels.* Retrieved July 2008, from www.mip-site.org

Opdahl, A. L., & Berio, G. (2007). A roadmap for UEML. In G. Doumeingts, J. Müller, G. Morel & B. Vallespir (Eds.), *Enterprise interoperability: New challenges and approaches* (pp. 169-178). London: Springer Verlag.

Pedersen, M. K., Fountain, J., & Loukis, E. (2006). Preface to the focus theme section: 'Electronic markets and e-government'. *Electronic Markets, The International Journal, 16*(4), 263-273.

Reich, B. H., & Benbasat, I. (2000). Factors that influence the social dimension of alignment between business and information technology objectives. *MIS Quarterly, 24*(1), 81-113.

Sabherwal, R., & Chan, Y. E. (2001). Alignment between business and IS strategies: a study of prospectors, analyzers, and defenders. *Information Systems Research, 12*(1), 11-33.

State Services Commission. (2007). *New Zealand e-government interoperability framework.*

Touzi, J., Lorré, J. P., Bénaben, F., & Pingaud, H. (2007). Interoperability through model-based generation: The case of the collaborative information system (CIS). In G. Doumeingts, J. Müller, G. Morel & B. Vallespir (Eds.), *Enterprise interoperability: New challenges and approaches* (pp. 407-416). London: Springer Verlag.

United Nations. (2008). *UN e-government survey. From e-Government to connected governance* (No. ST/ESA/PAD/SER.E/112). New York: Department of Economics and Social Affairs, Divison for Public Administration and Development Management.

Walker, L. (2007). IBM business transformation enabled by service-oriented architecture. *IBM Systems Journal, 46*(4), 651-667.

Wang, H., Song, Y., Hamilton, A., & Curwell, S. (2007). Urban information integration for advanced e-planning in europe. *Government Information Quarterly, 24*(4), 736-754.

Wilson, F., van Engers, T., & Peters, R. (2007). Training egovernment actors: Experience and future needs. *European Journal of ePractice, 1*(November), 36-47.

Chapter VII
Strategic Planning for Alignment

1.   STRATEGIC PLANNING FOR ALIGNMENT

Developing a strategy for E-Government interoperability is taken to mean thinking strategically and planning for the effective long-term application and optimal impact of electronic information to support knowledge work and service provision in government agencies. Strategy can simply be defined as principles, a broad based formula, to be applied in order to achieve a purpose. These principles are general guidelines guiding the daily work to reach business goals. Strategy is the pattern of resource development and application decisions made throughout the organization. These encapsulate both desired goals and beliefs about what are acceptable and, most critically, unacceptable means for achieving them.

This chapter starts discussing different strategy levels and elements. Then, we introduce the Y-model for IS/IT strategy work. Important step in the Y-model is to describe the current and the desired business situation, and we list some methods that can help us gaining this understanding. At the end of the chapter we describe stages of integration between business and IT strategy.

1.1   Strategy Levels and Elements

Strategy is both a plan for the future and pattern from the past, it is the match an organization makes between its internal resources and skills (sometimes collectively called competencies) and the opportunities and risks created by its external environment. Strategy is the long-term direction of an organization. Strategy is the course of action for achieving an organization's purpose. Strategy is the direction and scope of an organization over the long term, which achieves advantage for the organization through its configuration of resources within a changing environment and to fulfill stakeholders' expectations (Johnson & Scholes, 2002).

Business strategy is concerned with achieving the mission, vision and objectives of an organization, while IS strategy is concerned with use of IS/IT applications, and IT strategy is concerned with the technical infrastructure as illustrated in Figure 7.1. An organization has typically several intra-organizational as well as inter-organizational IS/IT applications. The connection between them is also of great interest, as interdependencies should prevent applications from being separate islands. Furthermore, the arrows in the illustration in the figure are of importance. Arrows from business strategy to IS strategy, and from IS to IT strategy represent the alignment perspective, they illustrate *what* before *how*. What do we want to achieve? How might we achieve it? Arrows from IT to IS strategy, and from IS to business strategy represent the extension from *what* to *how* to *what*. This is the impact perspective, representing the potential impacts of modern information technology on future business options. Necessary elements of a business strategy

Figure 7.1. Relationships between strategies at three levels

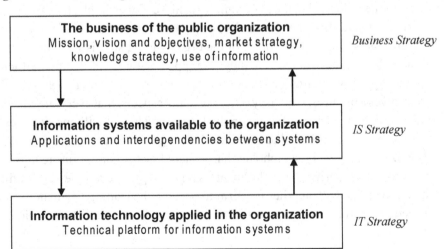

include mission, vision, objectives, market strategy, knowledge strategy, and our general approach to the use of information, information systems and information technology.

Mission describes the reason for firm existence. For example, the reason for law firm existence is client's needs for legal advice. The mission addresses the organization's basic question of 'What business are we in?' This single, essential, sentence should include no quantification, but must unambiguously state the purpose of the organization and should, just as carefully define what the organization does not do. According to Ward and Peppard (2002, p. 189), the mission is an unambiguous statement of what the organization does and its long-term, overall purpose:

Its primary role is to set a direction for everyone to follow. It may be short, succinct and inspirational, or contain broad philosophical statements that tie an organization to certain activities and to economic, social, ethical or political ends. Values are also frequently stated alongside the mission. Three widely-differing examples of missions are:

- *To be the world's mobile communications leader, enriching the lives of individuals and business customers in the networked society (large global telecommunication company)*
- *To eradicate all communicable diseases worldwide (World Health Organization)*
- *The company engages in the retail marketing on a national basis of petroleum products and the equitable distribution of the fruits of continuously increasing productivity of management, capital and labor amongst stockholders, employees and the public (a large public company).*

Vision describes what the firm wants to achieve. For example, the law firm wants to become the leading law firm in Norway. The vision represents the view that senior managers have for the future of the organization; so it is what they want it to become. This view gives a way to judge the appropriateness of all potential activities that the organization might engage in. According to Ward and Peppard (2002), the vision gives a picture, frequently covering many aspects, that everyone can identify with, of what the business will be in the future, and how it will operate. It exists to bring objectives to life, and to give the whole organization a destination that it can visualize, so that every stakeholder has a shared picture of the future aim.

Objectives describe where the business is heading. For example, the law firm can choose to merge with another law firm to become the leading law firm in Norway. Objectives are the set of major achievements that will accomplish the vision. These are usually small in number, but embody the most important aspects of the vision, such as financial returns, customer service, manufacturing excellence, staff morale, and social and environmental obligations.

Market strategy describes market segments and products. For example, the law firm can focus on corporate clients in the area of tax law. Public schools can focus on students and their learning material.

An important part of business strategy is concerned with knowledge strategy. According to Zack (1999, p. 135), a *knowledge strategy* describes the overall approach an organization intends to take to align its knowledge resources and capabilities to the intellectual requirements of its strategy:

It can be described along two dimensions reflecting its degree of aggressiveness. The first addresses the degree to which an organization needs to increase its knowledge in a particular area vs. the opportunity it may have to leverage existing but underutilized knowledge resources – that is, the extent to which the firm is primarily a creator vs. user of knowledge. The second dimension addresses whether the primary sources of knowledge are internal or external. Together these characteristics help a firm to describe and evaluate its current and desired knowledge strategy.

The business strategy part concerned with use of information and IT is sometimes called an information management strategy. The general approach to the use of information, information systems needs and information technology investments are described in this part. For example, the ambition level for IT in knowledge management is described, and the general approach to selection of ambition level and combination of ambition levels I – IV is discussed.

Necessary elements of an *IS strategy* include future IS/IT applications, future competence of human resources (IS/IT professionals), and future IS/IT organizational structure, and control of the IS/IT function. An important application area is knowledge management strategy. The future applications are planned according to priorities, how they are to be developed or acquired (make or buy), how they meet user requirements, and how security is achieved. The future competence is planned by types of resources needed, motivation and skills needed (managers, users, IS/IT professionals), salaries, and other benefits. The future IS/IT organization defines tasks, roles, management and possibly outsourcing.

Necessary elements of an *IT strategy* include selection of IT hardware, basic software, and networks, as well as how these components should interact as a technological platform, and how required security level is maintained. The IT platform consists of hardware, systems software, networks and communications, standards and support form selected vendors.

Figure 7.2. IS/IT strategy elements and interdependencies

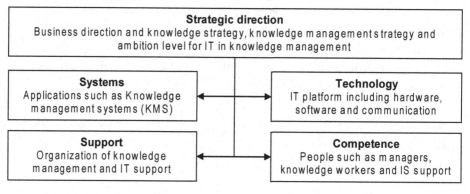

An *IS/IT strategy* is a combined strategy including business context, the IS in a narrow sense and the technological platform. Necessary elements of an IS/IT strategy include business direction and strategy (mission, vision, objectives, knowledge strategy), applications (knowledge management systems), people (future competence of human resources), organization (future organization and control of IT function), and IT platform (future technical infrastructure). Hence, IS/IT is quite a broad term. The term is broad to take care of all connections and interdependencies in a strategy, as changes in one element will have effect on all other elements, as illustrated in Figure 7.2.

Why is strategic IS/IT planning undertaken within business organizations? Hann and Weber (1996) see IS/IT planning as a set of activities directed toward achieving the following objectives:

1. Recognizing organizational opportunities and problems where IS/IT might be applied successfully
2. Identifying the resources needed to allow IS/IT to be applied successfully to these opportunities and problems
3. Developing strategies and procedures to allow IS/IT to be applied successfully to these opportunities and problems
4. Establishing a basis for monitoring and bonding IT managers so their actions are more likely to be congruent with the goals of their superiors
5. Resolving how the gains and losses from unforeseen circumstances will be distributed among senior management and the IT manager
6. Determining the level of decision rights to be delegated to the IT manager.

Based on the resulting strategy for interoperability in digital government, strategic management is important in participating agencies. Strategic management includes understanding the strategic position of an organization, strategic choices for the future, and turning strategy into action. Understanding the strategic position is concerned with the impact on strategy of the external environment, internal resources and competences, and the expectations and influence of stakeholders. Strategic choices involve understanding the underlying bases for future strategy at both higher and lower unit levels and the options for developing strategy in terms of both the directions in which strategy might move and the methods of development. Translating strategy into action is concerned with ensuring that strategies are working in practice. A strategy is not just a good idea, a statement, or a plan. It is only meaningful when it is actually being carried out (Johnson & Scholes, 2002).

1.2   The Y-Model for IS/IT Strategy Work

In the following, we present a model for development of an IS/IT strategy for knowledge management. However, we do not limit strategy work to knowledge management. Rather, we describe the complete IS/IT strategy work where knowledge management is a natural part of it. This is done to keep a complete strategy work process. A limited strategy only for knowledge management can cause sub-optimal solutions for the organization.

Empirical studies of information systems/information technology planning practices in organizations indicate that wide variations exist. Hann and Weber (1996) found that organizations differ in terms of how much IS/IT planning they do, the planning methodologies they use, the personnel involved in planning, the strength of the linkage between IS/IT plans and corporate plans, the focus of IS/IT plans (e.g., strategic systems versus resource needs), and the way in which IS/IT plans are implemented. It has been argued that the Internet renders strategic planning obsolete. In reality, it is more important than ever for companies to do strategic planning (Porter, 2001, p. 63):

Many have argued that the Internet renders strategy obsolete. In reality, the opposite is true. Because the Internet tends to weaken industry profitability without providing proprietary operational advantages, it is more important than ever for companies to distinguish themselves through strategy. The winners will be those that view the Internet as a complement to, not a cannibal of, traditional ways of competing.

In all kinds of strategy work, there are three steps. The first step is concerned with analysis. The second step is concerned with choice (selection and decision), while the final step is concerned with implementation. The model consists of seven stages covering analysis, choice and implementation. As illustrated in Figure 7.3 the stages are as follows:

1. **Describe current situation.** The current IS/IT situation in the business can be described using several methods. The benefits method identifies benefits from use of IS/IT in the business. Distinctions are made between rationalization benefits, control benefits, organizational benefits and market benefits. Other methods include the three-era model, management activities, and stages of growth.

2. **Describe desired situation.** The desired business situation can be described using several methods described in the first chapter. Value configurations, competitive strategy, management strategy, business process redesign, knowledge management, the Internet and electronic business, and information technology benefits.

3. **Analyze and prioritize needs for change.** After descriptions of the current situation and the desired situation, the needs for change can be identified. The gap between desired and current situation is called needs for change. Analysis is to provide details on needs, what change is needed, and how changes can take place. *What*-analysis will create an understanding of vision and goals, knowledge strategy, market strategy, and corporate problems and opportunities. *How*-analysis will create an understanding of technology trends and applications. These analyses should result in proposals for new IS/IT in the organization.

4. **Seek for alternative actions.** When needs for change have been identified and proposals for filling gaps have been developed, alternative actions for improving the current situation can be developed. New IS/IT can be developed, acquired, and implemented in alternative ways. For example, an information system can be developed in-house by company staff, it can be purchased as a standard application from a vendor, or it can be leased from an application systems provider (ASP).

5. **Select actions and make an action plan.** When needs for change and alternative actions have been identified, several choices have to be made and documented in an action plan. Important issues here include development process, user involvement, time frame and financial budget for IS/IT projects.

6. **Implement plan and describe results.** This is the stage of action. Technical equipment such as servers, PCs, printers and cables are installed. Operating systems are installed. Application packages, software programs, programming tools, end user tools and database systems are installed. Development projects are organized. Management and user training takes place. Document results over time.

7. **Evaluate results.** Implementation results are compared with needs for change. It is determined to what extent gaps between desired and current situation have

Figure 7.3. The Y-model for IS/IT strategy work

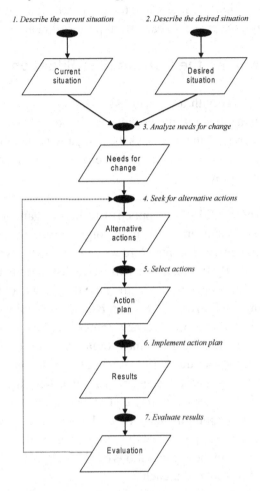

been closed. This is the beginning of the IS/IT strategy revision process, where a new process through the Y-model takes place. Typically, a new IS/IT strategy process should take place every other year in business organizations.

While stages 1 to 3 cover *analysis*, 4 and 5 cover *choice*, and 6 and 7 cover *implementatio*n. In some strategy models, stage 2 is listed as the first stage. It is here recommended to do stage 1 before stage 2. It is easier to describe the ideal situation when you know the current situation. If you start out with stage 2, it often feels difficult and abstract to describe what you would like to achieve. Having done stage 1 first makes the work more relevant. Stage 3 is a so-called gap analysis, looking at the difference between the desired and actual situation. This stage also includes prioritizing. Stage 4 is a creative session as it calls for ideas and proposals for alternative actions. Stages 5 and 6 are typical planning stages. The final stage 7 is important because we can learn from performing an evaluation.

1.3   Describing the Current IS/IT Situation

The Y-model starts with a description of the current situation. We focus on the IS/IT situation, as this will be the subject of change later in the model. First of all we have to understand in what ways the company is using IS/IT. Many approaches can help us gain an understanding of the present IS/IT situation. Some methods are listed in the following:

1. **Benefits of IS/IT.** IS/IT is applied in business organizations to achieve benefits. We can study current IS/IT in the organization to understand what benefits have been achieved so far. Here we can determine what main benefit categories is currently the case. We will make distinctions between rationalization benefits, control benefits, organizational benefits, and market benefits.

2. **Stages of IS/IT growth.** IS/IT in business organizations change over time. New hardware and software, new areas of applications, and new IS/IT support functions emerge. Most business organizations develop through stages over time. Here we can determine at what stage the business organization is for the time being. These stages are classified into three eras: data processing, information systems and information networks.

3. **IS/IT in management activities.** Management activities can be studied in a hierarchical perspective of operational, tactical and strategic management. Current IS/IT in the organizations can be assigned to these levels to determine the extent of support at each level.

4. **IS/IT in business processes.** In a company, many business processes take place at the same time. Some of the processes may rely heavily on IS/IT, while others are mainly manual at the current point in time.

5. **IS/IT support for value configuration.** We make distinctions between value chain, value shop and value network. In each of these value configurations, IS/IT can support activities. The current IS/IT situation is described by identifying activities in the value configuration depending on the extent of technology support.

6. **Strategic integration.** Business strategy and IT strategy have for a long time suffered from lack of coordination and integration in many organizations. Here we measure the current IS/IT situation by use of ten integration mechanisms to determine integration stage in an organization.

7. **IS/IT in e-business.** For most firms, becoming an e-business is an evolutionary journey. We introduce six stages to describe the evolving e-business: external communications, internal communications, e-commerce, e-business, e-enterprise, and transformation.

8. **IS/IT enabled business transformation**. IT-enabled transformation can include business direction change, but more often we find examples at lower levels, such as business design change and business process change.

9. **IS/IT support for knowledge management.** The stages of growth model for knowledge management technology can be applied, where the current IS/IT situation is described by the stage at which the firm currently is performing.

Description of the current situation assumes that we have been able to define borders for our study. Borders exist for both breath and depth. Breath is a question of whether the whole company or only one division should be studied. Depth is a question of whether all aspects such as technology, marketing, management and finance should be included in the study. We recommend both extensive breath and thorough depth to ensure that a wide range of alternative solutions and alternative actions can be identified in later stages of the Y-model. In the case of breath, this may imply that both suppliers and customers are included because there may be electronic market places used by our suppliers and customers. In the case of depth, this may imply that analysis of top management is included because management competence in the area of IS/IT can influence both management attitudes and ambitions concerning future applications of IS/IT.

Description of the current IS/IT situation should focus on issues of importance in technology and knowledge management. Less emphasis should be put on technology itself, such as drawings of company networks and servers. Technology management is focused on the management of information technology, while knowledge management is focused on knowledge strategy and knowledge management systems.

1.4   Describing the Current and Desired Business Situation

We have used some of the nine methods to describe the current situation of IS/IT. Now we have to consider whether the current IS/IT applications are what the company needs or if there might be changes needed. We use the Y-model as our guiding approach. We compare the present business situation (with its support from IS/IT) with the desired business situation. If the current IS/IT applications are not able to serve the needs of the future desired business, then there are needs for change in IS/IT applications and the way we do business. At this point we are moving into stage 2 of the Y-model.

There are many techniques for business analysis. Some are general, while others are more specific. General analysis techniques include SWOT analysis and the X-model. Specific analysis techniques include business direction (mission, vision, and objectives), market strategy, value system, competitive forces and product life cycle. Some of these analytical tools are listed in the following:

1. *SWOT analysis* is an analytical tool for assessing the present and future situation focusing on strengths (S), weaknesses (W), opportunities (O) and threats (T). The whole company may be the object of analysis, but also a department in a company or a project in a company may be the study object. How can IS/IT exploit our strengths, compensate our weaknesses, use opportunities and avoid threats? How can IS/IT help make it happen?

2. *X model.* The X model is a tool for description and analysis of both the current and a desired situation. It is a method for assessing the situation within a company, a project, or a department. The situation consists of a time period in which work is done. In the beginning of the time period, there are both factual and personal inputs, and at the end of the period, there are both factual and personal outputs. How can IS/IT improve factual and personal outputs? How can IS/IT help make it happen?

3. *Business direction.* Important business concepts are mission, vision and objectives. How can IS/IT make the firm achieve its vision? How can IS/IT make the firm reach its objectives? How can IS/IT help make it happen?

4. *Market strategy.* The market strategy shows our position and ambition in the market place. We can either have the same product as our competitors, or we can have a different product. If we have the same product as everyone else, it has to be sold at the same price as all the others (as in a vegetable market or through the Internet). It is not possible for an Internet bookstore to sell at a higher price than others, when there is perfect information and information searching is associated with no costs. This is called the law of indifference. In order to survive, the company must have a cost advantage that will give higher profits and result in higher earnings for the owners. How can IS/IT cause a cost advantage? How can IS/IT help make it happen? If we are selling a product that our customers perceive to be different from our competitors' product, then we have differentiation. A service may in its basic form be the same for all companies, like an airline travel, in the sense that all airlines are supposed to bring you safely to your destination. The product is differentiated by supplementary services. How can IS/IT make our customers perceive our products and services to be different from our competitor's? How can IS/IT help make it happen?

5. *Competitive forces.* The basis of this method is that a company exists within an industry and to succeed, it must effectively deal with the competitive forces that exist within the particular industry. For example, the forces in an emerging industry such as mobile communication are considerably different from those of established industries such as financial services. The company interacts with its customers, suppliers and competitors. In addition, there are potential new entrants into the particular competitive marketplace and potential substitute products and services. To survive and succeed in this environment, it is important to understand these interactions and the implications in terms of what opportunities or competitive advantage can occur. How can IS/IT reduce the threat of new entrants, reduce the bargaining power of suppliers, reduce the bargaining power of buyers, reduce the threat of substitute products and services, and reduce the rivalry among existing competitors? How can IS/IT help make it happen?

6. *Product portfolio analysis.* There are a number of approaches that aim to re-late the competitive position of an organization to the maturity of its product. The models assume there is a basic S-shaped curve description to the growth phenomenon of products. Four stages in the life cycle of any product can be identified as introduction, growth, maturity, and decline. When we look at the life cycle of all products in the firm, we can apply product portfolio analysis. This method shows the relationship between a product's current or future revenue potential and the appropriate management stance. The two by two matrix names the products in order to chart symptoms into a diagnosis so that effective management behavior can be adopted. The matrix classifies products according to the present market share and the future growth of that market. A successful product that lasts from emergent to mature market goes around the matrix. This strategy is simply to milk the cows, divest the dogs, invest in the stars and examine the wild cats. How can IS/IT get more milk for a longer period of time from the cows? How can IS/IT explore and exploit the stars? How can IS/IT eliminate the dogs? How can IS/IT develop the wild cats into stars? How can IS/IT help make it happen?

7. *Environmental analysis.* Environmental analysis is concerned with the external corporate environment. An analysis of the environment is important because it increases the quality of the strategic decision making by considering a range of the relevant features. The organization identifies a threats and opportunities facing it, and those factors that might assist in achieving objectives and those that might act as a barrier. The strategy of the organization should be directed at exploiting the environmental opportunities and blocking environmental threats in a way that is consistent with internal capabilities. This is a matter of environmental fit that allows the organization to maximize its competitive

position.   An external analysis can investigate politics, the economy, the society and the technology. This is sometimes called PEST analysis. If we include the study of legal and environmental matters, we call it PESTLE. The analytical work that has to be done in the company when doing environmental analysis is concerned with questions such as: What are the implications of the trends (changes in the environment)? What can the company do in order to meet the opportunities and threats that follow? How can knowledge management meet the opportunities and threats that follow? How can IS/IT help make it happen? For example, how can IS/IT help in global competition (politics)? How can IS/IT help in alliances and partnerships (economy)? How can IS/IT help serve an increasing number of older people (society)?

8.   *External knowledge analysis.* Distinctions can be made between core knowledge, advanced knowledge and innovative knowledge. While core knowledge is required to stay in business, advanced knowledge makes the firm competitively visible, and innovative knowledge allows the firm to lead its entire industry. The knowledge map can be applied to identify firm position. The map in terms of the strategic knowledge framework illustrates firm knowledge levels compared with competitors' knowledge levels.

9.   *Internal knowledge analysis.* While the knowledge map represents an external analysis of the firm's current knowledge situation, the knowledge gap represents an internal analysis of the firm's current knowledge situation. The knowledge gap is dependent on business strategy. What the company does is different from what the company will do, creating a strategy gap. What the company knows is different from what the company has to know, creating a knowledge gap. Two important links emerge: the strategy-knowledge-link and the knowledge-strategy-link.

1.5   Strategic Alignment

IT is recognized as a critical business discipline because it is central to all business activities of modern enterprises in the creation of organizational and customer value. To create business value from IT, business needs to understand the role IT plays, not only in supporting the running of the business in such back-office functions as HR, finance, inventory control, but more importantly the special and competitively differentiated ways that IT plays in delivering products and services to the cooperating agencies and citizens. The integral role that IT has enmeshed into all business functions today means that IT has become a central nervous system of the business. In particular, information *is* the blood stream of business, which flows through all business functions (processes) supported by the IT nervous system. Business value is created by each business function or process through dynamic consumption (processing) of input information and creation of new output information, which in turn will be 'consumed' by another business function (process) as defined by the value configuration of the business.

The fundamental principle of all the critical success factors of IT strategy is therefore IT and business acting as one. This requires each IT task to be aligned with and 'justified' by the business function it is designed to contribute, for and based on which its business value is measured.

IT and business acting as one is easier said than done, however. In reality not many enterprises have yet fully mastered the practice of the fundamental principle of IT and business acting as one. This is because of the bad old tradition of IT in the past (and even today for some enterprises) working (either being treated or wanted to be treated) as the 'back-office techie guys' who seemed to do as they were told (or requested) by the business without having any concern for the end-customers or indeed the business purpose of the tasks being requested. In the past, IT saw themselves as the technical guys who would do whatever technical task is requested of them by the business. There was no need to understand the business, let alone the business strategy or points of differentiation. The 'us-versus-them' working relationship or company culture permeates between IT and business in most enterprises in the past, and indeed even till today.

While this scenario may be an extreme example for today's enterprises, it is nonetheless still a common issue for most enterprises today that some degree of misalignment still exists between business and IT. The varying degrees of organizational misalignment and functional disconnect between business and IT have been the key inhibitor of value creation by IT in all enterprises, past and present. Despite rigorous and diligent attempts by researchers and practitioners alike, in the past twenty years, various surveys have shown that business-IT alignment remains a strategically critical priority for business and IT leaders to manage and achieve.

In a classical study of alignment, King and Teo (1997) investigated the degree of alignment and integration between business strategy and IT strategy in enterprises as illustrated in Table 7.1. They found that companies go through four stages of strategic integration with increasing degree of integration as the company becomes excellent (mature) in exploiting and managing IT for business differentiation. The first stage is separate planning with *administrative integration*. The second is one-way linked planning with *sequential integration*, while the third is two-way linked planning with *reciprocal integration*. The fourth stage is *fully integrated* business and IT planning – the most mature level of business and IT acting as one.

There are many factors affecting the ability of business and IT acting as one. The combination of these factors defines the level at which business functions and IT functions do act as one in strategy formulation, planning and execution. King and Teo (1997) identify ten factors affecting business-IT partnership in business-

Table 7.1. Stages of integration between business strategy and IT strategy, adapted from King & Teo (1997)

Benchmark Variables	Stage 1 Administrative Integration	Stage 2 Sequential Integration	Stage 3 Reciprocal Integration	Stage 4 Full Integration
Purpose of integration	Administrative and nonstrategic	Support business strategy	Support and influence business strategy	Joint development of business and IT strategies
Role of the IT function	Technically oriented and nonstrategic	Resource to support business strategy	Resource to support and influence business strategy	Critical to long-term survival of organization
Primary role of the IT executive	Functional administrator responsible for back room support	IT expert who formulates IT strategy to implement business strategy	IT expert who provides valuable inputs during strategy formulation and implementation	Formal and integral member of top management who is involved in many business matters
Performance criteria for the IT function	Operational efficiency and cost minimization	Contribution to business strategy implementation	Quality of IT inputs into business strategy formulation and implementation	Long-term impact on organization
Triggers for developing IS applications	Need to automate administrative work processes	Business goals considered first	Business goals and IT capabilities considered jointly	IT applications are critical to success of business strategy
Top management participation in IT planning	Seldom	Infrequent	Frequent	Almost always
User participation in IT planning	Seldom	Infrequent	Frequent	Almost always
IT executive participation in business planning	Seldom	Infrequent	Frequent	Almost always
Assessment of new technologies	Seldom	Infrequent	Frequent	Almost always
Status of IT executive (Number of levels below the CEO)	Four or more	Three	Two	One

IT strategic management. They call these factors benchmark variables. The four stages of integration can be described in terms of benchmark variables as shown in Table 7.1. Benchmark variables indicate the theoretical characteristics at each stage of integration. For example, organizations at Stage 1 can theoretically be expected to conform to values of benchmark variables listed under Stage 1. However, this does not mean that it is not possible for organizations at Stage 1 to have values of benchmark variables applicable to other stages. Each of the ten benchmark variables can be explained more in detail as follows (King & Teo, 1997):

1. **Purpose of integration.** At Stage 1, integration focuses primarily on the support of administrative work processes. IT is still a commodity service and not critical for business strategy. This gradually changes as the IT function begins to support business strategy (Stage 2) or influence business strategy (Stage 3). At Stage 4, there is joint strategy development for both business and IT strategies – at which business and IT truly acting as one with strategic influences going both directions.

2. **Role of the IT function.** The general transition from being technically oriented to business oriented is a trend for most IT functions. At Stage 1, the IS function is viewed as being primarily technically oriented. Gradually, this role changes when the IT function is used as a resource to support the implementation (Stage 2) and formulation (Stage 3) of business strategies. At Stage 4, the IS function is viewed as critical to the long-term success of the organization. To be able to act as one with the business IT acts and thinks like a business with strong business skills. Similarly business becomes very IT savvy.

3. **Primary role of the IT executive.** There seems to be a general decrease in the size of the central IS function. This may have resulted in a shift in the responsibilities of the IS function from systems design to systems integration, and from the role of a developer to that of an advisor. Due to increasing decentralization, the IT function may assume a staff role similar to a federal government in coordinating dispersed IT resources. The skill requirements of the senior executive have also changed over the years with increasing emphasis on both knowledge about changing technology and knowledge about the business. In addition, significant political and communication skills are required. The role of the IT executive gradually changes from being a functional administrator responsible for providing back room support (Stage 1), to being an IT expert who formulates IT strategy to implement business objectives (Stage 2). As the organization begins to apply IT for strategic purposes, the role of the IS executive becomes more important. He or she begins to play a major role in facilitating and influencing the development and implementation of IT applications to achieve business objectives (Stage 3). Finally, in Stage 4, the

IT executive becomes a formal and integral member of the top management team, and provides significant inputs in both IT and non-IT related matters.

4. **Performance criteria for the IT function.** As the IT function matures in terms of alignment to business needs and influence on business solutions, performance criteria for the IT function change from a structured focus on operational efficiency to a more unstructured concern for the impact of IT on strategic direction. The early performance criteria (Stage 1) for the IT function are primarily concerned with operational efficiency, technical quality and cost minimization. When the IT function begins to play a more strategic role by adapting to and influencing business processes, the emphasis gradually shifts to effective strategy implementation (Stage 2), and then to the quality of IT inputs into business strategy formulation and implementation (Stage 3). Ultimately, the performance criteria for the IT function is its long-term impact on the organizational performance (Stage 4) where IT is becoming a business transformer to create a sustainable strategic advantage.

5. **Triggers for developing IT applications.** Initially, triggers for development of new IT applications are opportunities for achieving greater efficiencies through process automation. As IT applications begin to be increasingly used to support business direction, business goals become trigger mechanisms in deciding appropriate IT applications to be developed (Stage 2). At Stage 3, joint considerations of business goals and as well as IT capabilities become important as the organization attempts to develop systems for sustainable competitive advantage. Finally, in Stage 4, IT applications are developed because they are critical to the success of the organization's strategy and the creation of business value for sustained superior performance.

6. **Top management participation in IT planning.** Traditionally, as in Stage 1, top management did not pay great attention to the IT function because it was considered to be an overhead function that generated only cost. Top management's concern was only what IT did cause in terms of technology expenditures, not what kind of benefits were achieved from applying information and communication technologies and systems. At Stage 2, greater top management participation in IT planning begins when IT strategies come to be used to support business strategies rather than just specifying technical solutions. The realization that strategic IT planning can also influence business strategy motivates top management to participate more actively in this kind of strategy work by applying a business language rather than a technical language (Stage 3). For example, e-business influences the way government works in terms of E-Government. Finally, in Stage 4, when the IT function becomes critical for the survival or sustainable superior performance of the organization, top management and senior IT executives jointly formulate business and IT plans – business and IT truly acting as one.

7. **User participation in IT planning.** Before the availability of end-user computing, user management was generally not significantly involved – they were mainly complaining when something went wrong (Stage 1). However, as end-user systems and tools begin to dominate individual work, and the IT function begins to influence functional units in terms of its effects on everyday work as well as business strategies, participation of users becomes more important and natural in order to fully exploit the potential of information technology. User participation gradually increases through the stages, until at Stage 4, where users participate and contribute extensively in IT planning.

8. **IT executive participation in business planning.** The other side of business management alignment in IT planning is having IT executives participate in business planning. The traditional role of the IT function in providing administrative support does not assume the senior IT executive to participate in business planning (Stage 1). The senior IT executive reacts to business plans and does not have any influence on their formulation. Often, the IT executive simply does not understand the business plan and is unable to translate business strategy into IT solutions. At Stage 2, senior IT executive participation is initiated. As the IT function in the eyes of business executives becomes more important in achievement of business objectives, it becomes necessary and smart to include more frequent participation of the senior IT executive in business planning because the traditional participants are relatively unfamiliar with the potential of information technology (Stage 3). With greater participation, the senior IT executive learns the business, becomes more informed about business objectives and is better able to provide higher quality inputs into the planning process. At Stage 4, the senior IT executive becomes an integral member of the top management team and participates extensively in both business planning and IT planning based on alignment expertise acquired at earlier stages.

9. **Assessment of new technologies.** During IT planning, new technologies, which can impact on IT operations as well as business operations, are usually assessed. The level of expertise and sophistication involved in assessing new technologies is the basis for this ninth benchmark variable. In the early stages of IT planning (Stages 1 and 2), assessment of functionality as well as impact of new technologies, if any, is usually done rather informally and infrequently. At Stage 3, the need for formal, knowledge-based and frequent procedures for assessing new technologies becomes apparent as the IT function begins to play a more important role in business planning. At Stage 4, assessment of the impact of new technologies becomes an integral part of business planning and IT planning when the CIO (chief information officer) and the CEO (chief executive officer) have established a mutual communication platform.

The business and IT executives are constantly seeking out potential disruptive technologies to transform the business with.

10. **Status of IT executive.** The responsibilities of the IT function have changed over the years due to technological and conceptual changes that made information technology more important to organizations. IT line responsibilities are being rapidly distributed in many organizations as the IT function begins to take on more staff responsibilities. With these changing responsibilities of the IT function, the status of the senior IT executive is likely to become higher. The position of the senior IT executive - in terms of the number of levels below the CEO - can serve as an indication of the importance of the IT function to the organization's strategy.

So what must business and IT do to act as one – resonating harmonically even in the event of changing business environment? In addition to the mutual understanding of business and IT roles and capabilities in customer value creation described above, two more ingredients are required: Behavioral and Organizational.

The behavioral component deals with establishment of strong relationship and trust between business and IT. This component requires IT to work proactively to engage the business. It requires strong leadership and communications skills, as well as business skills. IT is a means to a business end. IT executives must therefore have a deep understanding of their company business and master the art of business communication. All IT activities and service performance levels must be explained in terms of business context. For instance, instead of saying IT has improved the order management process by implementing a business process management platform using the state of the art service oriented architecture, we say that the order management process has been redesigned with in-built flexibility for ease of adaptation for future business change and has reduced the order-to-cash from x days to y hours. This business context communication will improve the business understanding of IT role, and indeed IT value to business.

The organizational process deals with the mutually dependent nature of business and IT accountabilities in setting strategic direction and planning for, and execution and value-delivery of IT-dependent business programs (and projects). This is known as IT governance, part of corporate governance as described in the next chapter.

CONCLUSION

Resource-based strategy is concerned with development and application of resources. While the business strategy is the broadest pattern of resource decisions, more specific decisions are related to information systems (IS) and information technology (IT).

IS must be seen both in a business and an IT context. IS is in the middle because IS supports the business while using IT. As part of a resource-based strategy, both IS and IT represent capabilities and resources that have to be developed.

The Y-model is presented as a tool for development of an IS/IT strategy. The model consists of seven stages covering analysis, choice and implementation. The stages are describe current solution, describe desired solution, analyze and prioritize needs for change, seek for alternative actions, select actions and make an action plan, implement plan and describe results, evaluate results.

REFERENCES

Hann, J., & Weber, R. (1996). Information systems planning: a modern and empirical test. *Management Science, 42*(7), 1043-1063.

Johnson, G., & Scholes, K. (2002). *Exploring corporate strategy*. Harlow, UK: Pearson Education, Prentice Hall.

King, W. R., & Teo, T. S. H. (1997). Integration between business planning and information systems planning: Validating a stage hypothesis. *Decision Science, 28*(2), 279-308.

Porter, M. E. (2001). Strategy and the Internet. *Harvard Business Review, 79*(3), 62-78.

Ward, J., & Peppard, J. (2002). *Strategic planning for information systems*. Chichester, NY: Wiley.

Zack, M. H. (1999). Developing a knowledge strategy. *California Management Review, 41*(3), 125-145.

Chapter VIII
Governance Structure for Alignment

1.   GOVERNANCE STRUCTURE FOR ALIGNMENT

Given the political nature of back-office integration, should cross-organizational back-office integration be seen as a command and control challenge or a process management challenge? This question was phrased by Bekkers (2007), who found that comparative case studies primarily have shown that integration is the outcome of a process, in which offices have been able to create a shared understanding about the necessity of integration and in which conflicting rationalities, with their own core values, internal logic and legitimacy, have to be weighted against each other. Bekkers (2007) argues that it is a goal-searching, incremental process, which should anticipate a changing political agenda in order to gain support. Understanding is reached through the ongoing recognition of the interdependencies among back-offices, and as a result of a focus on the content of the problem and not on jurisdictions and costs. Trust and political and legal pressure are the drivers that facilitate this process. Co-ordination in terms of governance has to consider a mix of conflict and co-operation.

We start this chapter trying to answer *what is IT governance*. We take look at the broader issue of organizational governance and contracts in governance, and we list reasons why IT governance is important. Other topics covered are such as decision makers and decision rights, categories of decisions, stakeholders and distribution of decision rights.

1.1 What is IT Governance?

IT governance can be defined as specifying decision rights and accountability framework to encourage desirable behavior in the use of IT (Weill & Ross, 2004).

This is the definition we will use here.

Other definitions are for example: (i) IT governance is the structures and processes that ensure that IT supports the organization's mission. The purpose is to align IT with the organization, maximize the benefits of IT, use IT resources responsibly and manage IT risks, (ii) A structure of relationships and processes to direct and control the organization in order to achieve the organization's goals by adding value while balancing risk versus return over IT and its processes, (iii) IT governance is the responsibility of the board of directors and executive management. It is an integral part of organizational governance and consists of the leadership and organizational structures and processes that ensure that the organization's IT sustains and extends the organization's strategies and objectives, and (iv) IT governance is the system by which an organization's IT portfolio is directed and controlled. IT Governance describes (a) the distribution of decision-making rights and responsibilities among different stakeholders in the organization, and (b) the rules and procedures for making and monitoring decisions on strategic IT concerns (Peterson, 2004).

An extensive definition was presented by the IT Governance Institute (2004) as follows. It is a board or senior management responsibility in relation to IT to ensure that:

- IT is aligned with the business strategy, or in other words, IT delivers the functionality and services in line with the organization's needs, so the organization can do what it wants to do.
- IT and new technologies enable the organization to do new things that were never possible before.
- IT-related services and functionality are delivered at the maximum economical value or in the most efficient manner. In other words, resources are used responsibly.
- All risks related to IT are known and managed and IT resources are secured.

A distinction has to be made between IT management as discussed previously in this book and IT governance that we introduce here. IT management is focused

Figure 8.1. Distinction between IT management and IT governance

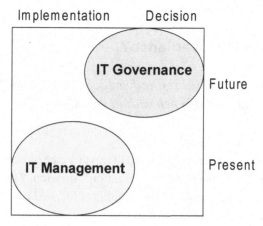

on the internal effective supply of IT services and products and the management of present IT operations (Grembergen, Haes, & Guldentops, 2004). IT Governance in turn is much broader, and concentrates on performing and transforming IT to meet present and future demands of the business (internal focus) and the business' customers (external focus).

The difference between IT management and IT governance is illustrated in Figure 8.1. While IT management is concerned with implementing IT services at the present, IT governance is concerned with making decisions for the future.

Whereas the domain of IT management focuses on the efficient and effective supply of IT services and products, and the management of IT operations, IT Governance faces the dual demand of (1) contributing to present business operations and performance, and (2) transforming and positioning IT for meeting future business challenges. This does not undermine the importance or complexity of IT management, but goes to indicate that IT Governance is both internally and externally oriented, spanning both present and future time frames. One of the key challenges in IT Governance is therefore how to simultaneously perform and transform IT in order to meet the present and future demands of the business and the business' customers in a satisfying manner (Peterson, 2004).

IT governance is important because it encourages desirable behavior in the use of IT by identifying and allowing relevant executives to make qualified decisions. A desirable behavior is one that is consistent with the organization's mission, strategy, values, norms and culture, such as behavior promoting successful entrepreneurs and their entrepreneurship. IT governance is not about what specific decisions are made in terms of choices between alternative infrastructures or applications. Rather, governance is about systematically determining who makes each type of decision (labelled decision right), who has input to a decision (labeled input right), and how these people (or groups) are empowered and held accountable for their role (Weil, 2004).

Effective IT governance draws on general organizational governance principles such as transparency to manage and use IT to achieve corporate performance goals. Effective IT governance encourages and leverages the potential of all organization personnel in using IT, while ensuring compliance with the organization's overall vision and principles of conduct. Weill (2004) suggests that as a result of this, good IT governance can achieve a management paradox: simultaneously empowering and controlling.

All organizations have implicitly some form of IT governance. The difference is that organizations with effective governance have actively designed a set of IT governance mechanisms (e.g., actors, topics, areas, committees, budgets, processes, approvals, IT organizational structure, chargeback, etc.) that encourage behaviors consistent with the organization's ambitions, values, norms and culture. In these organizations, when the perceived desirable behavior changes, IT governance also changes (Weil, 2004). IT governance cannot be considered in isolation because it links to the governance of other key organizational assets such as knowledge, procedures, money, customer relations, etc.). Governance of key assets, in turn, links to desirable behavior and hence organizational performance (Weil, 2004).

In the models of *organizational governance* one can organize the variety of variables and concepts used to describe the complexity of organizational governance mechanisms into two main categories: capital-related and labor-related. The capital-related aspects contain, among others, variables like ownership structure, corporate voting, the identity of owners, and the role of institutional owners. The labor-related aspects refer mainly to the stakeholding position of labor in organizational governance. Here one could mention employee involvement schemes, participatory management, co-determination, etc. (Cernat, 2004).

1.2   Organizational Governance

Before we dive into IT governance, we must look at the broader issue of organizational governance in organizations. Organizational governance is concerned with governing key assets, such as (Weill & Ross, 2004):

- **Human assets:** People, skills, career paths, training, reporting, mentoring, competencies and so on.
- **Financial assets:** Cash, investments, liabilities, cash flow, receivables and so on.

- **Physical assets:** Buildings, plant, equipment, maintenance, security, utilization, and so on.
- **IP assets:** Intellectual property (IP), including product, services, and process know-how formally patented, copyrighted, or embedded in the organizations' people and systems.
- **Information and IT assets:** Digitized data, information, and knowledge about customers, processes performance, finances, information systems, and so on.
- **Relationship assets:** Relationships within the organization as well as relationships, brand, and reputation with customers, suppliers, business units, regulators, competitors, channel partners, and so on.

As we can see from this list, IT governance includes not only information and IT assets. IT governance is concerned with several of these assets, sometimes even all of these assets. In this perspective, IT governance may be as comprehensive in scope as organizational governance.

In governing IT, we can learn from good financial and organizational governance. For example, the CFO (chief financial officer) does not sign every check or authorize every payment. Instead, he or she sets up financial governance specifying who can make the decisions and how. The CFO then oversees the organization's portfolio of investments and manages the required cash flow and risk exposure. The CFO tracks a series of financial metrics to manage the organization's financial assets, intervening only if there are problems or unforeseen opportunities. Similar principles apply to who can commit the organization to a contract or a partnership. Exactly the same approach should be applied to IT governance (Weill & Ross, 2004).

The dichotomy market or hierarchy has exercised a dominant influence on the study of forms of governance and their operation for some time. However, in the past two decades there have been large numbers of investigations of intermediate forms of governance. Subsequently it has been recognized that the behavior that occurs within exchanges is not necessarily determined by the forms of governance used, and this points to a need to understand behavior within a variety of exchanges (Blois, 2002).

1.3   Contracts in Governance

Blois (2002) defines governance as the institutional framework in which contracts are initiated, monitored, adapted, and terminated. An exchange occurs between two organizations when resources are transferred from one party to the other in return for resources controlled by the other party.

The arrangement of inter-organizational exchanges has become of critical importance in today's government. Many scholars have criticized the inadequacies of legal contracts as mechanisms for governing exchange, especially in the face of uncertainty and dependence. Other scholars argue that it is not the contracts per se but the social contexts in which they are embedded that determine their effectiveness. Cannon, Achrol and Gundlach (2000) investigated the performance implications of governance structures involving contractual agreements and relational social norms, individually and in combination (plural form) under varying conditions and forms of transactional uncertainty and relationship-specific adaptation. Their research is presented in the following. Hypotheses were developed and tested on a sample of buyer-seller relationships. The results provide support for the plural form thesis – increasing the relational content of a governance structure containing contractual agreements enhanced performance when transactional uncertainty was high, but not when it was low.

Cannon et al. (2000) applied the term legal bonds to refer to the extent to which detailed and binding contractual agreements were used to specify the roles and obligations of the parties. To the extent contracts were characterized in this way, they were less flexible and therefore more constrained in their adaptive properties. Highly detailed contracts were also less likely to possess the kinds of general safeguards that are more effective in thwarting self-interest-seeking behavior under circumstances of ambiguity.

Various perspectives on the nature of contracts as a mechanism of governance may be found in the literature. According to the original transaction cost framework (Williamson, 1979), formal contingent claims contracts (i.e., classical contracts) are inefficient mechanisms of governance in the face of uncertainty because organizations are bounded in their rationality and find it impossible to contemplate all possible future contingencies. For exchanges involving high levels of idiosyncratic investments and characterized by uncertainty, internal organization or hierarchy is predicted to be a more efficient form of governance than the market (Cannon et al., 2000).

However, neoclassical contract law argues that contracts can provide useful governance in exchange relationships even in the face of uncertainty and risk. This tradition of contract law is marked by doctrine and rules that attempt to overcome the difficulties posed by the classical tradition's emphasis on discreteness and presentation of exchange. The new doctrines enable parties to respond to unforeseen contingencies by making adjustments to ongoing exchange and ensuring continuity in their relationships. For example, concepts such as "good faith" and "reasonable commercial standards of fair dealing in the trade" are recognized under the Uniform Commercial Code (UCC) of 1978 in the US as general provisions for contracting behavior that also help to ensure continuity in exchange relationships. Similarly, "gap filler" provisions of the UCC rely on "prior dealings" between parties and "customary practices" across an industry or trading area for completing contract terms intentionally left open or omitted, thus allowing for adjustments to contingencies (Cannon et al., 2000).

However, neoclassical contracts are not indefinitely elastic (Williamson, 1991). Many scholars remain skeptical of how effective even the most carefully crafted contracts can be. It is argued that the scope for drafting rules in contracts to address changing or ambiguous conditions, or the ability to rely on general legal safeguards for controlling commercial conduct, is limited by both practicality and the law itself.

Drawing on these views, Cannon et al. (2000) argue that when a transaction involves relationship-specific adaptations and is (1) subject to dynamic forces and future contingencies that cannot be foreseen or (2) involves ambiguous circumstances where tasks are ill-defined and prone to exploitation, the difficulty of writing, monitoring, and enforcing contracts is increased, and their overall governance effectiveness weakened. In each case, efforts to govern the relationship on the basis of detailed and formal contracts—without the benefit of some additional apparatus—are not likely to enhance performance.

Social or relational norms are defined generally as shared expectations regarding behavior. The norms reflect expectations about attitudes and behaviors parties have in working cooperatively together to achieve mutual and individual goals. The spirit of such sentiments is captured by many overlapping types of relational contracting norms. These can be reduced to a core set of five (Cannon et al., 2000):

- **Flexibility.** The attitude among parties that an agreement is but a starting point to be modified as the market, the exchange relationship, and the fortunes of the parties evolve.
- **Solidarity.** The extent to which parties believe that success comes from working cooperatively together versus competing against one another. It dictates that parties stand by one another in the face of adversity and the ups and downs of marketplace competition.
- **Mutuality.** The attitude that each party's success is a function of everyone's success and that one cannot prosper at the expense of one's partner. It expresses the sentiment of joint responsibility.
- **Harmonization of conflict.** The extent to which a spirit of mutual accommodation toward cooperative ends exists.
- Restraint in the use of power. Forbearance from taking advantage of one's bargaining position in an exchange. It reflects the view that the use of power not only exacerbates conflict over time but also undermines mutuality and solidarity, opening the door to opportunism.

Together, these cooperative norms define relational properties that are important in affecting adaptations to dynamic market conditions and safeguarding the continuity of exchanges subject to task ambiguity.

According to Cannon et al. (2000), norms represent important social and organizational vehicles of control in exchange where goals are ill defined or involve open-ended performance. Norms provide a general frame of reference, order, and standards against which to guide and assess appropriate behavior in uncertain and ambiguous situations. In such situations contracts are often incomplete, and legal remedies can undermine relationship continuity. In contrast, norms motivate performance through focusing attention on the shared values of the partners to safeguard and rely on peer pressure and social sanctions to mitigate the risk of shirking and opportunistic expropriation. Because they involve expectations rather than rigid requirements of behavior, they create a cooperative as opposed to a confrontational environment for negotiating adaptations, thus promoting continuity in exchange.

1.4 Why is IT Governance Important?

IT Governance matters because it influences the benefits received from IT investments. Through a combination of practices (such as redesigned business processes and well-designed governance mechanisms) and appropriately matched IT investments, top-performing organizations generate superior returns on their IT investments (Weil, 2004). Weill and Ross (2004, p. 22) list the following reasons why IT governance is important:

- **Good IT governance pays off.** Among the for-profit firms we studied, the ones pursuing a specific strategy (for example, customer intimacy or operational excellence) with above-average IT governance performance had superior profits as measured by a three-year industry adjusted return on assets.
- **IT is expensive.** The average enterprise's IT investment is now greater than 4.2 percent of annual revenues and still rising. This investment results in IT exceeding 50 percent of the annual total capital investment of many enterprises. As IT has become more important and pervasive, senior management teams are increasingly challenged to manage and control IT to ensure that value is created. To address this issue, many enterprises are creating or refining IT governance structures to better focus IT spending on strategic priorities.
- **IT is pervasive.** In many enterprises, centrally managed IT is no longer possible or desirable. There was a time when requests for IT spending came only from the IT group. Now IT spending originates all over the enterprise. Some estimates suggest that only 20 percent of IT spending is visible in the IT budget. The rest of the spending occurs in business process budgets, prod-

uct development budgets, and every other type of budget. Well-designed IT governance arrangements distribute IT decision making to those responsible for outcomes.

- **New information technologies bombard enterprises with new business opportunities.** Foresight is more likely if an enterprise has formalized governance processes for harmonizing desirable behaviors and IT principles.

- **IT governance *is* critical to organizational learning about IT value.** Effective governance creates mechanisms through which enterprises can debate potential value and formalize their learning. Governance also facilitates learning by formalizing exception processes. Enterprises often learn through exceptions – where a different approach from standard practice is used for good reasons. Effective governance makes learning via exceptions explicit and shares any new practices across the enterprise if appropriate.

- **IT value depends on more than good technology.** In recent years there have been spectacular failures of large IT investments – major enterprise resource planning (ERP) systems initiatives that were never completed, e-business initiatives that were ill-conceived or poorly executed, and data-mining experiments that generated plenty of data but few valuable leads. Successful firms not only make better IT decisions, they also have better IT decision-making processes. Specifically, successful firms involve the right people in the process. Having the right people involved in IT decision making yields both more strategic applications and greater buy-in.

- **Senior management has limited bandwith.** Senior management does not have the bandwith to consider all the requests for IT investments that occur in a large enterprise let alone get involved in many other IT-related decisions. If senior managers attempt to make too many decisions, they become a bottleneck. But decisions throughout the enterprise should be consistent with the direction in which senior management is taking the organization. Carefully designed IT governance provides a clear, transparent IT decision-making process that leads to consistent behavior linked back to the senior management vision while empowering everyone's creativity.

- **Leading enterprises govern IT differently.** Top performing firms balancing multiple performance goals had governance models that blended centralized and decentralized decision making. All top performers' governance had one aspect in common. Their governance made transparent the tensions around IT decisions such as standardization versus innovation.

1.5 Governance of Resources

According to the resource-based theory of the organization, performance differences across organizations can be attributed to the variance in the organizations' resources and capabilities. The essence of the resource-based theory of the organization lies in its emphasis on the internal resources available to the organization, rather than on the external opportunities and threats dictated by industry conditions. An organization's resources are said to be a source of competitive advantage to the degree that they are scarce, specialized, appropriable, valuable, rare, and difficult to imitate or substitute.

As presented earlier in this book, Wade and Hulland (2004) developed a typology of IT resources, where resources held by an organization can be sorted into three types of processes: inside-out, outside-in, and spanning. Inside-out resources include IS infrastructure, IS technical skills, IS development, and cost effective IS operations.

1.6 Decision Makers and Decision Rights

Weill and Ross (2004, p. 58) use political archetypes (monarchy, feudal, federal, duopoly, anarchy) to describe the combinations of people who have either decision rights or input to IT decisions:

1. **Business Monarchy.** In a business monarchy, senior business executives make IT decisions affecting the entire enterprise. It is a group of business executives or individual executives (CxOs), including committees of senior business executives (may include CIO). It excludes IT executives acting independently.
2. **IT Monarchy.** In an IT monarchy, IT professionals make IT decisions. It is a group of IT executives or individual CIOs.
3. **Feudal.** The feudal model is based on traditions where the princes and princesses or their designated knights make their own decisions, optimizing their local needs. It is business unit leaders, key process owners or their delegates.
4. **Federal.** The federal decision-making model has a long tradition in government. Federal arrangements attempt to balance the responsibilities and accountability of multiple governing bodies, such as country or states. It is c-level executives and business groups (e.g., business units or processes). It may also include IT executives as additional participants. It is equivalent of the central and state governments working together.
5. **IT Duopoly.** The IT duopoly is a two-party arrangement where decisions represent a bilateral agreement between IT executives and one other group (e.g., CxO or business unit or process leaders). The IT executives may be a

central IT group or team of central and business unit IT organizations.

6.   **Anarchy.** Within an anarchy, individuals or small groups make their own decisions based only on their local needs. Anarchies are the bane of the existence of many IT groups and are expensive to support and secure. It can be each individual user.

Peterson (2004) discusses decision makers and decision rights in terms of centralization versus decentralization. Over the past decade, organizations have set out to achieve the best of both worlds by adopting a *federal* IT governance structure. In a federal IT governance model, IT infrastructure decisions are centralized, and IT application decisions are decentralized. The federal IT governance model thus represents a hybrid model of both centralization and decentralization.

The discussion of whether to centralize or decentralize IT governance is based on a rational perspective of the organization, in which choices are reduced to one of internal efficiency and effectiveness. This view assumes a system of goal consonance and agreement on the means for achieving goals, i.e., rational and logical trade-off between (a) efficiency and standardization under centralization, versus (b) effectiveness and flexibility under decentralization.

In general, it is assumed that centralization leads to greater specialization, consistency, and standardized controls, while decentralization provides local control, ownership and greater responsiveness and flexibility to business needs. However, flexibility under decentralization may lead to variable standards, which ultimately result in lower flexibility, and specialization under centralization incurs risks due to bounded rationality and information overload (Peterson, 2004).

A federal approach towards IT governance challenges managers in local business units to surrender control over certain business-specific IT domains for the well-being of the enterprise, and to develop business-to-corporate and business-to-IT partnerships. The potential risk in contemporary business environments is that either centralization or decentralization fit the organization into a fixed structure. The challenge is therefore to balance the benefits of decentralized decision-making and business innovation and the benefits of central control and IT standardization (Peterson, 2004).

1.7   Categories of Decisions

Weill and Ross (2004, p. 27) defined the following five decision categories:

1.   *IT Principles* are a related set of high-level statements about how IT is used in the business. Once articulated, IT principles become part of the enterprise's management lexicon and can be discussed, debated, supported, overturned,

and evolved. The hallmark of an effective set of IT principles is a clear trail of evidence from the business to the IT management principles. IT principles can also be used as a tool for educating executives about technology strategy and investment decisions.

2. *IT Architecture* is the organizing logic for data, applications, and infrastructure, captured in a set of policies, relationships, and technical choices to achieve desired business and technical standardization and integration. By providing a road map for infrastructure and applications (and consequently investment decisions), architecture decisions are pivotal to effective IT management and use. By clarifying how IT supports business principles, IT principles state – implicitly or explicitly – the requirements for process standardization and integration. The key to process standardization is discipline – adherence to a single, consistent way of doing things. Process integration allows multiple business units to provide a single face to a customer or to move seamlessly from one function to another.

3. *IT Infrastructure* is the foundation of planned IT capability (both technical and human) available throughout the business as shared and reliable services and used by multiple applications. Foresight in establishing the right infrastructure at the right time enables rapid implementation of future electronically enabled business initiatives as well as consolidation and cost reduction of current business processes. Overinvesting in infrastructure – or worse, implementing the wrong infrastructure – results in wasted resources, delays, and system incompabilities with business partners. Infrastructure base are the technology components, such as computers, printers, database software packages, operating systems, and scanners. The technology components are converted into useful shared services by a human IT infrastructure composed of knowledge, skills, standards, and experience.

4. *Business Applications Needs* often has two conflicting objectives – creativity and discipline. Creativity is about identifying new and more effective ways to deliver customer value using IT. Creativity involves identifying business applications that support strategic business objectives and facilitate business experiments. Discipline is about architectural integrity – ensuring that applications leverage and build out the enterprise architecture rather than undermine architectural principles. Discipline is also about focus – committing the necessary resources to achieve project and business goals. Business application needs decisions require reconciling complex change and opposing organizational forces. Managers responsible for defining requirements must distinguish core process requirements from nonessentials and know when to live within architectural constraints. They must design experiments knowing that actual benefits could be different from anticipated benefits – or if there are

no benefits, they must pull the plug. Most importantly, they must know how to design organizational change and then make it happen. Business application needs decisions require creative thinkers and disciplined project managers and are probably the least mature of the five IT decisions.

5. *IT Investment and Prioritization* is often the most visible and controversial of the five key IT decisions. Some projects are approved, others are bounced, and the rest enter the organizational equivalent of suspended animation with the dreaded request from the decision makers to "redo the business case" or "provide more information". Enterprises that get superior value from IT focus their investments on their strategic priorities, cognizant of the distinction between "must have" and "nice to have" IT capabilities. IT investment decisions address three dilemmas: (a) how much to spend, (b) where to spend it, and (c) how to reconcile the needs of different constituencies. Probably the most important attribute of a successful IT investment process is ensuring that the enterprise's IT spending reflects strategic priorities. Investment processes must reconcile the demands of individual business units as well as demands to meet enterprise wide needs. Many enterprises value the interdependence of their business units and support their efforts to invest in IT according to business unit strategy. Most enterprises also emphasize the importance of enterprise wide efficiencies and even integration. Enterprises that attempt to persuade independent business units to fund shared infrastructure are likely to experience resistance. Instead, business leaders must articulate the enterprise wide objectives of shared infrastructure and provide appropriate incentives for business unit leaders to sacrifice business unit needs in favor of enterprise wide needs.

1.8   Stakeholders

An important task in establishing and designing IT governance is to identify stakeholders. Stakeholders may be assigned input rights and decision rights.

The stakeholder approach to strategic management was introduced by Freeman (1984). According to Freeman a stakeholder is any group or individual who can affect, or is affected by, the achievement of a corporation's purpose. Stakeholders include employees, customers, suppliers, stockholders, banks, environmentalists, government and other groups who can help or hurt the corporation. For each category of stakeholders groups can be broken down into several useful smaller categories. Freeman's focus was to show how executives could use the stakeholder approach to manage their organization more effectively. In instrumental stakeholder theory, the role of management is seen as achieving a balance between the interests of all stakeholders. For each major strategic issue we must think through the effects on a number of stakeholders, and therefore, we need processes that help take into account the concerns of many groups. It is argued that maintaining an appropriate balance between the interests of all stakeholder groups is the only way to ensure survival of the organization and the attainment of other performance goals. The normative condition is that managers must provide economic and otherwise returns to stakeholders in order to continue engaging in wealth creating activities by virtue of the critical resources stakeholders provide to the organization.

Stakeholder theory is justified on the basis that organizations have responsibilities to stakeholders for moral reasons, and that there is no priority of one set of interests over another. Upholding four principles: 1) honoring agreements, 2) avoiding lying, 3) respecting the autonomy of others, and 4) avoiding harm to other, are necessary precondition for efficient working. And thus, stakeholder theories of the firm establish economic relationships within a general context of moral management. Contrary to the traditional understanding of the principal-agent relationship, used in several IT outsourcing studies, a stakeholder orientation will include at least two new dimensions: 1) a number of stakeholder groups, and 2) the interpretation of the four moral principles that underlie stakeholder theory. Neglecting these dimensions, organizations will have less satisfied stakeholders, and will show financial performance that is consistently below industry average (Shankman, 1999).

The term stakeholder is a powerful one. This is due, to a significant degree, to its conceptual breath. The term means many different things to many different people and hence evokes praise and scorn from a wide variety of scholars and practitioners of myriad academic disciplines and backgrounds. Such breadth of interpretation, though one of stakeholder theory's greatest strengths, is also one of its most prominent theoretical liabilities as a topic of reasoned discourse. Much of the power of stakeholder theory is a direct result of the fact that, when used unreflectively, its managerial recommendations and implications are merely limitless. When discussed in instrumental variation (i.e., that managers should attend to stakeholders as a means to achieving other organizational goals such as profit or shareholder wealth maximization) stakeholder theory stands virtually unopposed. Stakeholder theory is a theory of organizational management and ethics. Indeed all theories of strategic management have some moral content, though it is often implicit. Moral content in this case means that the subject matter of the theories is inherently moral topics (i.e., they are not amoral). Stakeholder theory is distinct because it addresses morals and values explicitly as a central feature of managing organizations. The ends of cooperative activity and the means of achieving these ends are critically examined in stakeholder theory in a way that they are not in many theories of strategic management (Phillips, Freeman, & Wicks, 2003).

Managing stakeholders involves attention to more than simply maximizing shareholder wealth. Attention to the interests and well being of those who can assist or hinder the achievement of the organization's objectives is the central admonition of the theory. In this way, stakeholder theory is similar in large degree with alternative models of strategic management, such as resource-based theory. However, for stakeholder theory, attention to the interests and well being of some non-shareholders is obligatory for more than the prudential and instrumental purposes of wealth maximization of equity shareholders. While there are still some stakeholder groups whose relationship with the organization remains instrumental (due largely to the power they wield) there are other normatively legitimate stakeholders than simply equity shareholders alone. According to Phillips et al. (2003), stakeholder theory may be undermined from at least two directions – critical distortion and friendly misinterpretations – at its current stage of theoretical development. Critical distortions include arguments that stakeholder theory is an excuse for managerial opportunism and that stakeholder theory cannot provide sufficiently specific objective function for the corporation. Friendly misinterpretations include arguments that stakeholder theory requires changes to current law and that stakeholder theory is socialism and refers to the entire economy.

According to Phillips et al. (2003), it is commonly asserted that stakeholder theory implies that all stakeholders must be treated equally irrespective of the fact that some obviously contribute more than others to the organization. Prescriptions of equality have been inferred from discussions of balancing stakeholder interests and are in direct conflict with the advice of some experts on organizational design and reward systems. However, corporations should attempt to distribute the benefits of their activities as equitably as possible among stakeholders in light of their respective contributions, costs, and risks. This interpretation of balance is called meritocracy, where benefits are distributed based on relative contribution to the organization. In addition to meritocracy, it has been suggested that stakeholders may usefully be separated into normative and derivative stakeholders. Normative stakeholders are those to whom the organization has a direct moral obligation to attend to their well-being. They provide the answer to seminal stakeholder query "For whose benefit ought the organization be managed?" Typically normative stakeholders are those most frequently cited in stakeholder discussions such as financiers, employees, customers, suppliers and local communities. Alternatively, derivative stakeholders are those groups or individuals who can either harm or benefit the organization, but to whom the organization has no direct moral obligation as stakeholders. This latter group might include such groups as competitors, activists, terrorists, and the media. The organization is not managed for the benefit of derivative stakeholders, but to the extent that they may influence the organization or its normative stakeholders, managers are obliged to account for them in their decision-making. Far from strict equality, therefore, there are a number of more convincing ways that stakeholder theory may distinguish between and among constituency groups.

Stakeholder theory is a managerial conception of organizational strategy and ethics. The central idea is that an organization's success is dependent on how well it manages the relationships with key groups such as customers, employees, suppliers, communities, financiers, and others that can affect the realization of its purpose. The manager's job is to keep the support of all of these groups, balancing their interests, while making the organization a place where stakeholder interests can be maximized over time. The identification of stakeholder groups is currently among the central debates in the scholarly and popular (Freeman & Phillips, 2002).

Lacity and Willcocks (2000) define a stakeholder as a group of people with aligned interests. The term is widely used and accepted by IT outsourcing practitioners and researchers. However, as indicated by some of the reviewed literature above, stakeholder is defined and used differently in finance (issue of CEO responsibility to shareholders or stakeholders), law (requires ownership), and gaming (person who holds the bets). According to Lacity and Willcocks (2000) there is four distinct client IT stakeholder groups and three distinct supplier IT stakeholder groups. The groups identified are customer senior business managers, customer senior IT managers, customer IT staff, customer IT users, and supplier senior managers, supplier account managers, supplier IT staff. An additional group is the subcontractors. All stakeholder groups are presumed to have significant differences in expectations and goals regarding IT outsourcing. Thus, it is reasonable to propose that upholding the interest of these different stakeholder groups with the principles of moral management will affect the success of IT outsourcing.

1.9 Decision Rights Distribution

Weill and Ross (2004) studied both who made each of the five decisions and who provided input to those decisions. They then categorized the enterprise's approach by archetypes of decision makers. Table 8.1 shows a combination of decision makers

Table 8.1. How enterprises govern

	IT Principles	IT Architecture	IT Infrastructure	Business Applications	IT Investments
Business Monarchy					X
IT Monarchy		X	X		
Feudal					
Federal				X	
IT Duopoly	X				
Anarchy					

and categories of decisions. The most frequent decision maker for each category found by Weill and Ross (2004) is indicated with an X in the table.

IT principles, which set the strategic role for IT across the enterprise, were decided in a variety of ways. Thirty-six percent of enterprises used a duopoly approach (usually IT professionals and the CxOs in a T-shaped duopoly), but business and IT monarchies and federal approaches were also regularly used. Duopolies in general and senior management IT duopolies in particular seem to have gained favor in IT principles decisions because senior managers sense that they must take the lead to ensure that IT aligns with business strategies. Working in partnerships with IT leaders in decision processes establishes realistic expectations for IT and forces clarification of business strategy. The most frequent input to IT principles came from federal management.

Over 70 percent of enterprises relied on IT monarchies to choose *IT architecture*, suggesting that senior managers view architecture more as a technical than strategic issue. Most enterprises attempt to incorporate business strategy considerations into architecture decisions via inputs from federal and duopoly arrangements.

Like architecture, *IT infrastructure* decisions are often made within the IT unit. Almost 60 percent of enterprises used IT monarchies to make infrastructure decisions. This arrangement gives IT independence in designing and pricing service offerings. Input to IT infrastructure decisions typically come from federal arrangements.

People who make *business applications needs* decisions specify the business needs for systems to be acquired or built in the next year or so. Enterprises studied by Weill and Ross (2004) displayed a wide variety of approaches to these decisions. Federal approaches were slightly more popular than duopolies, and there were also substantial numbers of enterprises using feudal and business monarchies. Input to business applications needs decisions were mostly provided through federal arrangements as well.

Three approaches dominated *IT investment and prioritization* decision-making: business monarchies, federal, and duopolies. The there approaches were almost equally popular, but they offer different views of how enterprises ensure maximum value from IT investments. That only nine percent of enterprises place IT investment decisions in the hands of IT professionals reflects the growing awareness that IT investment decisions involve business tradeoffs - decision makers determine which business processes will and will not receive IT support. Input to IT investment and prioritization decisions was mostly provided by federal arrangements.

Nielsen (2004) suggested decision rights distribution as indicated in Table 8.2. This is a sample effective IT governance arrangement matrix.

Weill and Ross (2004) found significant variation in IT governance arrangements among the 256 organizations studied. Each of the five key IT decisions has a choice of six governance archetypes, yielding very many possible combinations. The ten

Table 8.2. Sample effective IT governance arrangements matrix

	IT Principles	IT Architecture	IT Infrastructure	Business Applications	IT Investment
Business Monarchy					Executive committee subgroup, includes CIO
IT Monarchy		CIO IT leadership (CIO, CIO's office and business unit CIOs)	CIO IT leadership (CIO, CIO's office and business unit CIOs)		
Feudal					
Federal					
IT Duopoly	Executive committee at C levels (CxOs). IT leadership (CIO, CIO's office and business unit CIOs)			Business unit heads (presidents) Business process owners	
Anarchy					

most popular combinations accounted for twenty-five percent of the enterprises. Within these ten, Weill (2004) identified the three most effective arrangements, as measured by IT governance performance. These three top governance performers are illustrated in Table 8.3.

Organizational arrangement A uses duopolies for principles and investment, IT monarchies for infrastructure and architecture, and federal management for business application needs. This kind of arrangement needs IT groups that are well tuned to business needs, preferably with a high level of trust between business and IT management. The federal model for application needs can benefit from potential synergies (such as common work processes and customers) across business units.

Organizational arrangement B is similar, using a duopoly for prioritizing application needs and a business monarchy for investment decisions. For enterprises with few potential synergies, using a duopoly for application needs can work well because there is less need to coordinate across business units. Arrangements A and B seem both to be good starting points for enterprises since they are balancing growth and profitability according to Weill (2004), because the tensions of business units seeking to meet their local customer needs might be balanced with senior managers governing IT investments.

Table 8.3. Top three overall governance performers (Weil, 2004)

	IT Principles	IT Architecture	IT Infrastructure	Business Applications Needs	IT Investment and Prioritization
Business Monarchy	C	C	C		B C
IT Monarchy		A B	A B		
Feudal					
Federal				A C	
IT Duopoly	A B			B	A
Anarchy					

Organizational arrangement C is much more centralized, with business monarchies making all decisions except business application needs, which is federal. More centralized approaches are typically used in organizations with single business units which have the value configuration of a value chain. Arrangement C requires business leaders who are interested and knowledgeable about IT issues – often the result of CIOs and vendors educating and working closely with the senior management team. Arrangement C seems also sensible when major changes are occurring, such as mergers, crime internally, major cost cutting, crises etc., and then decision rights must be tightly held.

According to Weill (2004), Table 8.3 illustrates how, in the three top performing patterns, the five decision-making approaches fit together to create a total governance design that is reinforcing and balancing the tensions inherent in large enterprises. For example, an IT monarchy for IT architecture can be very effective if the architecture is guided by IT principles set by a business monarchy or a duopoly. However, if IT monarchy is unable to translate IT principles into IT architecture decisions, tensions will emerge again. The IT decision makers need to focus on creating an integrated and flexible IT architecture guided by the business-driven IT principles set by the senior leaders in the business monarchy.

According to Weill (2004), organizations wanting to lead on asset utilization can learn from these top performers and consider:

- Setting IT principles with a strong focus on asset utilization and using an IT duopoly consisting of CxOs and the corporate IT group.
- Empowering business/IT relationship managers who focus on achieving business value from IT in their business unit and exploring and exploiting the enterprise-wide infrastructure.

- Establishing a technical core of infrastructure and architecture providers who design and implement the government organization's technology platform and interact with the business/IT relationship managers.
- Involving IT architects and systems designers on business unit projects to facilitate IT education of the business leaders and effective use of the shared infrastructure and architecture standards.
- Developing a simple chargeback system and a regular review process to help business unit leaders see the costs and benefits of shared services.

To analyze IT governance, Weill (2004) suggests that managers map their enterprise's current IT governance onto a matrix similar to the table used here. Then it can be subjectively assessed whether or not IT governance is encouraging desirable behaviors for the enterprise's performance goals. If not, the appropriate top performers' governance (best practice) can be used as starting-point templates to create a new governance model that is then tailored to the enterprise's culture, structure, strategy and goals.

CONCLUSION

IT governance matters because it influences the benefits received from IT investments. Through a combination of practices, such as redesigning business processes and well-designed governance mechanisms, and appropriately matched IT investments, top-performing organizations generate superior returns on their IT investments (Weil, 2004).

The governance aspect of interoperability includes four types of key factors according to Archmann and Kudlacek (2008): political (policy and institutional issues), legal (intellectual property rights, digital signatures and electronic identities), managerial (willingness for cultural change) and economic (funding and financial schemes).

Grant, McKnight, Uruthirapathy and Brown (2007) stress the importance of insight when designing governance for shared services organizations in the public sector. As shared services organizations become more popular as a service management and delivery option in government, properly defining and setting up the governance structure continues to be a key success factor. In many organizations, information technology has become crucial in the support, the sustainability and the growth of the business. This pervasive use of technology has created a critical dependency on IT that calls for a specific focus on IT governance. IT governance consists of the leadership and organizational structures and processes that ensure that the organization's IT sustains and extends the organization's strategy and objectives (Grembergen et al., 2004).

REFERENCES

Archmann, S., & Kudlacek, I. (2008). Interoperability and the exchange of good practice cases. *European Journal of ePractice, 2*(February), 3-12.

Bekkers, V. (2007). The government of back-office integration. Organizing co-operation between information domains. *Public Management Review, 9*(3), 377-300.

Blois, K. (2002). Business to business exchanges: A rich descriptive apparatus derived from MacNail's and Menger's analysis. *Journal of Management Studies, 30*(4), 523-551.

Cannon, J. P., Achrol, R. S., & Gundlach, G. T. (2000). Contracts, norms, and plural form governance. *Journal of the Academy of Marketing Science, 28*(2), 180-194.

Cernat, L. (2004). The emerging European corporate governance model: Anglo-Saxon, Continental, or still the century of diversity. *Journal of European Public Policy, 11*(1), 147-166.

Freeman, R. E. (1984). *Strategic management: A stakeholder approach.* Boston: Pitman Publishing Inc.

Freeman, R. E., & Phillips, R. A. (2002). Stakeholder theory: A libertarian defense. *Business Ethics Quarterly, 12*(3), 331-349.

Grant, G., McKnight, S., Uruthirapathy, A., & Brown, A. (2007). Designing governance for shared services organizations in the public service. *Government Information Quarterly, 24*(3), 533-538.

Grembergen, W. V., Haes, S. D., & Guldentops, E. (2004). Structures, processes and relational mechanisms for IT governance. In W. V. Grembergen (Ed.), *Strategies for information technology governance* (pp. 1-36). Hershey, PA: IGI Global Publishing.

IT Governance Institute. (2004). *IT Governance Global Status Report.* Rolling Meadows, Il: IT Governance Institute.

Lacity, M. C., & Willcocks, L. P. (2000). Relationships in IT outsourcing: A stakeholder perspective. In R. W. Zmud (Ed.), *Framing the domains of IT management: Projecting the future through the past.* Cincinnati, OH: Pinnaflex Educational Resources.

Nielsen, K. B. (2004). *Reality of IS Lite - and more.* Gartner Group, EXP client presentation.

Peterson, R. R. (2004). Integration strategies and tactics for information technology governance. In W. V. Grembergen (Ed.), *Strategies for information technology governance* (pp. 37-80). Hershey, PA: IGI Global Publishing.

Phillips, R., Freeman, R. E., & Wicks, A. C. (2003). What stakeholder theory is not. *Business Ethics Quarterly, 13*(4), 479-502.

Shankman, N. A. (1999). Reframing the debate between agency and stakeholder theories of the firm. *Journal of Business Ethics, 19*(4), 319-334.

Wade, M., & Hulland, J. (2004). Review: The resource-based view and information systems research: Review, extension, and suggestions for further research. *MIS Quarterly, 28*(1), 107-142.

Weil, P. (2004). *Don't just lead, govern: How top-performing firms govern IT* (No. CISR WP No. 341): Center for Information Systems Research, Sloan School of Management, Massachusetts Institute of Technology.

Weill, P., & Ross, J. W. (2004). *IT governance.* Boston: Harvard Business School Press.

Williamson, O. E. (1979). Transaction-cost economics: The governance of contractual relations. *The Journal of Law and Economics, 22*(2), 233-261.

Williamson, O. E. (1991). Comparative economic organization: The analysis of discrete structural alternatives. *Administrative Science Quarterly, 36*(2), 269-296.

Chapter IX
The Role of the CIO

1. THE ROLE OF THE CIO

The CIO can be defined as the highest-ranking IT executive who typically exhibits managerial roles requiring effective communication with top management, a broad corporate perspective in managing information resources, influence on organizational strategy, and responsibility for the planning of IT. This definition is in line with research; which applied the following criteria when selecting CIOs for empirical observation: i) highest-ranking information technology executive; ii) reports no more than two levels from the CEO, that is, either reports to the CEO or reports to one of the CEOs direct reports, iii) areas of responsibility include information systems, computer operations, telecommunications and networks, office automation, end-user computing, help desks, computer software and applications; and iv) responsibility for strategic IS/IT planning. The CIO plays a vital role in every interoperability project in digital government. There may be a CIO in each involved public agency as well as a CIO for the whole of government. For example in Hong Kong, there is an office of the government chief officer, which developed the interoperability framework for all agencies and other public organizations to follow (2007).

In this chapter we start by defining the position of the CIO. CIOs are playing a key role sourcing IT resources and enabling IT governance. These topics are covered in the next sections. Then, we continue discussing CIO leadership roles. As organizations expand their use of the Internet, the CIO emerges as an important executive for developing digital government, competitive strategy and Internet strategy. We are also looking into the CIO selecting e-business model.

1.1 The CIO Position

The CIO position emerged in the 1970s as a result of increased importance placed on IT. In the early 1980s, the CIO was often portrayed as the corporate savior who was to align the worlds of business and technology. CIOs were described as the new breed of information managers who were businessmen first, managers second, and technologists third. It was even postulated that in the 1990s, as information became an organization's critical resource, the CIO would become the logical choice for the chief executive officer (CEO) position.

Job advertisements for information systems positions from 1970 to 1990 were reviewed by Todd, McKeen and Gallupe (1995). They investigated specific positions related to programmers, systems analysts and information systems managers. It is the latter position that is of interest here. At the time of the research, it was considered that successful information systems managers should have a blend of technical knowledge and sound business related skills. Further, in general, they should possess effective interpersonal skills. Over the twenty-year period, Todd et al. (1995) determined that there had not been much change in the required skills indicated in job advertisements.

Benjamin, Dickinson and Rockart (1985) suggested that the emergence of the CIO role represented the recognition of the importance of the role to be played within the organization. Kaarst-Brown (2005), however, suggested it is unfortunate that twenty years later, in 2005, the CIO is still held in lower regard than those senior managers of other more traditional business units. Kaarst-Brown (2005) suggested the reasons for this gap might be attributed to some of the items on the following list:

- Personality conflicts
- Lack of corporate technology vision
- Poorly aligned IT goals
- Lack of business knowledge
- Lack of IT awareness among the business executives
- Incorrect formal structure and reporting relationships

However, Kolbasuk (2005) reported that the perception of CIOs within organizations may be evolving. She suggests they may finally be getting the respect they deserve as they become members of the board of directors of large companies.

This movement to the board level in the organization indicates the perception of the CIO role is evolving from a manager primarily focused on regulations, back office operations, and administrative duties to applying information technology at a strategic level to facilitate competitive advantage through an understanding of how business processes function and may be adapted to a changing corporate environment.

As a manager of people, the CIO faces the usual human resource roles of recruiting, staff training, and retention, and the financial roles of budget determination, forecasting and authorization. As the provider of technological services to user departments, there remains a significant amount of work in publicity, promotion, and internal relations with user management. As a manager of an often-virtual information organization, the CIO has to coordinate sources of information services spread throughout and beyond the boundaries of the organization. The CIO is thus concerned with a wider group of issues than are most managers.

While information systems executives share several similarities with the general manager, notable differences are apparent. The CIO is not only concerned with a wider group of issues than most managers, but also, as the chief information systems strategist, has a set of responsibilities that must constantly evolve with the corporate information needs and with information technology itself. It has been suggested that the IT director's ability to add value is the biggest single factor in determining whether the organization views information technology as an asset or a liability. According to Earl and Feeny (1994, p. 11), chief information officers have a difficult job:

Chief information officers have the difficult job of running a function that uses a lot of resources but that offers little measurable evidence of its value. To make the information systems department an asset to their companies – and to keep their jobs – CIOs should think of their work as adding value in certain key areas.

Creation of the CIO role was driven in part by two organizational needs. First, accountability is increased when a single executive is responsible for the organization's processing needs. Second, creation of the CIO position facilitates the closing of the gap between organizational and IT strategies which has long been cited as a primary business concern.

Alignment of business and IT objectives is not only a matter of achieving competitive advantage, but is essential for the organization's very survival. Though the importance of IT in creating competitive advantage has been widely noted, achieving these gains has proven elusive. Sustained competitive advantage requires not only the development of a single system, but the ability to consistently deploy IT faster, cheaper, and more strategically than one's competitors. IT departments play

Figure 9.1. Sourcing options for IT resources and services

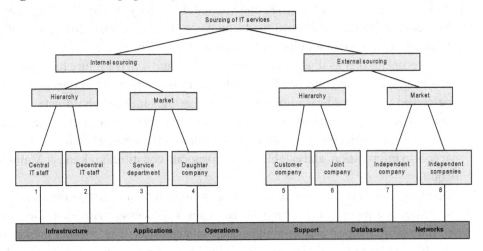

a critical role in realizing the potential of IT. The performance of IT functions, in turn, often centers on the quality of leadership, i.e., the CIO.

1.2   The CIO Sourcing IT Resources

IT sourcing is concerned with defining, planning and managing how an enterprise deploys internal and external resources and services to ensure the continuous fulfillment of its business objectives. A variety of sources have emerged. This variety is illustrated in Figure 9.1. Here we find internal sourcing and external sourcing. Both can be managed either through organizational hierarchy or through market mechanism.

In general, organizations have three basic alternatives for acquiring technological know-how. They can (1) develop the technology independently, (2) acquire another company that already has the technology, or (3) enter into a technology-sourcing arrangement. If a firm lacks the capabilities needed to develop a technology independently and other organizations already have the technology, management can consider external sourcing. There is a continuum of external sourcing methods based on the level of mutual commitment between the firm that has the technology (the source firm) and the firm that desires the know-how (the sourcing firm). These methods range from arms-length licensing contracts, through more tightly coupled co development partnerships and joint ventures, to the outright acquisition of the source firm (Steensma & Corley, 2001).

Steensma and Corley (2001) focused on the two polar extremes in their study of technology sourcing: market contracting through licensing versus the use of firm hierarchy through acquisition. The polar cases are basic particles from which more elaborate arrangements are constructed. Hierarchy implies that the sourcing firm can hierarchically control the technology, personnel, and other assets of the IT function and apply it to its current needs at its discretion.

Internal market as illustrated with numbers 3 and 4 in the figure has a different sourcing logic. The concept of internal market is not new. The concept was first perceived to have radical implications eliminating superior-subordinate relationships, organizing all activity in terms of self-responsible profit centers, determining compensation objectively, eliminating internal monopolies, allowing freedom of access to information, and establishing a corporate constitution (King & Malhotra, 2000).

These appear to be less radical in today's environment of matrix organizations, self-managed teams, and re-engineered business processes. However, the notion of internal markets is not as simples as first suggested. The internal market is a mechanism for unleashing market forces inside the firm. Firms selecting this alternative might be able to retain control of the function while achieving the objectives of cost savings and service-responsiveness that are often ascribed to an external vendor (King & Malhotra, 2000).

According to King and Malhotra (2000), the internal market within an organization is characterized by a setup in which internal units are enabled to act autonomously by exerting self-control in conducting transactions with other internal units and with external entities within a framework of an overarching corporate vision, values and precepts. This notion of internal markets may be best understood in terms of its potential broad applicability in an organizational context.

Implementation of the internal market concept requires the creation of a market economy inside a firm. In this, organizational units buy and sell goods and services among themselves and to others outside the firm at prices established in the open market. In contrast, the transfer prices that are used for internal transactions often represent a simulation of a marketing-clearing mechanism (King & Malhotra, 2000).

1.3   The CIO Enabling IT Governance

Monnoyer and Willmott (2005) are skeptical of IT governance. They argue that something is gone very wrong with the structures, processes, and policies that govern how a business makes IT decisions and who within the organization makes them. They find that IT governance arrangements have become a substitute for real leadership. Companies are relying on tightly scripted meetings, analyses, and decision frameworks to unite CIOs and business executives around a common vision for IT. But committee meetings and processes are poor stand-ins for executives who can forge a clear agreement among their peers about IT investment choices and drive the senior-level conversations needed to make tough trade-offs. Monnoyer and Willmott (2005) find that in companies with strong IT leaders, governance constitutes a much more flexible set of managerial activities, involves fewer people and fewer meetings, and is typically tailored to fit the IT leader's style, much as executive committee activities often reflect a CEO's leadership approach.

To play a key role in developing IT governance arrangements is important for the CIO to increase his or her chances for becoming the next CEO. While corporate governance allocates decision rights in the overall company affecting the CEO position, IT governance allocates decisions rights in all IT-related dimensions affecting the CIO position.

In many organizations, information technology has become crucial in the support, the sustainability and the growth of the business. This pervasive use of technology has created a critical dependency on IT that calls for a specific focus on IT governance. IT governance consists of the leadership and organizational structures and processes that ensure that the organization's IT sustains and extends the organization's strategy and objectives (Grembergen, Haes, & Guldentops, 2004).

IT governance matters because it influences the benefits received from IT investments. Through a combination of practices (such as redesigning business processes and well-designed governance mechanisms) and appropriately matched IT investments, top-performing enterprises generate superior returns on their IT investments (Weil, 2004).

1.4 CIO Leadership Roles

One approach to understanding the CIO position is to study managerial roles. In this chapter, ten roles by Mintzberg and six roles by Grover (derived from Mintzberg) are presented to shed light on the various leadership roles for CIOs.

Mintzberg (1994) notes a number of different and sometimes conflicting views of the manager's role. He finds that it is a curiosity of the management literature that its best-known writers all seem to emphasize one particular part of the manager's job to the exclusion of the others. Together, perhaps, they cover all the parts, but even that does not describe the whole job of managing. Based on an observational study of chief executives, Mintzberg (1994) concluded that a manager's work could be described in terms of ten job roles. As managers take on these roles, they perform management functions. These ten roles consist of three interpersonal roles (figurehead, leader and liaison), three informational roles (monitor, disseminator, and spokesman), and four decisional roles (entrepreneur, disturbance handler, resource allocator, and negotiator):

- **Figurehead** performs some duties of a ceremonial nature. Examples are greeting visitors, responding to journalists' questions, and visiting customers and allies.

- **Personnel leader** is responsible for motivation of subordinates and for staffing and training. Examples are most activities involving subordinates, such as settling disagreements between subordinates.

- **Liaison** establishes a web of external relationships. Examples are attending conferences and giving presentations.

- **Monitor** seeks and receives information to understand and learn from the environment. Examples are reading journals and listen to external experts.

- **Disseminator** transmits information to other organizational members. Examples include forwarding reports and memos, making phone calls to present information, and holding informational meetings.

- **Spokesman** involves the communication of information and ideas. Examples are speaking to the board of directors and top management, and talking to users.

- **Entrepreneur** acts as initiator and designer of much of the controlled change in the organization. Examples are user ideas converted to systems proposals and management objectives transformed to infrastructure actions.

- **Disturbance handler** is responsible for solving conflicts in the organization.

- **Resource allocator** is responsible for allocation of human, financial, material, and other resources. Examples are working on budgets, developing project proposals, and monitoring information technology projects.

- **Negotiator** is responsible for representing the organization in negotiations. Examples are negotiations with unions concerning wages and with vendors concerning procurements.

According to Mintzberg (1994), these ten roles are common in all managerial jobs regardless of the functional or hierarchical level. However, differences do exist in the importance and effort dedicated to each managerial role based on job content, different skill levels, and expertise. Mintzberg (1994) states that managers are in fact specialists, required to perform a particular set of specialized managerial roles that are dependent upon the functional area and hierarchical level in which they work.

Grover, Jeong, Kettinger and Lee (1993) used the Mintzberg framework to study CIO roles. They selected six of ten roles, which they found relevant for CIOs: personnel leader, liaison, monitor, spokesman, entrepreneur and resource allocator. The four other roles (figurehead, disseminator, disturbance handler, and negotiator) were not operationalized because Grover et al. (1993) found that the activities constituting these roles were correlated with the activities of the other six roles and because they found that the activities that comprised those four roles were consistently important only for certain functions and levels of management. The six selected roles were related to information technology management by rephrasing them:

- As the *personnel leader*, the IS manager is responsible for supervising, hiring, training, and motivating a cadre of specialized personnel. Literature has emphasized the impact of this role on IS personnel. This role is mainly internal to the IS organization.
- The *spokesman* role incorporates activities that require the IS manager to extend organizational contacts outside the department to other areas of the organization. Frequently, he or she must cross traditional departmental boundaries and become involved in affairs of production, distribution, marketing, and finance. This role is mainly external in relation to the intra-organizational environment.
- As the *monitor*, the IS manager must scan the external environment to keep up with technical changes and competition. In acting as the firm's technical innovator, the IS manager uses many sources including vendor contacts, professional relationships, and a network of personal contacts. This role is mainly external in relation to the inter-organizational environment.
- As the *liaison*, the IS manager must communicate with the external environment including exchanging information with IS suppliers, customers, buyers, market analysts, and the media. This role is mainly external in relation to the inter-organizational environment.
- As the *entrepreneur*, the IS manager identifies business needs and develops solutions that change business situations. A major responsibility of the IS manager is to ensure that rapidly evolving technical opportunities are understood, planned, implemented, and strategically exploited in the organization.
- As the *resource allocator*, the IS manager must decide how to allocate human, financial, and information resources. The litany of past discussion on charge-back systems (users have to pay for IT services) and the importance of "fairness" in IS resource allocation decisions speak to the importance of this role. This role is mainly internal to the IS organization.

In Figure 9.2, the selected six CIO roles are illustrated. The roles of personnel leader and resource allocator are both internal to IT functions. The entrepreneur absorbs ideas from the intra-organizational environment, while the spokesman influences the intra-organizational environment. The liaison informs the external environment, while the monitor absorbs ideas from the external environment.

Figure 9.2. CIO roles on different arenas

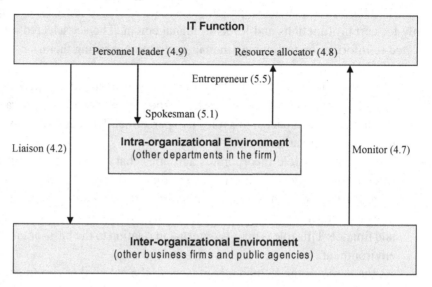

A survey was conducted in Norway to investigate CIO roles (Gottschalk, 2007). CIOs were asked questions about the importance of the different roles. Survey results indicate some variation in the importance of roles. Responding CIOs found the role of entrepreneur most important and the role of liaison least important. This is indicated with numbers in Figure 9.2, where the scale went from 1 (not important) to 6 (very important).

1.5   The CIO Developing Digital Government

As organizations expand their use of the Internet from electronic commerce to electronic business, the CIO emerges as the most important executive for performance improvements when selecting business models.

Electronic commerce (EC) is an important concept that describes the process of buying, selling, or exchanging products, services, and information, via computer networks, including the Internet (Turban, King, Lee, Warkentin, & Chung, 2002). From a communications perspective, EC is the delivery of goods, services, information, or payments over computer networks or by any other electronic means. From a business process perspective, EC is the application of technology toward the automation of business transactions and workflow. From a service perspective, EC is a tool that addresses the desire of firms, consumers, and management to cut service costs while improving the quality of goods and increasing the speed of service delivery. From an online perspective, EC provides the capability of buying and selling products and information on the Internet and other online services. From a collaboration perspective, EC is the framework for inter- and intra-organizational collaboration. From a community perspective, EC provides a gathering place for community members, to learn, transact, and collaborate.

Electronic commerce over large ubiquitous networks will soon be conducted in routine fashion. While some may question the timeframe involved, few will question its imminence. In this transient phase of rapid technological change, it is difficult to see the real implications of these changes for both business and society. Recent writings have elaborated on the power of information technologies to reduce the costs of coordination and transactions and consequently to influence governance structures between buyers and sellers. Much of the popular press is also fairly aggressive in providing anecdotes of innovative companies that have leveraged Web-based technologies by expanding, improving, or modifying product and service offerings. A subliminal theme in all this hyperbole is the notion that these technologies are good and will provide the consumer with many more options, services and advantages. Grover and Ramanlal (1999) challenged this theme by presenting alternative scenarios in which these technologies did not necessarily work in the best interest of the customer. For example, product customization, enabled by IT networks, can allow sellers to exploit buyers rather than benefit buyers.

The emergence of e-commerce is creating fundamental change to the way that business is conducted. These changes are altering the way in which every enterprise acquires wealth and creates shareholder value. The myriad of powerful computing and communications technology enabling e-commerce allow organizations to streamline their business processes, enhance customer service and offer digital products and services. This shift underlying marketing fundamentals is now the driving force that is luring many organizations to embrace e-commerce. However, as they are learning, organizations must proceed with caution, as the road to e-commerce is littered with failed initiatives (Chang, Jackson, & Grover, 2003).

While engaging in e-commerce undoubtedly has substantial benefits, this marketplace is also quite competitive. E-commerce reduces customer search and switching costs, has the ability to distribute information on new products, access new sales channels and reduce entry-level capital requirements, thereby lowering barriers to entry. Companies, which exhibit a market orientation, by being vigilant regarding the needs of customers and the actions of competitors, tend to achieve better performance. Over-emphasizing one dimension at the cost of the other tend to lead to sub-optimization in an environment that rewards the ability to sense and respond to a variety of information cues (Chang et al., 2003).

The term commerce is defined by some as describing transactions conducted between business partners. When this definition of commerce is used, some people find the term electronic commerce to be fairly narrow. Thus, many use the term

Figure 9.3. E-Commerce is part of E-business

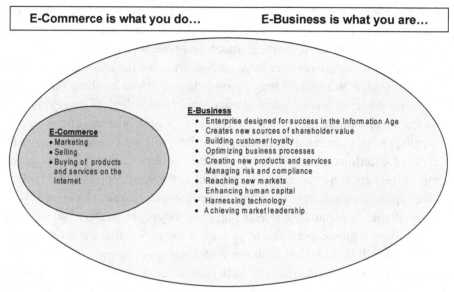

e-business. E-business refers to a broader definition of EC, not just the buying and selling of goods and services, but also servicing customers, collaborating with business partners, and conducting electronic transactions within an organization (Turban et al., 2002).

E-commerce is part of e-business, as illustrated in Figure 9.3. The difference can be demonstrated using a business example. The business example is concerned with handling of customer complaints. As long as customers do not complain, then e-commerce may be sufficient for electronic transactions with customers. The front end of the business is electronic, and this front end is the only contact customers have with the business. However, if a customer complains, then other parts of the business may have to get involved. For example, if the customer has received a computer which is found deficient. Then the customer gets in touch with the vendor. The vendor has to decide whether the complaint is justified. If it is, then the vendor has to decide whether to (a) fix the product, (b) replace the product, or (c) refund the money paid for the product.

This kind of decision-making will typically involve other departments in addition to marketing and sales departments. These other departments may be the technical department, the production department and the finance department. While the marketing and sales departments have electronic communication with the customer using information systems, other departments may not be connected to the same information systems. In this situation, the internal handling of a customer

Figure 9.4. Customer complaint handling business process in company with e-commerce but no e-business

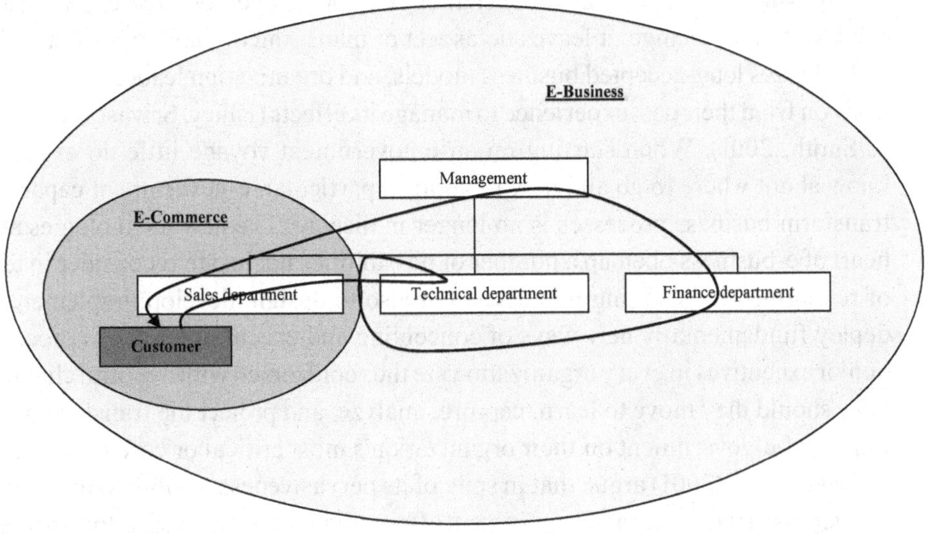

complaint in the business is not transparent to and accessible for the customer. The customer may experience time passing by, without any information from the vendor. A complaining customer was angry already at the time of the complaint. The anger and frustration are rising as the customer receives no response. The customer is unable to obtain information from the vendor by electronic means, since the vendor is doing e-commerce, not e-business.

If the vendor would be an e-business, then the business process of customer complaints handling would be an integrated information system to which the customer has access. Then it is possible for the customer to follow the complaint handling process, and it is possible for other departments than marketing and sales, to stay in direct contact with the complaining customer to resolve the issues. This business process is illustrated in Figure 9.4.

Weill and Vitale (2002) uses the following working definition of e-business: Marketing, buying, selling, delivering, servicing, and paying for products, services, and information across (nonproprietary) networks linking an enterprise and its prospects, customers, agents, suppliers, competitors, allies, and complementors. The essence of this definition is the conduct of business and business processes over computer networks based on nonproprietary standards. The Internet is the exemplar of a nonproprietary network used today for e-business. Given its low cost and universal access, the Internet will be the major infrastructure for the foreseeable future. However, new access technologies already on the horizon (e.g., use of wireless application protocol from mobile telephones) will supplement the Internet.

E-business embodies the most challenging, pervasive, disruptive, and disconcerting form of change: it leaves no aspect of managing organizations untouched, it challenges long-accepted business models, and organization leaders have little to draw on from their past experience to manage its effects (Fahey, Srivastava, Sharon, & Smith, 2001). When starting on an e-government voyage little do executives know about where to go and how to do it. In particular, e-government capacity to transform business processes is no longer in dispute. The new technologies at the heart of e-business open up a number of possibilities not just to reconsider in terms of re-engineering existing processes, but also to design, develop, implement and deploy fundamentally new ways of conceiving and executing business processes. Senior executives in every organization are thus confronted with a central challenge: How should they move to learn, capture, analyze, and project the transformational impact of e-government on their organization's most critical or core processes?

Fahey et al. (2001) argue that in spite of its pervasiveness, visibility, and impact, e-business in industries and government often remains a poorly understood phenomenon. E-government constitutes the ability of an agency or public service provider to electronically connect, in multiple ways, many organizations, both internal and external, for many different purposes. It allows an organization to execute electronic transactions with any individual entity along the value creation – authorities, citizens, municipalities, hospitals, police, and courts. Increasingly, e-business allows an organization to establish real-time connections simultaneously among numerous entities for some specific purpose, such as optimizing the flow of cases, document production and decision-making in the value shop configuration.

1.6   The CIO Developing Competitive Strategy

A study conducted by Chang et al. (2003) proposed that e-commerce initiatives are important strategic initiatives and that firms with a stronger e-commerce market orientation will be more successful. Content analysis of CEO's letter to shareholders of 145 Fortune 500 firms was conducted to evaluate the importance of e-commerce and strategic orientation. The results provide support to the studies proposition and indicate that e-commerce must be pursued carefully as a strategic initiative rather than as an appendage to an existing organization.

Strategy is an ongoing process of evaluating purpose as well as questioning, verifying and redefining the manner of interaction with the competitive environment. Complexity of the strategy process can be simplified by searching for patterns of behavior in organizations. These patterns of emergent behavior can be used to describe the underlying processes of organizational adaptation. Basic strategic orientation of organizations can be described in terms of a typology of defenders, prospectors, analyzers and reactors. Each orientation differs with respect to risk disposition, innovativeness and operational efficiencies. Strategic orientation such as low cost or differentiation is means of altering the firm's position vis-à-vis competitors and suppliers. Strategy involves mustering resources and creating capabilities that are difficult to imitate by competitors, resulting in superior rents. Strategic orientation is both an issue of how firms position themselves with respect to competitors and an issue of how firm-specific resources are exploited.

Much strategic management literature has been devoted to identifying attributes or dimensions of a company's strategic orientation. Internet-based businesses include portals, travel sites, e-tailers, and providers of financial and informational services. These businesses attempt to leverage the Internet infrastructure and digital economics in order to gain strategic positioning within the marketplace. For Internet-based businesses, four major dimensions of strategic orientation are particularly pertinent: risk disposition, innovativeness, operational efficiency and marketing intensity (Grover & Saeed, 2004).

1.7 The CIO Developing an Internet Strategy

Many of the pioneers of Internet business, both dot-coms and established companies, have competed in ways that violate nearly every precept of good strategy. There was for a long time an absence of strategy. According to Porter (Porter, 2001), the time has come to take a clearer view of the Internet. It is necessary to move away from rhetoric–such as Internet industries, e-business strategies, and a new economy–and see the Internet for what it is. It is an enabling technology, a powerful set of tools that can be used, wisely or unwisely, in almost any industry and as part of almost any strategy.

Strategy is neither the quest for the universally best way of competing nor an effort to be all things to every customer. It defines a way of competing that delivers unique value in a particular set of uses or for a particular set of customers. To establish and maintain a distinctive strategic positioning, a company needs to follow six fundamental principles (Porter, 2001):

- It must start with the *right goal*: superior long-term return on investment. Only by grounding strategy in sustained profitability will real economic value be generated. Economic value is created when customers are willing to pay a price for a product or service that exceeds the cost of producing it.
- A company's strategy must enable it to deliver a *value proposition*, or set of benefits, different from those that competitors offer.
- Strategy needs to be reflected in a *distinctive value configuration*. To estab-

lish a sustainable competitive advantage, a company must perform different activities than rivals or perform similar activities in different ways.

- Robust strategies involve *trade-offs*. A company must abandon or forgo some product features, services, or activities in order to be unique at others.
- Strategy defines how all the elements of what a company does *fit* together. A strategy involves making choices throughout the value configuration that are independent; all a company's activities must be mutually reinforcing.
- Strategy involves *continuity* of direction. A company must define a distinctive value proposition that it will stand for, even if that means forgoing certain opportunities.

The absence of strategy in many pioneering Internet businesses, have mislead them to focus on revenues rather than profits, indirect values rather than real value, every conceivable product rather than trade-offs, activities of rivals rather than tailor the value configuration, and rash of partnerships rather than build control. To capitalize on the Internet's strategic potential, executives and entrepreneurs alike will need to develop a strategy that exploits this potential. In some industries, the use of the Internet represents only a modest shift from well-established practices. Virtual activities do not eliminate the need for physical activities, but often amplify their importance. The complementarity between Internet activities and traditional activities arises for a number of reasons. First, introducing Internet applications in one activity often places greater demands on physical activities elsewhere in the value configuration. Second, using the Internet in one activity can have systemic consequences, requiring new or enhanced physical activities that are often unanticipated. Third, most Internet applications have some shortcomings in comparison with conventional methods, such as customers being unable to physically examine products (Porter, 2001).

1.8   The CIO Selecting E-Business Model

A business model can be defined as the method by which an organization builds and uses its resources to offer its customers better value than its competitors and to take money doing so. It details how a firm makes money now and how it plans to do so in the long run. The model is what enables a firm to have a sustainable competitive advantage, to perform better than its rivals in the long term. A business model can be conceptualized as a system that is made up of components, linkages between the components, and dynamics (Afuah & Tucci, 2003).

Weill and Vitale (2001) define an e-business model as a description of the roles and relationships among a firm's consumers, customers, allies, and suppliers that identifies the major flows of product, information, and money, and the major benefits to participants. There are many different ways to describe and classify e-business models. Weill and Vitale (2001) propose that there are a finite number of atomic e-business models, each of which captures a different way to conduct e-business. Firms can combine atomic e-business models as building blocks to create tailored e-business models and initiatives, using their competencies as their guide. Weill and Vitale (2001) identified a small number of 8 atomic e-business models, each of which describes the essence of conducting business electronically:

1. Direct to Customer. The distinguishing characteristic of this model is that buyer and seller communicate directly, rather than through an intermediary. The seller may be a retailer, a wholesaler or a manufacturer. The customer may be an individual or a business. Examples of the direct-to-customer model are Dell Computer Corporation (www.dell.com) and Gap, Inc. (www.gap.com).

Infrastructure. The direct-to-customer model requires extensive electronic connection with the customer, including online payment systems. Many direct-to-customer implementations include an extranet to allow customized Web pages for major B2B customers. Operating a direct-to-customer e-business requires significant investment in the equivalent of the store: the Web site. Direct-to-customer businesses spend millions of dollars developing easy-to-navigate and easy-to-use Web sites with the goal of improving the B2B or B2C shopping experience online. Lands End (www.landsend.com) has devised a feature by which women can build and store a three-dimensional model of themselves to "try on" clothes electronically. In their field research, Weill and Vitale (2001) found that firms with e-business initiatives containing the direct-to-customer e-business model needed and were investing more heavily in three areas of infrastructure services: application infrastructure, communications, and IT management. Direct-to-customer firms particularly needed payment transaction processing to process online customer payments, enterprise-wide resource planning (ERP) to process customer transactions, workflow infrastructure to optimize business process performance, communication network services linking all points in the enterprise to each other and the outside world (often using TCP/IP protocol), the installation and maintenance of workstations and local area networks supporting the large number of people required to operate a direct-to-customer model, and service-level agreements between the business and the IT group or outsourcer to ensure, monitor, and improve the systems necessary for the model.

Sources of Revenue. The main source of revenue in the direct-to-customer model is usually direct sales to customers. Supplemental revenues come from advertising, the sale of customer information, and product placement fees.

Critical Success Factors. Critical success factors are the things a firm must do well to flourish. The following list shows the critical success factors for the direct-to-customer model: create and maintain customer awareness, in order to build a critical mass of users to cover the fixed cost of building an electronic presence; reduce customer acquisition costs; strive to own the customer relationship and understand individual customer needs; increase repeat purchases and average transaction size; provide fast and efficient transaction processing, fulfillment, and payment; ensure adequate security for the organization and its customers; and provide interfaces that combine ease of use with richness of experience, integrating multiple channels.

2.   Full-Service Provider. A firm using the full-service provider model provides total coverage of customer needs in a particular domain, consolidated via a single point of contact. The domain could be any major area of customer needs requiring multiple products and services, for example, financial services, health care, or industrial chemicals. The full-service provider adds value by providing a full range of products, sourced both internally and externally, and consolidated them using the channel chosen by the customer. Examples of the full-service provider are the Prudential Advisor (www.prusec.com) and GE Supply Company (www.gesupply.com).

Infrastructure. Virtually all businesses aspire to getting hundred percent of their customers' business, or at least to getting as much of that business as they can profitably handle. Yet the number of full-service providers remains small. Part of the reason for this is required infrastructure. The missing piece of infrastructure in many businesses is often a database containing information about the customer and the products that the customer owns. Without owning these data, a provider does not own the customer relationship, and therefore some of the customer's transactions are likely to take place directly with other providers. All of the important interactions with customers occurring across any channel or business unit must be recorded in the firm wide customer database. Weill and Vitale (2001) identified in their field research databases and data warehouses as some of the most important infrastructure services associated with the full-service provider model. Other important infrastructure services included the following: the ability to evaluate proposals for new information systems initiatives to coordinate IT investments across a multi-business-unit firm with the goal of a single point of contact for the customer; centralized management of IT infrastructure capacity to integrate across multiple business units within the firm and third-party providers, the full-service provider model is not readily workable if each business unit optimizes its own IT needs; installation and maintenance of workstations and local area networks to operate the online business linking all the business units and third-party providers; electronic support for groups to coordinate the cross-functional teams required to implement this model; and the identification and testing of new technologies to find cost-effective ways to deliver this complex business model to the customer across multiple channels.

Sources of Revenue. A full-service provider gains revenues from selling its own products and those of others, and possibly also from annual membership fees, management fees, transaction fees, commissions on third-party products, advertising or listing fees from third-party providers, and fees for selling aggregated data about customers.

Critical Success Factors. One important critical success factor is the brand, credibility and trust necessary for a customer to look to the firm for its complete needs in an area. Another is owning the customer relationship in one domain and integrating and consolidating the offering of many third parties into a single channel or multiple channels. A third factor is owning more of the customer data in the relevant domain than any other player. A final factor is enforcement of policies to protect the interests of internal and external suppliers, as well as customers.

3. Whole of Enterprise. The single point of contact for the e-business customer is the essence of the whole-of-enterprise atomic business model. Although many of this model's breakthrough innovations have occurred in public-sector organizations, the model is applicable in both the for-profit and the public sectors. An example of this model is the Australian state of Victoria with its Business Channel (www.business.channel.vic.gov.au) and Health Channel (www.betterhealth.vic.gov.au).

Infrastructure. For the whole-of-enterprise model, infrastructure needs to link the different systems in the various business units and provide a firm wide perspective for management. The field research by Weill and Vitale (2001) revealed that the following infrastructure services are the most important for implementing this model: centralized management of infrastructure capacity to facilitate integration and capture economies of scale; identification and testing of new technologies to find new ways to integrate the often different systems in many business units into a single point of customer contact; management of key data independent of applications and the creation of a centralized repository for firm wide information; electronic means of summarizing data from different applications and platforms to manage the complexity arising from a single point of contact for multiple business units; development of an ERP service to process the transactions instigated by customers interacting with several different business units, often requiring consolidating or linking several ERPs in the firm; payment transaction processing, either on a firm wide basis or by linking several systems across the business units; large-scale data-processing facilities to process transactions from multiple business units, often centralized to achieve economies of scale; and integrated mobile computing applications, which provide another channel to the customer.

Sources of Revenue. In the for-profit sector, revenues are generated by provision of goods and services to the customer by the business units. There may also be the opportunity to charge an annual service or membership fee for this level of service.

In the government sector, the motivation is usually twofold: improved service and reduced cost. Service to the community is improved through continuous, round-the-clock operation and faster service times. Government costs can potentially be reduced by sharing more infrastructures and eliminating the need to perform the same transaction in multiple agencies.

Critical Success Factors. The following list details the critical success factors for the whole-of-enterprise model: changing customer behavior to make use of the new model, as opposed to the customer continuing to interact directly with individual units; reducing costs in the individual business units as the direct demands on them fall, and managing the transfer pricing issues that will inevitably arise; altering the perspective of the business units to take an enterprise-wide view, which includes broad product awareness, training, and cross-selling; in the integrated implementation, reengineering the business processes to link into life events at the front end and existing legacy processes and systems at the back end; and finding compelling and practical life events that customers can use as triggers to access the enterprise.

4. Intermediaries such as portals, agents, auctions, aggregators, and other intermediaries. E-business is often promoted as an ideal way for sellers and buyers to interact directly, shortening old-economy value chains by disintermediating some of their members. Yet some of the most popular sites on the Internet, both for consumers and for business users, are in fact intermediaries – sites that stand between the buyer and the seller. The services of intermediaries include search (to locate providers of products and services), specification (to identify important product attributes), price (to establish the price, including optional extras such as warranties), sale (to complete the sales transaction, including payment and settlement), fulfillment (to fulfill the purchase by delivering the product or service), surveillance (to conduct surveillance of the activities of buyers and sellers in order to report aggregate activity and prices and to inform and regulate the market), and enforcement (to enforce proper conduct by buyers and sellers). Examples of intermediaries are electronic malls, shopping agents, specialty auctions, electronic markets, electronic auctions and portals.

Infrastructure. Intermediaries generate value by concentrating information and bringing together buyers and sellers, operating entirely in space and thus relying on IT as the primary infrastructure. Weill and Vitale (2001) found in their field interviews that the most important infrastructure services for firms pursuing the intermediary atomic business model are the following: knowledge management, including knowledge databases and contact databases that enable the codification and sharing of knowledge in this highly information-intensive business; enforcing Internet and email policies to ensure proper and consistent use of electronic channels to buyers, sellers, and intermediaries; workstation networks to support the products and services of this all-electronic business model; centralized management of e-business applications, ensuring consistency and integration across product offerings; information systems planning to identify the most effective uses of IT in the business; and information systems project management to ensure that business value is achieved from IT investments.

Sources of Revenue. An intermediary may earn revenues from buyers, sellers, or both. Sellers may pay a listing fee, a transaction fee, a sales commission, or some combination. Similarly, buyers may pay a subscription fee, a success fee, or a sales commission.

Critical Success Factors. The chief requirement for survival as an intermediary is sufficient volume of usage to cover the fixed costs of establishing the business and the required infrastructure. Attracting and retaining a critical mass of customers is therefore the primary critical success factor. Another important critical success factor is building up infrastructure just quickly enough to meet demand as it increases.

5. Shared Infrastructure. The firm provides infrastructure shared by its owners. Other suppliers, who are users of the shared infrastructure, but not owners, can also be included. Customers who access the shared infrastructure directly are given a choice of suppliers and value propositions. The owner and the non-owner suppliers are generally represented objectively. In some situations, goods or services flow directly from the shared infrastructure to the customer. In other situations, a message is sent by the shared infrastructure to the supplier, who then completes the transaction by providing the goods or services to the customer. An example illustrating the features of the shared-infrastructure business model is the system from 2000 by America's largest automakers, some of their dealers, and IBM, Motorola, and Intel. The initiative was named Covisint (collaboration vision integrity). General Motors, Ford and DaimlerChrysler see stronger potential benefits from cooperating on supply-chain logistics than from competing.

Infrastructure. The shared-infrastructure business model requires competitors to cooperate by sharing IT infrastructure and information. This level of cooperation requires agreement on high-level IT architectures as well as operational standards for applications, data communications, and technology. Effective implementation of the shared-infrastructure model also requires enforcement of these standards, and most shared-infrastructure models have a joint committee to set and enforce standards. Another role of these committees is to implement the policies of the shared infrastructure about what information, if any, is hared and what information is confidential to partner firms. Weill and Vitale (2001) found in their field research that the most important infrastructure services required by firms implementing the shared-infrastructure atomic business model all concerned architectures and standards: specification and enforcement of high-level architectures for data, technology, applications, communications, and work that are agreed to by alliance partners; and specification and enforcement of detailed standards for the high-level architectures.

Sources of Revenue. Revenues can be generated both from membership fees and from transaction fees. The alliance may be run on a nonprofit basis or on a profit-making basis. Not-for-profit shared infrastructures are typically open to all eligible organizations and distribute any excess revenues back to their members. The for-profit models are typically owned by a subset of the firms in a given segment, which split up any profits among themselves.

Critical Success Factors. Critical success factors for the shared-infrastructure model include the following: no dominant partner that gains more than any other partner; an unbiased channel and objective presentation of product and service information; critical mass of both alliance partners and customers; management of conflict among the ongoing e-business initiatives of the alliance partners; compilation and delivery of accurate and timely statements of the services and benefits provided to each member of the alliance; and interoperability of systems.

6.   Virtual Community. Virtual communities deserve our attention, and not only because they are the clearest, and perhaps the last, surviving embodiment of the original intent of the Internet. By using IT to leverage the fundamental human desire for communication with peers, virtual communities can create significant value for their owners as well as for their members. Once established, a virtual community is less susceptible to competition by imitation than any of the other atomic business models. In this business model, the firm of interest – the sponsor of the virtual community – sits in the center, positioned between members of the community and suppliers. Fundamental to the success of this model is that members are able, and in fact are encouraged, to communicate with one another directly. Communication between members may be vial email, bulletin boards, online chat, Web-based conferencing, or other computer-based media, and it is the distinguishing feature of this model. Examples of this model are Parent Soup (www.parentsoup.com), a virtual community for parents, and Motley Fool (www.motleyfool.com), a virtual community of investors.

Infrastructure. Virtual communities depend on IT to exist. In particular, the creation and continual enhancement of an Internet site is essential if a virtual community is to survive. Many virtual-community sites include not just static content and links, but also tools of interest to potential members. Weill and Vitale (2001) found in their field research that the infrastructure services most important for the virtual-community business model are the following: training in the use of IT for members of the community; application service provision (ASP) to provide specialized systems virtual communities need such as bulletin boards, email, and ISP access; IT research and development, including infrastructure services for identifying and testing new technologies and for evaluating proposals for new information systems initiatives; information systems planning to identify and prioritize potential investments in IT in this completely online business; and installation and maintenance of workstations and local area networks to support the electronic world of the virtual community.

Sources of Revenue. A sponsoring firm can gain revenue from membership fees, direct sales of goods and services, advertising, clickthroughs and sales commissions. A firm sponsoring a virtual community as an adjunct to its other activities may receive no direct revenue at all from the virtual community. Rather, the firm receives less tangible benefits, such as customer loyalty and increased knowledge about its customer base.

Critical Success Factors. The critical success factors for a virtual community include finding and retaining a critical mass of members; building and maintaining loyalty with an appropriate mix of content and features; maintaining privacy and security for member information; balancing commercial potential and members' interests; leveraging member profile information with advertisers and merchants; and engendering a feeling of trust in the community by its members.

7. Value Net Integrator. Traditionally, most firms operate simultaneously in two worlds: the physical and the virtual. In the physical world, goods and services are created in a series of value-adding activities connecting the supply side (suppliers, procurement, and logistics) with the demand side (customers, marketing, and shipping). In the virtual world, information about the members of the physical value chain are gathered, synthesized, and distributed along the virtual value chain. E-business provides the opportunity to separate the physical and virtual value chains. Value net integrators take advantage of that split and attempt to control the virtual value chain in their industries by gathering, synthesizing, and distributing information. Value net integrators add value by improving the effectiveness of the value chain by coordinating information. A pure value net integrator operates exclusively in the virtual value chain, owning a few physical assets. To achieve the gathering, synthesizing, and distributing of information, the value net integrator receives and sends information to all other players in the model. The value net integrator coordinates product flows form suppliers to allies and customers. The product flows from the suppliers to customers may be direct or via allies. In some cases the value net integrator may sell information or other products to the customer. The value net integrator always strives to own the customer relationship with the other participants in the model, thus knowing more about their operations than any other player. Examples of value net integrators are Seven-Eleven Japan and Cisco Systems (www.cisco.com).

Infrastructure. The value net integrator succeeds in its role by gathering, synthesizing, and distributing information. Thus, for a value net integrator, data and electronic connectivity with allies and other players are very important assets. Field research carried out by Weill and Vitale (2001) suggests that the most important infrastructure services required for a value net integrator include middleware, linking systems on different platforms across the many players in the value net; a centralized data warehouse that collects and summarizes key information for analysis from decentralized databases held by several players across the value net; specification and enforcement of high-level architectures and detailed standards for data, technology, applications, and communications to link together different technology platforms owned by different firms; call centers to provide advice and guidance for partners and allies in getting the most value from the information provided by the value net generator; and high-capacity communications network service to support the high volumes of information flowing across the value net.

Sources of Revenue. In this model, revenues are generally earned by fees or margins on the physical goods that pass through the industry value net. By using information about consumers, the value net integrator is able to increase prices by meeting consumer demand. By using information about suppliers, the value net integrator reduces costs by cutting inventories and lead times.

Critical Success Factors. The critical success factors for the value net integrator atomic business model are as follows: reducing ownership of physical assets while retaining ownership of data; owning or having access to the complete industry virtual value chain; establishing a trusted brand recognized at all places in the value chain; operating in markets where information can add significant value, such as those that are complex, fragmented, regulated, multilayered, inefficient, and large with many sources of information; presenting the information to customers, allies, partners, and suppliers in clear and innovative ways that provide value; and helping other value chain participants capitalize on the information provided by the value net integrator.

8.   Content Provider. Like many terms associated with e-business, content provider has different meanings to different people. We define content provider as a firm that creates and provides content (information, products, or services) in digital form to customers via third parties. The physical-world analogy of a content provider is a journalist, recording artist, or stock analyst. Digital products such as software, electronic travel guides, and digital music and video are examples of content. A virtual-world example of a content provider is weather forecasters such as Storm Weather Center (www.storm.no).

Infrastructure. Content providers must excel at tailoring and manipulating their core content to meet the specific needs of customers. Content providers must categorize and store their content in well-indexed modules so it can be combined and customized to meet customer needs via a wide variety of channels. Customers and transactions tend to be relatively few, at least compared with the number of end consumers and their transactions. Often complex and unique IT infrastructures are needed to support the particular needs of the specialized professionals employed by the content provider. Field research by Weill and Vitale (2001) identified the most important infrastructure services: multimedia storage farms or storage area network infrastructures to deal with large amounts of information; a strong focus on architecture, including setting and enforcing standards particularly for work; detailed data architectures to structure, specify, link manipulate, and manage the core intellectual property; workstation network infrastructures to enable the fundamentally online business of a content provider; and a common systems development environment to provide compatible and integrated systems, ensuring the systems can provide content across multiple channels to their customers.

Sources of Revenue. The primary source of revenue for a content provider is fees from its third parties or allies. These fees may be based on a fixed price per month or year, or on the number of times the third party's own customers access the content. In some situations, the fees paid are lower for content branded by the provider, and higher for unbranded content, which then appears to the customer to have been generated by the third party itself.

Critical Success Factors. To succeed, a content provider must provide reliable, timely content in the right format and at the right price. The critical success factors

Figure 9.5. E-business models integration with customers versus partners

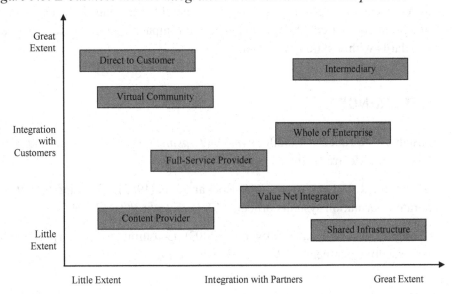

for this model include the following: branding (the value of content is due in part to reputation), recognized as best in class (the business of content provision will be global and competitive), and network (establishing and maintaining a network of third parties through which content is distributed.

One way of comparing these e-business models is to analyze to what extent each model creates integration with customers and to what extent each model creates integration with partners. As illustrated in Figure 9.5, the business model of Direct to Customer creates mainly integration with customers, while Shared Infrastructure creates mainly integration with partners.

CONCLUSION

As the highest-ranking IT executive the CIO has an important role in the organization requiring effective communication with top management. The CIO has to deal with sourcing options for IT resources and services. In an IT governance perspective the CIO must establish structures, processes, and politics that govern how and who within the organization that makes IT decisions. The CIO may take on different roles related to information technology management – as a personnel leader, spokesman, monitor, liaison, entrepreneur, and resource allocator. As organizations expand their use of the Internet, CIOs play a central role in selecting and developing business models.

In a survey of state government CIOs on collaborative government and e-government, Reddick (2008) found that collaboration stimulated and supported by CIOs is an important approach to enhance the successful adoption of electronic government and e-government projects. One of the findings indicates a high level of agreement that collaboration is having an impact on communication, trust and standards within state governments.

REFERENCES

Afuah, A., & Tucci, C. L. (2003). *Internet business models and strategies* (2nd ed.). New York: McGraw-Hill.

Benjamin, R. I., Dickinson, C., & Rockart, J. F. (1985). Changing tole of the corporate information systems officer. *MIS Quarterly, 9*(3), 177-197.

Chang, K., Jackson, J., & Grover, V. (2003). E-commerce and corporate strategy: An executive perspective. *Information & Management, 40*(7), 663-675.

Earl, M. J., & Feeny, D. F. (1994). Is your CIO adding value? *Sloan Management Review, 35*(3), 11-20.

Fahey, L., Srivastava, R., Sharon, J. S., & Smith, D. E. (2001). Linking e-business and operating processes: The role of knowledge management. *IBM Systems Journal, 40*(4), 889-907.

Gottschalk, P. (2007). *CIO and corporate strategic management: Changing role of CIO to CEO*. Hershey, PA:IGI Global Publishing.

Grembergen, W. V., Haes, S. D., & Guldentops, E. (2004). Structures, processes and relational mechanisms for IT governance. In W. V. Grembergen (Ed.), *Strategies for information technology governance* (pp. 1-36). Hershey, PA:IGI Global Publishing.

Grover, V., Jeong, S. R., Kettinger, W. J., & Lee, C. C. (1993). The chief information officer: A study of managerial roles. *Journal of Management Information Systems, 10*(2), 107-130.

Grover, V., & Ramanlal, P. (1999). Six myths of information and markets: Information technology networks, electronic commerce, and the battle for consumer surplus. *MIS Quarterly, 23*(4), 456-495.

Grover, V., & Saeed, K. A. (2004). Strategic orientation and performance of Internet-based businesses. *Information Systems Journal, 14*(1), 23-42.

King, W. R., & Malhotra, Y. (2000). Developing a framework for analyzing IS sourcing. *Information & Management, 37*(6), 323-334.

Kolbasuk, M. (2005). CIOs get respect. *Insurance and Technology, 30*(9), 18.

Kaarst-Brown, M. (2005). Understanding an organization's view of the CIO: The role of assumptions about IT. *MIS Quarterly Executive, 4*(2), 287-301.

Mintzberg, H. (1994). Rounding out the manager's job. *Sloan Management Review, 36*(1), 11-26.

Monnoyer, E., & Willmott, P. (2005). What IT leaders do [Electronic Version]. *McKinsey Quarterly*, 5 pages. Retrieved August, 2008 from www.mckinseyquarterly.com

Office of the Government Chief Information Officer. (2007). *The HKSARG Interoperability Framework*. Government of the Hong Kong Special Administrative Region.

Porter, M. E. (2001). Strategy and the Internet. *Harvard Business Review, 79*(3), 62-78.

Reddick, C. G. (2008). Collaborative management and e-government: A survey of state government CIOs. *Electronic Government, an International Journal, 5*(2), 146-161.

Steensma, H. K., & Corley, K. G. (2001). Organizational context as moderator of theories on firm boundaries for technology sourcing. *Academy of Management Journal, 44*(2), 271-291.

Todd, P. A., McKeen, J. D., & Gallupe, R. B. (1995). The evolution of IS job skills: A content analysis of IS job advertisements from 1970 to 1990. *MIS Quarterly, 19*(1), 1-27.

Turban, E., King, D., Lee, J., Warkentin, M., & Chung, H. M. (2002). *Electronic commerce: A managerial perspective*. Sidney, Australia: Pearson Education, Prentice Hall.

Weil, P. (2004). *Don't just lead, govern: How top-performing firms govern IT* (No. CISR WP No. 341): Center for Information Systems Research, Sloan School of Management, Massachusetts Institute of Technology.

Weill, P., & Vitale, M. R. (2001). *Place to space. Migrating to eBusiness models.* Boston: Harvard Business School Press.

Weill, P., & Vitale, M. R. (2002). What IT infrastructure capabilities are needed to implement e-business models? *MIS Quarterly Executive, 1*(1), 17-34.

Chapter X

The Case of Police Investigations

1.   THE CASE OF POLICE INVESTIGATIONS

An investigation is an effective search for material to bring an offender to justice. Knowledge and skills are required to conduct an effective investigation. Investigative knowledge enables investigators to determine if a given set of circumstances amounts to a criminal offence, to identify the types of material that may have been generated during the commission of an offence and where this material may be found. It also ensures that investigations are carried out in a manner, which complies with the rules of evidence, thereby increasing the likelihood that the material gathered will be admitted as evidence.

In this chapter we use police investigations as an example to show interoperability at different levels. First, we give an introduction to how police investigation work. Then, we cover topics such as information systems in police investigations, stages of growth model, filtration of knowledge, value creation in investigations, and how detectives work.

1.1   The Case of Asset Recovery Investigations

Police investigations often require access to a variety of information sources to be successful. Some of these sources are manual, like when interviewing a suspect or a witness, or when collecting evidence at the crime scene. However, more and more information sources are becoming electronic in terms of digital information (Gottschalk, 2007).

For a criminal, it is impossible to move, to live, to operate at any level without leaving traces, bits, and seemingly meaningless fragments of personal information, fragments that can be retrieved and amplified. Successful asset recovery requires the combination of these information fragments. An information perspective on asset recovery recognizes that financially related, personal information is the raw material of successful investigations (Kennedy, 2007). While jurisdictions create rules to protect information pertaining to their citizens, criminals seek to benefit from those rules to prevent information regarding their criminal proceeds from falling into the possession of financial investigators. The result is according to Kennedy (2007) an information war.

Financial investigations are information intensive. They involve both public and private sector material, for example taxation records and bank account information, which demonstrate money movements, together with any relevant information as to lifestyle. Any record that provides information concerning money may be significant. The investigator seeks to discover where money came from, who obtained it, when it was received and where it was stored, deposited, or transformed into other forms of property (Kennedy, 2007).

While investigators will wish to obtain information, they must ensure that they do so in a lawful manner. There are a number of legal barriers, which restrict the transmission of information in most countries. The typical obstacle is some kind of confidentiality, often defined in terms of a human rights act and a data protection act (Kennedy, 2007).

According to Kennedy (2007), information from foreign jurisdictions is often a hurdle. Criminals may try to hide assets overseas, and crucial information may also reside overseas. Investigators therefore require a means of obtaining information from overseas. However, cross-border criminal organizations attempt to use legal and organizational gaps and inadequate communication between national authorities to their advantage. An example of such difficulties is that the courts in one jurisdiction are inevitably reluctant to enforce information-gathering orders issued by courts in another jurisdiction.

Shared databases have improved law enforcement access to information resources. In the past, public sector information was held on discrete databases, which were effectively isolated from other sources of information. It has been recognized that better sharing of information between government departments can lead to the identification and reduction of fraud. However, integrated law enforcement computer databases raise a "big brother" concern for others (Kennedy, 2007).

1.2 How Police Investigations Work

Knowledge assists investigators to make effective and accountable decisions during an investigation. It enables them to locate, gather and use the maximum amount of material generated by the commission of an offence to identify and bring offenders to justice. Centrex (2005b) has outlined the knowledge that investigators require to conduct competent criminal investigation. There are four areas of investigative knowledge required to conduct an effective investigation, these are: the legal framework, characteristics of crime, national and local force policies, and investigative skills.

Firstly, all investigators must have a current and in-depth knowledge of criminal law and the legislation, which regulates the process of investigation. Next, investigators need to understand the characteristics of crime. Crime can be placed into three broad categories: property crime, crimes against the person and crimes against society. An examination of the types of crime in each category shows that they vary widely in terms of the behaviors involved, the types of victims, the motives of offenders, the methods used to commit the crime, and the degree of planning involved. The differences between crimes are significant for investigators because the circumstances in which crimes are committed determine the volume and distribution of the material available for them to gather. The third area of investigative knowledge is national and local force policies. The police service is a complex organization with its procedures and resource management. Many of these policies have a direct bearing on the conduct of investigations, and investigators should have knowledge of these that are relevant to the type of investigations they are involved in. Finally, investigative skills are required. Investigations should be conducted with integrity, commonsense and sound judgment. Actions taken during an investigation should be proportionate to the crime under investigation and take account of local cultural and social sensitivities. The success of an investigation relies on the goodwill and cooperation of victims, witnesses and the community.

Although investigators can acquire knowledge from formal training courses and the literature that exists on criminal investigation, they also need practical experience of investigations to underpin this knowledge. Centrex (2005b) argues that investigators should never rely on experience alone. This is because experience is unique to the individual, people learn at different speeds, and each will learn something different from the process.

Table 10.1. Knowledge categories and dimensions of 12 organized crime cases in Norway

Knowledge Dimensions / Knowledge Categories	Identification	Damage	Reason	Connection
Activity Knowledge	**Credit card fraud:** *Import and export of credit cards for illegal use*	**Trafficking:** *Women forced to sex*	**Doping:** *Illegal drugs*	**Money fraud:** *Illegal income statements to get bank loans*
Structural Knowledge	**Albanians:** *Same ethnic background*	**Cars:** *Stolen cars are sold in Eastern Europe*	**Documents:** *False identification papers are produced for terrorists*	**Rents:** *Legal rent for illegal activities*
System Knowledge	**Narcotics:** *Cars on the road all the time with narcotics in spare wheels*	**Somaliens:** *Leakage will be punished*	**Homicide:** *Murders on demand*	**Money laundering:** *Stocks sold at high prices to stockbroker*

Effective practice is generally taken to mean simply what works, but often examples of effective practice are not detailed enough for practitioners to use successfully. Practitioners do not just need to know what works, but also how and why something works if they are to understand and use the information effectively. In addition to know-what, there is a need for know-how and know-why (Gottschalk, 2007). In Table 10.1, a total of twelve organized crimes in Norway are classified according to knowledge categories and crime characteristics.

Investigation is the police activity concerned with (1) the apprehension of criminals by gathering of evidence leading to their arrest, and (2) the collection and presentation of evidence and testimony for the purpose of obtaining convictions. According to Smith and Flanagan (2000), the process begins with an initial crime scene assessment where sources of potential evidence are identified. The information derived from the process then has to be evaluated in order to gauge its relevance to the investigation. During the next stage, the information is interpreted to develop inferences and initial hypotheses. The senior investigating officer (SIO) can then develop this material into appropriate and feasible lines of enquiry. The SIO will have to prioritize actions, and to identify any additional information that may be required to test that scenario. As more information is collected, this is the fed back into the process until the objectives of the investigation are achieved. Providing a suspect is identified and charged, the investigation then enters the post-charge stage, where case papers are compiled for the prosecution. Subsequently, the court process will begin.

Police investigation units represent a knowledge-intensive and time-critical environment. Successful police investigations are dependent on efficient and effective knowledge sharing. Furthermore, Lahneman (2004) argues that successful knowledge management in law enforcement depends on developing an organizational culture that facilitates and rewards knowledge sharing. In this context, detectives as knowledge workers are using their brains to make sense of information. Knowledge is often defined as information combined with interpretation, reflection and context. This combination takes place in the brains of detectives.

1.3   Information Systems in Police Investigations

Law enforcement agencies need advanced knowledge about crimes and criminal organizations to fight organized crime. In addition, they need knowledge of tools for analysis of organized crime. For example, geographic information systems (GIS) can help identify hot-spots and simulate activities of criminal organizations. Another example is network analysis. Xu and Chen (2004) demonstrate how network analysis might be applied by using shortest-path algorithms to identify associations in criminal networks. Effective and efficient link analysis techniques are needed to help law enforcement and intelligence agencies fight organized crimes such as narcotics violation, terrorism, and kidnapping.

Knowledge organizations apply knowledge management systems in their knowledge work. Several knowledge management systems support detectives. One example is geographic information systems. In Sweden, the Hobit system is a geographic occurrences and crime information system used within the Swedish police. The system gives the police an improved opportunity to map out crimes. When and where crimes are committed can be processed and sought out faster thanks to the new system.

The use of geographic information systems by crime analysts in law enforcement is growing. In England and Wales, Weir and Bangs (2007) report that the large majority of crime analysts surveyed used GIS in their analysis. Analysis used in crime reduction and community safety can extend beyond crime data alone. Analysts make use of a large number of multi-agency datasets in order to better understand crime problems and more effectively target interventions. Similarly, Johnson, Birks, McLaughlin, Bowers and Pease (2007) report the use of GIS in crime mapping, where they found that crime (burglary and other types) clusters in space and time.

1.4   Stages of Growth for Police Investigation

Knowledge management is concerned with simplifying and improving the process of sharing, distributing, creating, capturing and understanding knowledge. Information technology can play an important role in successful knowledge management initiatives. The extent of information technology can be defined in terms of growth stages for knowledge management systems. Here, a model consisting of four stages is presented: officer-to-technology systems, officer-to-officer systems, officer-to-information systems and officer-to-application systems as illustrated in Figure 10.1.

Stage 1: Officer-to-Technology Stage. Tools for end users are made available to knowledge workers. In the simplest stage, this means a capable networked PC on every desk or in every briefcase, with standardized personal productivity tools (word processing, presentation software) so that documents can be exchanged easily throughout a company. More complex and functional desktop infrastructures can also be the basis for the same types of knowledge support. Stage 1 is recognized by widespread dissemination and use of end-user tools among knowledge workers in the company. For example, lawyers in a law firm will in this stage use word processing, spreadsheets, legal databases, presentation software, and scheduling programs.

Related to the new changes in computer technology is the transformation that has occurred in report writing and recordkeeping in police investigations. Every police activity or crime incident demands a report on some kind of form. The majority of police patrol reports written before 1975 were handwritten. Today, officers can write reports on small notebook computers located in the front seat of the patrol unit; discs are handed in at the end of the shift for hard copy needs. Cursor keys and spell-check functions in these report programs are useful timesaving features.

An example of an officer-to-technology system is the Major Incident Policy Document in the UK (Home Office, 2005). This document is maintained whenever a Major Incident Room using HOLMES system is in operation. Decisions, which should be recorded, are those which affect the practical or administrative features of the enquiry, and each entry has clearly to show the reasoning for the decision. When the HOLMES system is used, the SIO directs which policy decisions are recorded on the system. The basic information entered into HOLMES is location of incident, data and time of incident, victim(s), senior investigating officer, and date enquiry commenced. During the enquiry, which has been run on the HOLMES system, a closing report is prepared and registered as another document linked to a category of Closing Report. The report will contain the following information: introduction, scene, the victim, and miscellaneous.

Figure 10.1. The knowledge management systems stage model for police investigations

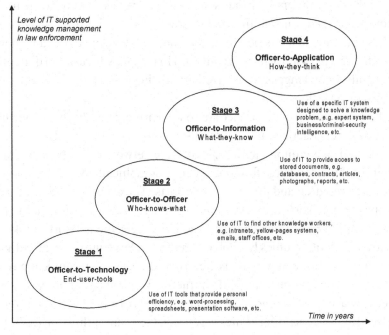

Stage 1 can be labeled *end-user-tools* or *people-to-technology* as information technology provide knowledge workers with tools that improve personal efficiency.

Stage 2: Officer-to-Officer Stage. Information about who knows what is made available to all people in the firm and to selected outside partners. Search engines should enable work with a thesaurus, since the terminology in which expertise is sought may not always match the terms the expert uses to classify that expertise.

According to Alavi and Leidner (2001), the creation of corporate directories, also referred to as the mapping of internal expertise, is a common application of knowledge management technology. Because much knowledge in an organization remains uncodified, mapping the internal expertise is a potentially useful application of technology to enable easy identification of knowledgeable persons.

Here we find the cartographic school of knowledge management, which is concerned with mapping organizational knowledge. It aims to record and disclose who in the organization knows what by building knowledge directories. Often called Yellow Pages, the principal idea is to make sure knowledgeable people in the organization are accessible to others for advice, consultation, or knowledge exchange. Knowledge-oriented directories are not so much repositories of knowledge-based information as gateways to knowledge, and the knowledge is as likely to be tacit as explicit.

At Stage 2, firms apply the personalization strategy in knowledge management. According to Hansen, Nohira and Tierney (1999), the personalization strategy implies that knowledge is tied to the person who developed it and is shared mainly through direct person-to-person contact. This strategy focuses on dialogue between individuals: knowledge is transferred mainly in personal email, meetings and one-on-one conversations.

Electronic networks of practice are computer-mediated discussion forums focused on problems of practice that enable individuals to exchange advice and ideas with others based on common interests. Electronic networks have been found to support organizational knowledge flows between geographically dispersed co-workers and distributed research and development efforts. These networks also assist cooperative open-source software development and open congregation on the Internet for individuals interested in a specific practice. Electronic networks make it possible to share information quickly, globally, and with large numbers of individuals.

Communication competence is important at stage 2. Communication competence is the ability to demonstrate skills in the appropriate communication behavior to effectively achieve one's goals. Communication between individuals requires both the decoding and encoding of messages. Lin, Geng and Whinston (2005) found that knowledge transfer depends on the completeness or incompleteness of the sender's and the receiver' information sets.

The dramatic reduction in electronic communication costs and ease of computer-to-computer linkages has resulted in opportunities to create new channel structures, fuelling interest in inter-organizational systems. Inter-organizational systems are planned and managed ventures to develop and use IT-based information exchange systems to support collaboration and strategic alliances between otherwise independent actors. These systems allow for the exchange of information between partners for the purpose of coordination, communication, and cooperation.

Whilst the access to organizational information and communication of knowledge with distant colleagues through mobile technology is an emerging phenomenon in the business world, the police have a long tradition of supporting geographically distributed work through the employment of state-of-the-art mobile technologies (Sørensen & Pica, 2005, p. 143):

Mobile technologies serve multiple purposes and generally extend the institution of the police to the situation of operational policing. This is constituted through a number of elements. The technologies provide legitimacy for the officers by symbolically representing the institution; they render the officers accountable through documentation and control of actions; they provide a sense of security through connecting to control rooms and colleagues, and they support some emancipation of officers through the ability to provide global and individually tailored views of police databases and activity logs. The technologies provide essential background information through polychromic temporal behavior, and serve as an essential "life-line" to colleagues and the control room during intense monochromic temporal behavior.

The typical system at stage 2 of knowledge management technology in police investigations is the intranet. Intranets provide a rich set of tools for creating collaborative environments in which members of an organization can exchange ideas, share information, and work together on common projects and assignments regardless of their physical location. Information from many different sources and media, including text, graphics, video, audio, and even digital slides can be displayed, shared, and accessed across an enterprise through a simple common interface. Stage 2 can be labeled *who-knows-what* or *people-to-people* as knowledge workers use information technology to find other knowledge workers.

Stage 3: Officer-to-Information Stage. Information from knowledge workers is stored and made available to everyone in the firm and to designated external partners. Data mining techniques can be applied here to find relevant information and combine information in data warehouses. On a broader basis, search engines are Web browsers and server software that operate with a thesaurus, since the terminology in which expertise is sought may not always match the terms used by the expert to classify that expertise.

An essential contribution that IT can make is the provision of shared databases across tasks, levels, entities, and geographies to all knowledge workers throughout a process. For example, Infosys Technologies – a US: $ 1 billion company with over 23,000 employees and globally distributed operations - created a central knowledge portal called KShop. The content of KShop was organized into different content types, for instance, case studies, reusable artifacts, and downloadable software. Every knowledge asset under a content type was associated with one or more nodes (representing areas of discourse) in a knowledge hierarchy or taxonomy.

Sifting though the myriad of content available through knowledge management systems can be challenging, and knowledge workers may be overwhelmed when trying to find the content most relevant for completing a new task. To address this problem, system designers often include rating schemes and credibility indicators to improve users' search and evaluation of knowledge management system content.

An enterprise information portal is viewed as a knowledge community. Enterprise information portals are of multiple forms, ranging from Internet-based data management tools that bring visibility to previously dormant data so that their users can compare, analyze, and share enterprise information to a knowledge portal, which enables its users to obtain specialized knowledge that is related to their specific tasks.

Electronic knowledge repositories are electronic stores of content acquired about all subjects for which the organization has decided to maintain knowledge. Such repositories can comprise multiple knowledge bases as well as the mechanisms for acquisition, control, and publication of the knowledge. The process of knowledge sharing through electronic knowledge repositories involves people contributing knowledge to populate repositories (e.g., customer and supplier knowledge, industry best practices, and product expertise) and people seeking knowledge from repositories for use.

Individuals' knowledge does not transform easily into organizational knowledge even with the implementation of knowledge repositories. According to Bock, Zmud and Kim (2005), individuals tend to hoard knowledge for various reasons. Empirical studies have shown that the greater the anticipated reciprocal relationships are, the more favorable the attitude toward knowledge sharing will be.

In Stage 3, firms apply the codification strategy in knowledge management. According to Hansen et al. (1999), the codification strategy centers on information technology: knowledge is carefully codified and stored in knowledge databases and can be accessed and used by anyone. With a codification strategy, knowledge is extracted from the person who developed it, is made independent from the person and stored in form of interview guides, work schedules, benchmark data etc; and then searched and retrieved and used by many employees.

Two examples of knowledge management systems at stage 3 in law enforcement are COPLINK and geodemographics. COPLINK has a relational database system for crime-specific cases such as gang-related incidents, and serious crimes such as homicide, aggravated assault, and sexual crimes. Deliberately targeting these criminal areas allows a manageable amount of information to be entered into a database (Chen, Zheng, Atabakhsh, Wyzga, & Schroeder, 2003). Geodemographic profiles of the characteristics of individuals and small areas are central to efficient and effective deployment of law enforcement resources. Geocomputation is based on geographical information systems.

Stage 3 can be labeled *what-they-know* or *people-to-documents* as information technology provides knowledge workers with access to information from people that is typically stored in electronic documents. Examples of documents are contracts and agreements, reports, manuals and handbooks, business forms, letters, memos, budgets, articles, drawings, blueprints, photographs, maps, e-mail and voice mail messages, video clips, script and visuals from presentations, policy statements, computer printouts, and transcripts from meetings.

At stage 3, police management gets access to electronic information that can be used for managing police performance. At this stage, sufficient information is electronically stored to apply performance management systems. An example of such a system is iQuanta in the UK, which is a Web based data analysis tool that provides its users with easy access to unified policing performance information based on common data and agreed analysis. iQuanta arose from a system developed to provide the Home Office with accurate and timely assessment of police performance at different organizational levels. The system iQuanta supports the comparison of performance in three main ways, (i) comparison with peers (similar areas elsewhere), (ii) comparison across time, and (iii) progress towards targets/direction of travel.

Another example from the UK is the CORA system. CORA (Crime Objective Results & Analysis) is implemented at the Lancashire Police for performance management. CORA provides access to crime and detection data at several organizational levels. Several comparisons and forecasts are made and presented using a variety of different graphical displays. Navigation between views and drilling into the data is a matter of on-screen button presses. Printable versions of the views have been predefined (Home Office, 2004).

Stage 4: Officer-to-Application Stage. Information systems solving knowledge problems are made available to knowledge workers and solution seekers. Artificial intelligence based on computational rules and procedures is applied in these systems. For example, neural networks are statistically oriented tools that proceed at using data to classify cases into one category or another. A different example is expert systems that can enable the knowledge of one or a few experts to be captured and used by a much broader group of workers requiring the knowledge. Officer-to-application systems will only be successful if they are built on a thorough understanding of the relevant field of expertise and access to knowledgeable experts in the field.

Artificial intelligence (AI) is an area of computer science that endeavors to build machines exhibiting human-like cognitive capabilities. Most modern AI systems are founded on the realization that intelligence is tightly intertwined with knowledge. Knowledge is associated with the symbols we manipulate.

Knowledge-based systems deal with solving problems by exercising knowledge. The most important parts of these systems are the knowledge base and the inference engine. The former holds the domain-specific knowledge whereas the latter contains the functions to exercise the knowledge in the knowledge base. Knowledge can be represented as either rules or frames. Rules are a natural choice for representing conditional knowledge, which is in the form of if-when statements. Inference engines supply the motive power to the knowledge. There are several ways to exercise knowledge, depending on the nature of the knowledge. For example, backward-chaining systems work backward from the conclusions to the inputs. These systems attempt to validate the conclusions by finding evidence to support them. In law enforcement this is an important system feature, as evidence determines whether a person is charged or not for a crime.

Case-based reasoning systems are a different way to represent knowledge through explicit historical cases. This approach differs from the rule-based approach because the knowledge is not complied and interpreted by an expert. Instead, the experiences that possibly shaped the expert's knowledge are directly used to make decisions. Learning is an important issue in case-based reasoning, because with the mere addition of new cases to the library, the system learns. In law enforcement police officers are looking for similar cases to learn how they were handled in the past, making case-based reasoning systems an attractive application in policing.

Use of expert systems in law enforcement includes systems that attempt to aid in information retrieval by drawing upon human heuristics or rules and procedures to investigate tasks. The AICAMS project is a knowledge-based system for identifying suspects. AICAMS also includes a component to fulfill the needs for a simple but effective facial identification procedure based on a library of facial components. The system provides a capability for assembling an infinite number of possible facial composites by varying the position and size of the components. AICAMS also provides a geomapping component by incorporating a map-based user interface (Chen et al., 2003).

Another example is the SSMT (Scientific Support Modeling Tool) in the UK. This tool is aimed at enabling rapid process analysis and improvement of scientific support processes. The SSMT comprises two linked modules. First, the identification module covers the process from scene attendance through to generating a fingerprint or DNA match. Next, the detections module covers the steps after an incident has been generated through to detection of the crime. SSMT is a simulation tool applied to different situations, such as testing the impact of alternative scene attendance policies on resource requirements and identifying bottlenecks in the process (Chainey & Smith, 2006).

Stage Four can be labeled *how-they-think* or *people-to-application* where the system is intended to help solve a knowledge problem.

Knowledge management systems stage model. Information technology to support knowledge work of police officers is improving. For example, new information systems supporting police investigations are evolving. Police investigation is an information-rich and knowledge-intensive practice. Its success depends on turning information into evidence. However, the process of turning information into evidence is neither simple nor straightforward. The raw information that is gathered through the investigative process is often required to be transformed into usable knowledge before its value as potential evidence can be realized. Hence, in an investigative context, knowledge acts as an intervening variable in this transformative process of converting information via knowledge into evidence.

In relation to knowledge sharing in a policing context, Luen and Al-Hawamdeh (2001) reinforced the crucial point that tackling the willingness of police officers to create and share knowledge is a most difficult task. It is clear in the management literature that to create a knowledge-sharing environment, leadership by mangers, especially middle management, is of critical importance (Bock et al., 2005).

1.5   Filtration of Knowledge

Modern information systems provide police management with information about operations. ICT enables access to predefined sources and types of information. Because of the predefined nature of police systems, such systems also contribute to filtration of knowledge in the organization. Holgersson, Gottschalk and Dean (2008) explored how an information technology system might contribute to the filtration of knowledge in an organization. Filtration has an impact on the quality of decision-making and analysis, especially when information from an IT system plays a central role when compared to other sources of knowledge.

Individuals in an organization can interpret and describe conditions differently. Descriptions often vary between different groups of actors. In a small organization it is not unusual to find that most of the tasks are done by the same actors. If the organization grows in size, it will be natural with a specialization. For example, there may be one or more persons working only with IT related matters.

Accordingly, the risks are obvious that separate groups interpret the organization, its goals and problems differently. The probability of such diversity in views will likely increase as the organization grows older. In a new organization, which has grown, there is a possibility that actors in different positions have been involved with most of the tasks before there was a specialization. The conditions will therefore be better in terms of different groups of actors having a similar understanding.

Information technology has received a more central and critical role in the distribution of information. It is important to see an information system in a communicative perspective. The information system might be viewed as a social agent that can be both a sender and a receiver of information. Therefore, an information system has a central role to play in terms of quality of the communication between the sender and the person who tries to interpret the information. Output from an IT system causes often a precise and reliable impression, and it is often easier to acquire information from an IT system than to collect knowledge about an activity in other ways. These are two reasons why IT systems relatively one-sidedly are used to decide the outcome from a work process.

An example may illustrate our point. Organized pocket thefts in the city of Oslo were and are a problem. While 40% of the cases were solved in 2002, only 20% were solved in 2007. This is the kind of information police executives receive from the computer system. Based on this information, the attorney general concluded that police work has deteriorated. Top management in Norwegian police agreed. At the same time, patrolling police officers find the situation has improved. While there were 5000 pocket thefts in 2002, there were only 2000 in 2007. Hence, the number of unsolved cases dropt from 3000 (60% of 5000) to 1600 (80% of 2000). Street-level officers perceive that the situation has improved, and they are satisfied with their own work.

Patrolling officers had analyzed pocket theft patterns and found that the University Street in Oslo had particularly many thefts. They had visited restaurants and bars in that street and encouraged owners to install wardrobe and other measures to improve safety. Because of this kind of problem-oriented policing (POP), the number of pocket thefts dropped. This kind of information never reached the executive level of Norwegian police. Instead, police executives perceived the situation even worse than just the drop into half from 40% to 20%. Because police officers

Figure 10.2. The knowledge organization of police investigations as value shop activities

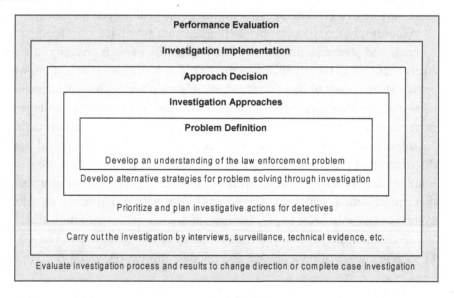

had taken off their uniforms to analyze crime patterns in the office, to identify hot spots, Oslo newspapers started to write about the lack of visible officers in the street. As executives generally are very worried about news in media, executives started to question why local police stations did not order officers back into the street. The message of declining crime because of POP never reached the executive floor, because such information was filtered away in ICT based reporting systems.

1.6   The Investigative Value Shop

Police investigations have the value configuration of a value shop (Gottschalk, 2007) 2007). As can be seen in Figure 10.2, the five activities of a value shop are interlocking and while they follow a logical sequence, much like the management of any project, the difference from a knowledge management perspective is the way in which knowledge is used as a resource to create value in terms of results for the organization. Hence, the logic of the five interlocking value shop activities in this example is of a police organization and how it engages in its core business of conducting reactive and proactive investigations.

The sequence of activities starts with problem understanding, moves into alternative investigation approaches, investigation decision, and investigation implementation, and ends up with criminal investigation evaluation. However, these five sequential activities tend to overlap and link back to earlier activities, especially in relation to activity 5 (control and evaluation) in police organizations when the need for control and command structures are a daily necessity because of the legal obligations that police authority entails. Hence, the diagram is meant to illustrate the reiterative and cyclical nature of these five primary activities for managing the knowledge collected during and applied to a specific police investigation in a value shop manner. Furthermore, Figure 10.2 illustrates the expanding domain of the knowledge work performed in police investigations, starting in the centre with problem understanding and ending at the edge with evaluation of all parts of the investigation process.

These five primary activities of the value shop in relation to a police investigation unit can be outlined as (Gottschalk, 2007):

1. **Problem definition.** This involves working with parties to determine the exact nature of the crime and hence how it will be defined. For example, a physical assault in a domestic violence situation depending on how the responding officers choose and/or perceive to define it can be either upgraded to the status of grievous bodily harm to the female spouse victim or it may be downgraded to a less serious common, garden variety assault where a bit of rough handing took place towards the spouse. This concept of making crime,

a term used on how detectives choose to make incidents into a crime or not, is highly relevant here and is why this first activity has been changed from the original problem finding term used in the business management realm to a problem definition process here in relation to police work. Moreover, this first investigative activity involves deciding on the overall investigative approach for the case not only in terms of information acquisition but also as indicated on Figure 10.2 in undertaking the key task, usually by a senior investigative officer in a serious or major incident, of forming an appropriate investigative team to handle the case.

2.   **Investigation approaches.** This second activity of identifying problem solving approaches involves the actual generation of ideas and action plans for the investigation. As such it is a key process for it sets the direction and tone of the investigation and is very much influenced by the composition of the members of the investigative team. For example, the experience level of investigators and their preferred investigative thinking style might be a critical success factor in this second primary activity of the value shop.

3.   **Approach decision.** This solution choice activity represents the decision of choosing between alternatives generated in the second activity. While the least important primary activity of the value shop in terms of time and effort, it might be the most important in terms of value. In this case, trying to ensure as far as is possible that what is decided on to do is the best option to follow to get an effective investigative result. A successful solution choice is dependent on two requirements. First, alternative investigation steps were identified in the problem solving approaches activity. It is important to think in terms of alternatives. Otherwise, no choices can be made. Next, criteria for decision-making have to be known and applied to the specific investigation.

4.   **Investigation implementation.** As the name implies, solution execution represents communicating, organizing, investigating, and implementing decisions. This is an equally important process or phase in an investigation as it involves sorting out from the mass of information coming into the incident room about a case and directing the lines of enquiry as well as establishing the criteria used to eliminate a possible suspect from further scrutiny in the investigation. A miscalculation here can stall or even ruin the whole investigation. Most of the resources spent on an investigation are used here in this fourth activity of the value shop.

5.   **Performance evaluation.** Control and evaluation involves monitoring activities and the measurement of how well the solution solved the original problem or met the original need. This is where the command and control chain of authority comes into play for police organizations and where the determina-

tion of the quality and quantity of the evidence is made as to whether or not to charge and prosecute an identified offender in a court of law.

1.7   Knowledge Workers in Investigations

Policing is generally viewed as a highly stressful and demanding profession. Considerable research has examined stress in policing. According to Richardsen, Burke and Martinussen (2006), most of this work has focused on the effects of the distress of police officers, the impact of police work on officers' spouses and families, police suicide, police drinking, police mortality, police fatigue, posttraumatic stress disorder, and the effects of shift work schedules on police performance and health. Although it is not clear whether police work is inherently more demanding than other professions, police officers experience work events that are associated with psychological distress.

Richardsen et al. (2006) studied the mediating role of both negative (cynicism) and positive (work engagement) work attitudes in the relationship between work events and work and health outcomes. The cynicism theory proposes that police officers come into the occupation with idealistic notions, but quickly come to realize the hard realities of the world and of police work. Over time, they then become increasingly intolerant of faults and mistakes in others and may lose a sense of purpose. Cynicism may be a way to cope with what is perceived to be an unfriendly, unstable, and insecure world, providing a convenient explanation for constant disillusionment and a way of acting out anger and resentment in the work place.

Richardsen et al. (2006) found that cynicism and engagement were highly correlated with both work and health outcomes in the expected direction; that is, cynicism was associated with increased health complaints and reduced commitment and efficacy, and engagement was associated with reduced health complaints and increased commitment and efficacy.

1.8   How Detectives Work

According to Tong (2007), the secretive nature of the detective world has attracted little attention from researchers. However, competing perspectives about detective work can be discerned from available literature. Detective work has been characterized as an art, a craft, a science, and a combination of all three. The old regime of the seasoned detective highlighted the notion of detective work as a craft. An alternative perspective highlights the scientific nature of detective work, which focuses on the skills needed for crime scene management, the use of physical evidence, investigative interviewing, informant handling, offender profiling, management of the investigative process, and knowledge management.

It is important for detectives to be effective in their work, as new public management is focusing closely on the effective use of resources. However, measuring effectiveness is no easy task. Measurement, in an investigative context, has focused upon the outcome of cases, often at the expense of evaluating the process of the investigation and quality of its outputs. Tong (2007) argues that not only have the police been subject to inadequate measurement criteria such as clear-up rates, there has also been a lack of recognition of good quality police work. The task of recognizing good detective work involves more than providing an appropriate method of measurement; it also implies an awareness of the impact of practice as well as an awareness of the knowledge accumulation, sharing and reuse.

It follows that the most useful approach to measuring detective effectiveness will not necessarily be the measurement of specific outcomes, although such measures will be useful for resource management. Tong (2007) argues that effectiveness in the context of detective work is best measured by focusing on the key processes and decisions in which detectives engage to encourage a professional working culture based on how detectives come to decisions. In the context of the value shop for knowledge work, decisions are made in all five primary activities: understanding the problem, identifying problem solutions, prioritizing actions, implementing investigation, and evaluating and controlling detective work.

Tong (2007) constructed the following profile of an effective detective after analyzing the academic literature relating to detective skills and abilities:

1. **Personal qualities.** Intelligence, common sense, initiative, inquisitiveness, independence of thought, commitment, persistence, ability to talk to people, flexibility, ability to learn, reflexivity, lateral thinking, creative thinking, patience, empathy, tolerance and interpreting uncertain and conflicting information, ability to work away from family and home, interpreting feelings, ideas and facts, honesty and integrity.
2. **Legal knowledge.** Knowledge of the law referring to police powers, procedure, criminal justice process, a good grounding in criminal law, awareness of changes to legislation, courtroom protocol, rules of disclosure, use of evidence, format of case file and awareness of defense arguments.
3. **Practical knowledge.** Technology available to detectives and used by criminals, understanding the context in which crime is committed and awareness of investigative roles of different functions of the police organization and specialist advisors. Recognition that crime changes with time and place and may require police responses that are tailored to specific context. Forensic awareness and practical expertise (e.g. crime scene preservation and packaging of evidence).

4. **Generic knowledge.** Recognition that knowledge changes, awareness of developments in practice will allow the detective to remain up to date.

5. **Theoretical knowledge.** Understanding of theoretical approaches to investigative reasoning and theories of crime.

6. **Management skills.** The management and control of case information, implementing investigative action, formulating investigative strategies, verify expert advice, prioritize lines of enquiry, formulate media strategies, awareness of resource availability and knowledge of roles of personnel available to the investigation. Manage knowledge and learning through the use of research skills to enable the detective to remain up to date.

7. **Investigative skills.** Interview technique, presenting evidence, cultivating informants, extracting core information (from files, reports, victims and witnesses), file construction, appraising and evaluating information, ability to absorb and manage large volumes of information, statement taking, problem-solving, formulating lines of enquiry, create slow time, assimilate information from crime scene, continually review lines of enquiry, question and challenge legal parties.

8. **Interpersonal skills.** Ability to communicate and establish a rapport with a range of people, remain open minded, awareness of consequences of actions and avoid speculation.

Stelfox and Pease (2005) argue that there has been surprisingly little empirical research into the way in which individual officers approach the task of investigating crime. In their own research they found that investigators are practical people. Assuming that the cognitive abilities of the average investigator are no more nor less than the population as a whole, it can be anticipated that he or she will remain liable to make the same cognitive errors as the rest of us. Assuming also that the decision-making environment the detective works in is unlikely to change much, it can be anticipated that errors will recur.

The national intelligence model (NIM) in the UK is a business model for law enforcement. It became the policy of the Association of Chief Police Officers (ACPO), and many forces underwent major restructuring and were allocated new resources in order to implement it. NIM takes an intelligence-led approach to policing. The UK government acknowledged its benefits, and all forces in England and Wales were required to implement NIM to national minimum standards from 2004. NIM consists of nine individual elements (Centrex, 2005a):

1. **Crime pattern analysis** is a generic term for a number of related analytical disciplines such as crime, or incident series identification, crime trend analysis, hot spot analysis and general profile analysis.

2.   **Market profile** is an assessment, continually reviewed and updated, that surveys the criminal market around a particular commodity, such as drugs or stolen vehicles, or of a service, such as prostitution, in an area.

3.   **Demographic/social trend analysis** is centered on an examination of the nature of demographic changes and their impact on criminality, as well as on the deeper analysis of social factors such as unemployment and homelessness, which might underlie changes or trends in offenders or offending behavior.

4.   **Criminal business profile** contains detailed analysis of how criminal operations or techniques work, in the same way the legitimate businesses may be explained.

5.   **Network analysis** describes not just the linkages between people who form criminal networks, but also the significance of the links, the roles played by individuals and the strengths and weaknesses of a criminal organization.

6.   **Risk analysis** assesses the scale of risks posed by individual offenders or organizations to individual potential victims, the public at large, and also to law enforcement agencies.

7.   **Target profile analysis** embraces a range of analytical techniques, which aim to describe the criminal, his or her criminal activity, lifestyle, associations, the risk the person poses, and personal strengths and weaknesses in order to give focus to the investigation targeting each person.

8.   **Operational intelligence assessment** maintains the focus of an operation on the previously agreed objectives, particularly in the case of a sizeable intelligence collection plan or other large scale operation.

9.   **Results analysis** evaluates the effectiveness of law enforcement activities, for example the effectiveness of patrol strategies, crime reduction initiatives or a particular method of investigation.

Element 4 in NIM is of particular interest when focusing on criminal organizations. This element acknowledges the enterprise paradigm of organized crime, where legal and illegal businesses share some common features. A criminal business profile might focus on primary and secondary activities of criminal organizations similar to non-criminal organizations. The profile might examine all aspects of activities, such as how victims are selected, the technical processes involved in the crimes, methods of removing, disposing of or laundering proceeds, and weaknesses in systems or procedures that the criminal business exploits. Similarly, element 5 supports the enterprise paradigm for criminal organizations.

Element 3 in NIM is often concerned with designing geo-demographic classification. Geo-demographics is a field of study, which involves the classification of persons according to the type of neighborhood in which they live. As a method of segmenting people it has long been of value to direct marketers who, being often unable to identify the age, marital status or occupational status of people in mailing lists, found it a useful means of applying selectivity to their mail shots. By analyzing the behavioral characteristics of consumers in different types of neighborhoods they found they could improve business performance by targeting promotional activities to names and addresses failing within specific types of postcode.

One of the bottlenecks in international police cooperation is the targeting of the proceeds of crime. International agencies such as Interpol and Europol are sometimes involved in the interaction between the authorities and enforcement organizations of the countries concerned. Borgers and Moors (2007) studied bottlenecks in international cooperation for the Netherlands in targeting the proceeds of crime. While no bottlenecks were found in cooperation with countries such as Belgium and the United Kingdom, bottlenecks were found in relation with countries such as Spain and Turkey. In relation to Turkey, the Netherlands acts mainly as the requesting state and not the requested state (Borgers & Moors, 2007, p. 8):

Regarding the cooperative relations with Turkey, Turkish respondents state that the framing of Dutch mutual assistance requests is inadequate. On the part of the Netherlands, there are different opinions on the depth of the investigation conducted at the request of the Netherlands. As far as the way in which people address one another is concerned, it is striking that the Turkish respondents sometimes consider the Dutch manner of operation as haughty and impatient. According to Dutch respondents, communication difficulties also occur if Dutch police officials directly contact the Turkish judges involved.

To fight organized crime, law enforcement in the UK reorganized. The United Kingdom's Serious Organized Crime Agency (SOCA) commenced operations in 2006 with an annual budget of £400 million. SOCA amalgamates the National Crime Squad, the National Criminal Intelligence Service (NCIS), and investigators from Customs and the Home Office's Immigration Service.

1.9   The Case of a Pedophile "Pocket Man"

One of the longest, highest-profile manhunts in Norwegian history may have succeeded Friday, January 11, 2008, when police arrested a suspect they call "The Pocket Man" in the sexual abuse of 300 to 400 young boys over three decades. Police said the suspect, identified only as a 55-year-old businessman from the western city of Bergen, was linked to five of the assaults through his DNA and that they expected to prove more cases. "The Pocket Man has finally been captured," Arne Joergen Olafsen, chief of police in the south-eastern Norway town of Ski, says at a news conference. "This is a relief for many, including the police."

Figure 10.3. Police have been working from this sketch of the suspect, as they tracked his movements based on children's reports of attacks all over southern Norway

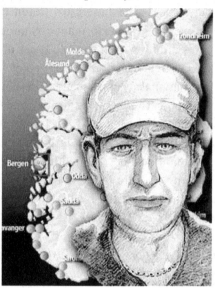

"The Pocket Man" — name stems from the man cutting off the bottoms of his pants pockets so they would be open. He then traveled the country, and induced young boys, all between age six and 12, to reach into a pocket on the pretence of helping him find an object. According to Norway's largest newspaper, Verdens Gang, he sometimes filed his pockets with sticky tape hoping the boys' hands would become stuck.

In 2000, police began publishing appeals for tips, police artist drawings of possible suspects and grainy photos taken from surveillance cameras. The national crime police established a special "Pocket Man" Internet site providing and seeking information about what they said were 300-400 assaults. At the news conference, police said a breakthrough in case came as a tip from a retired Bergen police officer, but gave no more details. Norwegian news media described the suspect, whose name was withheld, as a wealthy, divorced father of grown children. Police said they now believe the assaults started in 1976 and 1977. The suspect traveled through southern and western Norway, and varied the sites at which he abused the boys, including at swimming pools, public toilets and even at road intersections.

This case raises several interoperability issues. Considering the case took three decades for the police to solve, it makes sense to question whether or not an earlier solution to the case would have been possible given better interoperability. Here are some of the interoperability problems illustrated by this case:

- Norway is divided into several police districts. When a case occurs in one district, automatic links to similar unsolved cases in other districts are not established. This is mainly a problem of organizational interoperability.
- Since the pocket man turned out to be the brother of a police officer, the case was protected by insights from other officers to avoid internal gossip in the police force.
- A geographic information system was introduced late in the investigation.
- Several interesting sources for more information into the GIS were not available.

Olafsen said that geographic randomness meant each assault was reported to a different police station. It was not until the search was coordinated nationally that police saw the scope of the serial assault.

CONCLUSION

To succeed police investigations often require technical, Semantic and organizational interoperability. One important source of information for the police is digital information made accessible through various information systems, e.g. geographical information systems. Information technology can play an important role simplifying and improving the process of sharing, distributing, creating, capturing and understanding information. But, policing often requires interoperability with other districts, government departments, or even private organization.

REFERENCES

Alavi, M., & Leidner, D. E. (2001). Knowledge management and knowledge management systems: Conceptual foundation and research issues. *MIS Quarterly, 25*(1), 107-136.

Bock, G.-W., Zmud, R. W., & Kim, Y.-G. (2005). Behavioral intention formation in knowledge-sharing: Examining the roles of extrinsic motivators, social-psychological forces, and organizational climate. *MIS Quarterly, 29*(1), 87-111.

Borgers, M. J., & Moors, J. A. (2007). Targeting the proceeds of crime: Bottlenecks in international cooperation. *European Journal of Crime, Criminal Law and Criminal Justice, 15*(1), 1-22.

Centrex. (2005a). *Guidance on the national intelligence model.* Bedford, UK: National Centre for Policing Excellence.

Centrex. (2005b). *Practice advice on core investigative doctrine.* Bedford, UK: National Centre for Policing Excellence.

Chainey, S., & Smith, C. (2006). *Review of GIS-based information sharing systems* (Home Office Online Report No. 02/06). The Jill Dando Institute of Crime Science, University College London.

Chen, H., Zheng, D., Atabakhsh, H., Wyzga, W., & Schroeder, J. (2003). COPLINK: Managing law enforcement data and knowledge. *Communications of the ACM, 46*(1), 28-34.

Gottschalk, P. (2007). Information systems in police knowledge management. *Electronic Government, an International Journal, 4*(2), 191-203.

Hansen, M. T., Nohria, N., & Tierney, T. (1999). What's your strategy for managing knowledge? *Harvard Business Review, 77*(2), 106-116.

Holgersson, S., Gottschalk, P., & Dean, G. (2008). Knowledge management in law enforcement: knowledge views for patrolling police officers. *International Journal of Police Science and Management, 10*(1), 76-88.

Home Office. (2004). *Managing police performance: A practical guide to performance management*: Police Standards Unit & Accenture.

Home Office. (2005). *Guidance on statuary performance indicators for policing 2005/2006.* Police Standards Unit, Home Office, UK.

Johnson, S. D., Birks, D. J., McLaughlin, L., Bowers, K. J., & Pease, K. (2007). *Prospective crime mapping in operational context.* (Online report No. 19/07). Home Office, UK.

Kennedy, A. (2007). Winning the information wars. Collecting, sharing and analysing information in asset recovery investigations. *Journal of Financial Crime, 14*(4), 372-404.

Lahneman, W. J. (2004). Knowledge-sharing in the intelligence community after 9/11. *International Journal of Intelligence and Counterintelligence, 17*(4), 614-633.

Lin, L., Geng, X., & Whinston, A. B. (2005). A sender-receiver framework for knowledge transfer. *MIS Quarterly, 29*(2), 197-219.

Luen, T. W., & Al-Hawamdeh, S. (2001). Knowledge management in the public sector: principles and practices in police works. *Journal of Information Science, 27*(5), 311-318.

Richardsen, A. M., Burke, R. J., & Martinussen, M. (2006). Work health outcomes among police officers: The mediating role of police cynicism and engagement. *International Journal of Stress Management, 13*(4), 555-574.

Smith, N., & Flanagan, C. (2000). *The effective detective: Identifying the skills of an effective SIO* (Police Research Series Paper No. 122). London: Policing and Reducing Crime Unit.

Stelfox, P., & Pease, K. (2005). Cognition and detection: Reluctant bedfellows? In M. Smith & N. Tilley (Eds.), *Crime science: New approaches to preventing and detecting crime*. Willan Publishing.

Sørensen, C., & Pica, D. (2005). Tales from the police: Rhythms of interaction with mobile technologies. *Information & Management, 15*(2), 125-149.

Tong, S. (2007). *Training the effective detective: Report of recommendations.* Canterbury Christ Church University, Kent, UK.

Weir, R., & Bangs, M. (2007). *The use of geographic information systems by crime analysts in England and Wales.* (Online Report No. 03/07). Home Office.

Xu, J. J., & Chen, H. (2004). Fighting organized crimes: Using shortest-path algorithms to identify associations in criminal networks. *Decision Support Systems, 38*(3), 473-487.

Chapter XI
Levels of Organizational Interoperability

1.   LEVELS OF ORGANIZATIONAL INTEROPERABILITY

The most challenging of all interoperability issues seems to be related to organizational interoperability. While technical interoperability certainly represents
challenges of stretching current technology and waiting for more advanced technology in the future, we know that technology can be managed, and we know that
technology enjoys steady progress. Efforts at technical inter-connectivity have
been enhanced by significant developments in connectivity capabilities during the
past decade, such as increased availability of integrated technological solutions
and favorable cost-performance trends. While Semantic interoperability might
be a little more complicated, as it involves political and practical debates where
stakeholders have different agendas, we nevertheless expect continuous progress
in this area as well.

We start this chapter by discussing four levels of organizational interoperability
– business process interoperability, knowledge management interoperability, value
configuration interoperability, and strategy position interoperability. Then, we continue suggesting theory-based as well as general benchmark variables for measuring
organizational interoperability. Based on the levels of growth model with benchmark
variables, we are suggesting a stage hypothesis at the end of the chapter.

1.1 Level 1: Business Process Interoperability

Business process integration and interoperability are among the most significant factors driving electronic government today. In addressing the manifold technology challenges of integration and interoperability, new standardization efforts aim at improving the interoperability of businesses by moving toward a classification and specification of businesses processes, that is, one which describes alternative business processes and what each process does (Koehler, Hauser, Sendall, & Wahler, 2005).

A business process is a collection of interrelated tasks, which solve a particular work assignment. A business process is a structured, measured set of activities designed to produce a specific output for a particular function or client. It implies a strong emphasis on how work is done within an organization. A process is a specific ordering of work activities across time and space, where activities occur both in sequence and in parallel. A business process has a beginning and an end, and clearly defined inputs and outputs. It uses one or more resources and creates a result of value for the receiver in the organization or the client outside the organization. Activities in the business process are primarily important to the extent that they contribute to complete the process, i.e. that the business process delivers expected results in the form of governance and services.

This definition represents certain characteristics for a process. These characteristics focus on the business logic of the process (how work is done), such as having clearly defined boundaries, input and output, as well as activities ordered in time and space. Business processes are concerned with how work is organized, coordinated, staffed and focused on producing outputs. Business processes are workflows in the form of materials and information. Hence, business processes are collections of activities. Furthermore, business processes are the very special way the organization has chosen to coordinate work and knowledge, and the way management chooses to coordinate all production of services. Business processes do normally move across departmental borders. They may involve several levels in the hierarchy as well.

In an organization, many business processes take place at the same time. These processes are often dependent on each other, as they produce services through process interactions. The organization also interacts with its environment. The environment includes everything and everyone influencing the organization.

Today, executives are interested in identifying and improving business processes. This interest has emerged as executives realize that organizational success is dependent on the ability to deliver services at low costs, with high quality and professional performance. This interest has also emerged as more and more business processes have important interactions with the environment.

Information-intensive business processes will typically find intensive support by information systems. Business processes that were manual and inefficient may have been restructured, and activities in the processes may have been automated using information technology.

Efforts at business process interdependence have typically emphasized the view that the organization should develop its own vision for internal integration after assessing the benefits of integrating current business processes. If an organization deems the current processes to be effective, then it is important to articulate the specific objectives of internal integration: for instance, some organizations may seek to create cross-functional, horizontal business processes that are parallel to the traditional organization. Alternatively, the logic for internal integration may reflect a transition toward fundamentally redesigning the business processes over a period of time.

Efforts at business processes interdependence should then emphasize the need to ensure that inter-organizational needs guide internal integration efforts. Simply fine-tuning existing outmoded processes through current technological capabilities does not create the required organizational capabilities.

However, the benefits from information and communication technology are not fully realized if superimposed on the current business processes - however integrated they might be. This is because the current business processes subscribe to a set of organizational principles that responded to the bureaucratic era. Organizational concepts such as centralization versus decentralization, span of control, line versus staff, functional specialization, authority-responsibility balance, and administrative mechanisms for coordination and control are all derived from the general principles. Although these concepts are still valid, ICT functionality can significantly alter some of these old principles. Some modes of organizing may be rendered relatively inefficient. In the opinion of professionals and academics, the new logic of organization should be predicated on current and emerging ICT capabilities. ICT functionality should not simply be overlaid on existing business processes, but should be used as a lever for designing the new organization and associated business processes in a networked digital government.

Three critical questions for exploiting ICT-related benefits at the level of business process redesign are: (i) what is the rationale for the current organizational design? (what are the strengths and limitations?); (ii) what significant changes in business processes are occurring in the government sector? (what are the likely impacts?); what are the costs of continuing with the status quo? (when should we redesign the business process? what should be our pace of redesign?).

A government agency should initiate business process redesign after ascertaining the significant changes in its key allies' business processes – especially those of leading organizations – so that it can formulate appropriate responses beforehand.

Benefits from business process redesign are limited in scope if the processes are not extended outside the focal organizational boundary to identify options for re-designing relationships with the other organizations that participate in ultimately delivering government value.

Distinctions can be made between platform independent and platform specific integration of business processes. In the case of platform specific integration, reverse engineering, compilation and other transformations are needed to enable interoperability. Koehler et al. (2005) suggest a declarative approach to such transformations, where the goal is described in terms of relations between the initial and final states. The declarative approach is contrasted to the imperative approach, which defines explicit intermediate steps to reach the goal. Declarative approaches may have an advantage in that they can be analyzed, reused, and reversed.

1.2   Level 2: Knowledge Management Interoperability

Inter-organizational business processes are dependent on knowledge sharing and knowledge creation. There is a need for know-what, know-how, as well as know-why in cooperating organizations to be able to explore and exploit information exchanges. According to Kutvonen (2007), the main challenge for the interoperability knowledge management is to provide an extensible discipline to capture detailed enough ontology of business network models, service types, and service offers for automated use in the interoperability checking both at establishment and operational time. This discipline provides the inter-enterprise collaborations a kind of interoperability safety.

By ontology is meant a conception of reality. It seeks to describe or posit the basic categories and relationships of being or existence to define entities and types of identities within its framework. In an interoperability context, ontology is concerned with knowledge creation and sharing to the extent that it can make information exchanges safe, correct and efficient. The business network models define the structure of the collaboration, while the service types provide a bridging concept between the service offers and roles. Service offers provide knowledge about the actual services.

Kutvonen (2007) had chosen to use the defined business network models as the topmost level of ontologies. Each business network model gives a root for naming scheme within the ontology. The relevant knowledge includes knowledge about each enterprise, knowledge about exchanges, and knowledge about mutual concepts.

Organizational transformation and inter-organizational collaboration is founded on knowledge management, which in turn rests on trust. With trust identified as a common enabler in both processes and outputs of joint activities, open knowledge exchanges require declarations of intent from all parties (Mason & Lefrere, 2003).

1.3   Level 3: Value Configuration Interoperability

Information resource integration in cooperating organizations is dependent on value configurations involved. Information is applied in primary and secondary activities, where primary activities vary among value configurations.

Organizations that seek information resource integration with their business partners typically need to establish higher levels of external coordination. For example, increasing levels of external collaboration require agencies to systematically plan, implement and monitor their cooperation with external partners and to co-define cooperation targets (Greiner, Lippe, Kahl, Ziemann, & Jäkel, 2007). Coupling between primary activities in cooperating value configurations has to adhere to business processes in both organizations.

Since value configuration is more about value creation and less about value extraction, a strong relationship between knowledge and value emerges (Mason & Lefrere, 2003). In knowledge-based government enterprises, value arises from the effective application of knowledge and the efficient application of information technology.

1.4   Level 4: Strategy Position Interoperability

Interoperability strategy is concerned with agreeing to common goals and ground rules for achieving mutual benefits. The decision to make information resources more widely available has implications for the organizations concerned (where this may be seen as a loss of control or ownership), their staff (who may not possess the skills required to support more complex systems and a newly dispersed user community), and the end users (Mason & Lefrere, 2003).

Over the last several decades, strategy researchers have devoted attention to the question of how organizational elites (i.e., agency executives and directors) affect corporate strategy. The CEO as a person in position shapes the scope of the organization, while the CIO as a person in another position shapes the scope of IT in the organization. Jensen and Zajac (2004) proposed and tested the notion that while differences in individual characteristics of organizational elites may imply different preferences for particular business strategies such as diversification and expansions, these basic preferences, when situated in different agency contexts (e.g., CIO, CEO) generate very different strategic outcomes.

Therefore, we focus on the individual at the top of each government organization to understand the extent to which organizational interoperability is on the strategic agenda. We label the top executive CEO. The CEO is the only executive at level 1 in the hierarchy of an organization (Carpenter & Wade, 2002). All other executives in the organization are at lower levels. At level 2, we find the most senior executives. Level 3 includes the next tier of executives. Organizational interoperability is dependent on executives at all these levels who are willing to cooperate with executives in other organizations for mutual benefits. The most important executive role is the CEO.

Being a CEO involves handling exceptional circumstances and developing a high level of tacit knowledge and expertise; these characteristics and experiences contribute to the accumulation of organization-specific human capital. The time a CEO spends in the position represents a significant investment in organization-specific human capital for both the individual and the agency. The organization is investing its resources to compensate the CEO, and the CEO is investing his or her productive time. Both make these investments with the expectation of future return, and so age is a major factor determining the level of organization-specific human capital investment (Buchholtz, Ribbens, & Houle, 2003).

Being a CEO means bearing full responsibility for an organization's success or failure, but being unable to control most of what will determine it. It means having more authority than anyone else in the organization, but being unable to wield it without unhappy consequences. Porter, Lorsch and Nohira (2004) make this sound like a very tough job. They argue that this comes as a surprise to CEOs who are new to the job.

Some of the surprises for new CEOs arise from time and knowledge limitations—there is so much to do in complex new areas, with imperfect information and never enough time. Others stem from unexpected and unfamiliar new roles and altered professional relationships. Still others crop up because of the paradox that the more power you have, the harder it is to use. While several of the challenges may appear familiar, Porter et al. (2004) discovered that nothing in a leader's background, even running a large business within his organization, fully prepare him or her to be CEO.

CEOs have long been recognized as the principal architects of corporate strategy and major catalysts of organizational change, and the extent to which CEOs can effect change in corporate strategy is thought to be determined largely by the power they possess and how they decide to wield it (Bigley & Wiersema, 2002).

Bigley and Wiersema (2002) argued that CEO's cognitive orientations should influence how they wield their power to affect corporate strategy. On the one hand, predictions about a CEO's use of power require an understanding of the CEO's cognitive orientation toward his or her organization's strategy, because power is simply the ability to bring about a preferred or intended effect. On the other hand, hypothesized associations between a CEO's cognitive orientation and corporate strategy presuppose that the CEO has sufficient power to bring about the preferred or intended effects.

CEOs' strategic beliefs are likely to be instantiated to a significant degree in their organizations' current strategies. When a top executive seeking advice confirms and/or restores his or her confidence in the correctness of strategic beliefs, the CEO will be less likely to change firm strategy. McDonald and Westphal (2003) theorized that relatively poor organizational performance can prompt chief executive officers to seek more advice from executives of other organizations who are their friends or similar to them and less advice from acquaintances or dissimilar others and suggests how and why this patters of advice seeking could reduce organizations' propensity to change corporate strategy in response to poor performance.

McDonald and Westphal (2003) tested their hypotheses with a large sample. The results confirm their hypotheses and show that executives' social network ties can influence firms' responses to economic adversity, in particular by inhibiting strategic change in response to relatively poor firm performance. Additional findings indicate that CEOs' advice seeking in response to low performance may ultimately have negative consequences for subsequent performance, suggesting how CEOs' social network ties could play an indirect role in organizational decline and downward spirals in corporate performance.

1.5   Interoperability Benchmark Variables

In Table 11.1, some potential benchmark variables for the interoperability levels are suggested. This table might be applied in several ways. First, for one specific government agency, the level for each benchmark variable can be determined. While the result will not be consistent for one level, the average level might nevertheless be computed, thereby identifying the average level at which the organization is currently. Second, when two cooperating agencies do this exercise for themselves, results might be compared. Typically, one agency will be at a higher level than the other. This insight is useful, as cooperation might be easier when becoming aware of differences. Finally, a wide distribution of answers (some at level 1, others at level 4) might indicate that the organization has a very unclear understanding of what and why in terms of integration efforts currently underway.

This way of measuring organizational interoperability by applying benchmark variables to levels represent a new approach in need of more research. Future research might look at conceptualization of benchmark variables as well as empirical testing.

Each of the eight benchmark variables can be explained more in detail as follows:

- **Purpose of integration.** At Level 1, integration focuses primarily on solving administrative problems and irritation related to re-entering of data and

Table 11.1. Benchmark variables at levels of interoperability in digital government

Benchmark Variables	Level 1 Business Process Interoperability	Level 2 Knowledge Management Interoperability	Level 3 Value Configuration Interoperability	Level 4 Strategy Position Interoperability
Purpose of integration	Administrative efficiency when doing the things rights	Administrative effectiveness when doing the right things	Functional effectiveness when adding value to the work	Organizational effectiveness when adding business value
Role of information systems	Support for inter-organizational workflow	Mobilization of information resources	Integrating primary and secondary activities	Enabling mutual organizational benefits
Primary task for the CIO	Transformation of business process design into IT solutions	Establishing electronic knowledge exchanges	Transformation of value logic into IT solutions	Translation of strategic vision into implications for information systems
Primary role of the CIO	Monitor learning from the environment	Resource allocator prioritizing initiatives	Entrepreneur understanding inter-organizational business needs	Architect linking IT to business value of cooperating organizations
Main governance challenge	Standardization of work processes	Standardization of information systems	Integration of value creation activities	Common architecture and infrastructure
Design focus	Information exchange	Knowledge exchange	Service exchange	Benefits exchange
Top management role	Decisions on solutions	Stimulation of knowledge exchange	Communicating business value	Clear strategic direction

misunderstandings of information content. Avoiding mistakes and doing things right the first time is important at this stage. This gradually changes as information systems begin to support new ways of doing the work based on knowledge and learning (Level 2) or influence value creation (Level 3). At Level 4, there is joint strategy development for collaborating organizations – at which business and IS truly acting as one with strategic influences going both directions.

- **Role of information systems.** While each system will only do what it is supposed to do, it will nevertheless change its role in an inter-organizational setting. At Level 2 for example, an environment of knowledge sharing is created around the information system, enabling knowledge workers in different organizations to learn from each other.
- **Primary task for the CIO.** This is the most critical success factor for the IT manager. At Level 1, the most critical success factor is to establish inter-organizational workflow in an efficient and secure way. At Level 4, a very different success factor can be found. It is concerned with the CIO's ability to translate strategy into action. While a mutual strategy might be concerned with overall goals, the strategy does not always tell how those goals might be reached and how information systems might support the effort. Therefore, the CIO must be capable of translating general statements into detailed specifications of future systems.
- **Primary role of the CIO.** The CIO must initially get used to the idea of not having his or her 'kingdom' of systems anymore. Now systems become part of relationships with other 'kingdoms'. Thus, the CIO needs to develop relationships and cooperative arrangements with collaborating organizations to work for interoperability. At Level 4, all CIOs involved become members of a group of architecture, who work together to create the joint architecture.
- **Main governance challenge.** IT governance is concerned with decision rights related to key IT management areas. Initially, decisions should be made concerning standardization. At higher levels, architectural decisions are more important.
- **Design focus.** When information systems are designed, focus will change from standardization at lower levels to exchanges at higher levels.
- **Top management role.** The chief executive might find it difficult to 'let others into' his or her organization, as strengths and weaknesses become visible to outsiders. Especially at Level 2, where openness concerning operations and problems is a prerequisite for inter-organizational knowledge management.

1.6   Theory-Based Benchmark Variables

One of the theories presented in this book is *transaction cost theory*. When applying this theory to levels of organizational interoperability, we find different costs at different levels, as described in Table 11.2.

Another theory is *agency theory*, where the agency problem occurs when cooperating parties have different goals and division of labor. The cooperating parties are engaged in an agency relationship defined as a contract under which one or more organizations (the principal(s)) engage another organization (agent) to perform some electronic information service on their behalf, which involves delegating some decision making authority to the agent (Jensen & Meckling, 1976). According to Eisenhardt (1985), agency theory is concerned with resolving two problems that can occur in agency relationships. The first is the agency problem that arises when the desires or goals of the principal and agent conflict and it is difficult or expensive for the principal to verify what the agent is actually doing. The second is the problem of risk sharing that arises when the principal and agent have different risk preferences. The first agency problem arises when the two parties do not share productivity gains. The risk-sharing problem might be the result of different attitudes towards the use of new technologies. As illustrated in Table 11.2, agency problems can be defined as conflicts in the interoperability stage model.

Alliance theory is concerned with partnership, often referred to as alliance. Das and Teng (2003) discussed partner analysis and alliance performance. An important stream of research in the alliance literature is about partner selection. It emphasizes the desirability of a match between the partners, mainly in terms of their resource profiles. The approach is consistent with the resource-based theory of the firm, which suggests that organizations are defined by their resources profiles.

Relational exchange theory is based on relational norms. Norms of importance to interoperability include:

- **Flexibility**, which defines a bilateral expectation of the willingness to make adaptations as circumstances change
- **Solidarity**, which defines a bilateral expectation of a high value placed on the relationship.
- **Trust**, which defines an expectation of a predictable and desirable behavior in the future.

More theories could be added to this table, such as network theory, contractual theory, theory of core competencies, stakeholder theory, theory of organizational boundaries, production cost theory, and social exchange theory.

Table 11.2. Theory-based variables at levels of interoperability in digital government

Benchmark Variables	Level 1 Business Process Interoperability	Level 2 Knowledge Management Interoperability	Level 3 Value Configuration Interoperability	Level 4 Strategy Position Interoperability
Transaction cost theory	Information interpretation costs as well as business process understanding costs	Communication costs as well as disagreement costs	Management costs associated different and conflicting value creation logic	Executive costs associated with conflicting ambitions, visions and goals
Agency theory	Conflict between risk-seeking and risk-aversive government organizations when applying new technologies	Conflict between open and closed government organizations when sharing knowledge	Conflict between efficiency oriented value chains and problem solution oriented value shops	Conflict between collaborating government organizations about sharing productivity gains and results
Alliance theory	Partner organizations approach each other to establish information exchanges	Partner organizations implement all agreements of the alliance and the alliance grows rapidly	Alliance performance produces benefits for partner organizations	Partner organizations join forces by establishing joint goals for mutual benefits
Relational exchange theory	Flexibility by adapting to collaborating organizations' work processes	Solidarity by helping collaborating organizations	Profitability by aligning value creation to collaborating organizations	Positioning by joining forces with collaborating organizations

1.7   The Stage Hypothesis

Stages of growth models have been presented in various forms throughout this book. Models have been labeled maturity models, development models and stage models. The basic idea is the same: An evolution in terms of aggregation and accumulation. What we are suggesting here by means of the levels of growth model with benchmark variables is a stage hypothesis. Only empirical research can validate such a stage model, which is outside the scope of this book.

A stage model is based on a number of assumptions and that is why it is called a stage hypothesis. It assumes that predictable patterns (conceptualized in terms of stages) exist in the growth of a phenomenon such as inter-organizational interoperability. It assumes that stages are sequential in nature, occur as a hierarchical progression that is not easily reversed, and evolve a broad range of organizational activities and structures (King & Teo, 1997).

The following level in this model does not only represent a progression and an improvement when compared to the previous level. The next level also involves new kinds of challenges for the organization. The kinds of problems to be solved at the next level are different from those problems solved at the previous level. Problems, challenges and solutions change as an organization moves from one level to the next in Figure 11.1.

Benchmark variables should involve activities and structures that are characteristic for each stage of maturity. Relationships at Stage 1 can theoretically be expected to conform to values of benchmark variables listed under Stage 1. It is possible for relationships at Stage 1 to have values of benchmark variables applicable to other stages. However, the values of benchmark variables indicate the most likely theoretical characteristics of each stage of interoperability.

The stage hypothesis suggested here might be formulated in two parts:

- **Hypothesis A:** Values of benchmark variables for organizational interoperability will significantly correspond with their conceptual stage formulations given.
- **Hypothesis B:** The stages of organizational interoperability shows predictable patterns of growth from aligning work processes, knowledge sharing, to value creation, and into strategic alignment.

Figure 11.1. Stage model for organizational interoperability

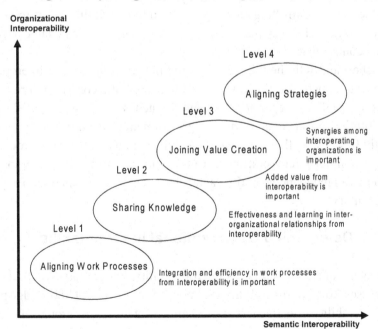

The stage hypothesis is based on the following implications when moving from one stage to the next stage. Stating that organizations suffer under lack of interoperability in electronic government means that interoperability research efforts should be spent in finding out which level of interoperability an organization might strive for. To guide developmental energies at lower levels of orientation, which provide additional understanding of the transitional events, individuals and organizations have to accumulate experience in order to move and grow from one stage of development to the next. The stages of growth are sequential in nature, occur as a hierarchical progression that is not easily reversed, and involve a broad range of organizational activities and structures.

In future research, the model has to be verified by testing content validity. Next, scales applied in the stage model have to be defined. Finally, it should be possible to empirically test the stage model. This is, however, outside the scope of this book.

The optimal level of interoperability is not necessarily the highest Level 4. As pointed out by transaction cost theory, infrequency of transactions might cause transaction costs to remain high, not justifying comprehensive extensive strategic alignment between interoperating organizations. Stating that organizations suffer under lack of interoperability in electronic government means that interoperability research efforts should be spent in finding out which level of interoperability an organization should strive for (Legner & Lebreton, 2007).

The 'optimal' level of interoperability for one organization when dealing with other government organizations is dependent on a number of factors, not just transaction costs. For example, legal issues are of importance: When one agency has the role of controlling another agency, interoperability needs to be limited and restricted in such a way that the controlled agency remains unable to involve itself in the control work.

Scholl and Klischewski (2007) ague that integration and interoperation may be outright unconstitutional because the democratic constitution requires powers to be divided into separate levels and branches of government. Since under the constitution, governmental and non-governmental constituencies operate independently from each other and own their information and business processes, neither integration nor interoperation, nor information sharing can be imposed on them, rather as an independent entity each constituency's participation in any interaction is voluntary.

1.8   Determining Organizational Interoperability

At Level 1 of business process interoperability, integration and efficiency in work processes from interoperability is important. At Level 2 of knowledge management interoperability, effectiveness and learning in inter-organizational relationships from

Figure 11.2. Benchmark variables are used to indicate characteristics at each stage level

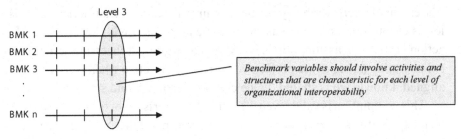

interoperability is important. At Level 3 of value configuration interoperability, added value from interoperability is important, while at Level 4 of strategy position interoperability, synergies among interoperating organizations is important as illustrated in Figure 11.2.

Benchmark variables are used to indicate characteristics at each stage of growth. Measurement is carried out using Guttman scales. The purpose is to identify the average level at which the organization is currently. A wide distribution of answers might indicate that the organization has a very unclear understanding of what and why efforts currently are underway in their relationship with other organizations. Two co-operating agencies might compare their results in terms of level and benchmark values.

For many government organizations, it is crucial and critical to be moving from one level to the next level:

- Efforts should be spent finding out which level of interoperability the organization should strive for.
- Individuals and organizations have to accumulate experience in order to move and grow from one level of development to the next.
- The levels of maturity are sequential in nature, they occur as a hierarchical progression that is not easily reversed, and involve a broad range of organizational activities and structures.

We leave to future research to verify the model by testing content validity. Furthermore, scales applied in the stage model have to be defined. Finally, it should be possible to empirically test the stage hypothesis.

1.9   Measuring Transaction Costs

The extent of interoperability can be measured in terms of transaction costs. Higher levels of interoperability are assumed to be associated with lower levels of transaction costs. This assumption is based on the argument that transactions between collaborating agencies are performed more cost-effective when work processes are aligned, knowledge is shared, value creation is joined, and strategies are aligned.

This assumption is valid given the same characteristics of transaction volume and form. Typically, however, higher levels of interoperability will be associated with higher transaction intensity, as transactions have become easier to carry out between cooperating agencies. Five attributes are associated with transaction costs:

1. The necessity of investment in durable, specific assets: If transacting organizations need investments in assets to carry out their inter-organizational transactions, then investment costs are part of transaction costs.

2. Infrequency of transaction: Cost estimate for each transaction has to be higher and included as part of transaction costs.

3. Task complexity and uncertainty: Cost estimate is dependent on complexity judgment and risk assessment.

4. Difficulty in measuring task performance: Transaction cost has to take into account the hidden costs associated with invisible inefficiency in task performance.

5. Interdependencies with other transactions: Transaction cost has to include changes in other transactions as a consequence of inter-organizational transactions.

These five attributes determine transaction costs for all participating agencies (Williamson, 2000). In addition some agencies may suffer from additional transaction costs because of opportunistic behavior by other agencies. Opportunism is self-interest seeking with guile and includes overt behaviors such as lying, cheating and stealing, as well as subtle behaviors such as dishonoring an implicit contract, shirking, failing to fulfill promises, and obligations. To measure transaction costs, then, is a matter of estimating certain cost elements and changing the size of these elements according to certain factors.

According to Anderson, Glenn and Sedatole (2000), empirical research indirectly tests transaction cost theory by relating observed information sourcing decisions to transaction attributes that proxy for transaction costs. Evidence on the relation between transaction-specific investments, contract duration, and technological uncertainty generally supports the theory. The consistency of the empirical results seems startling in light of two problems with the hypothesis that organizations take sourcing decisions to minimize the sum of production and transaction costs. First, production and transaction costs are rarely neatly separable. For example, the choice of production technology (and subsequent production costs) is often inextricably linked with production volume, which in turn depends on whether the organization produces some or all products internally. Second, decision-makers are likely to be affected by wealth effects associated with sourcing, and thus are unlikely to take decisions that strictly maximize organization profit.

Anderson et al. (2000) argue that because production costs are objectively calculated by the accounting system, while transaction costs are assessed subjectively through indirect indicators, functional managers are likely to differ in the importance that they assign to reducing transaction costs. Consequently, the effect transaction costs have on a make-or-buy choice can partly reflect the influence exerted by the purchasing manager. Production cost differences seems more influential in sourcing decisions than transaction cost differences, and experience of the decision-maker is related to assessments of technological uncertainty. Profit center managers engage in influence activities that increase the costs of price renegotiations above the level that is observed in comparable external market transactions. Managers sometimes seem more reluctant to make their organizations dependent on other organizations in an information exchange when investments in specific assets are necessary; and contrary to theory, managers sometimes consider previous internal investments in specific assets a reason to keep complete and independent internal work processes. In certain circumstances decision-makers systematically misestimate (or fail to consider) transaction costs.

CONCLUSION

An area where future progress is quite uncertain is the area of organizational interoperability. In this area, conflicting goals, hidden agendas, strong and weak stakeholders, competent and not-so-competent managers, lack of strategy, political rivalry, and other issues all meet to complicate the matter of interoperability. Furthermore, the concept of 'organizational' interoperability is complicated, as we have indicated in our discussions of organizational structure and organizational culture. Organizational interoperability is focusing on the ability of two or more units to provide services to and accept services from other units, and use the services so exchanged to enable them to operate effectively together (Legner & Lebreton, 2007).

We have in this chapter presented levels of organizational interoperability, interoperability benchmark variables, the stage hypothesis, theory-based as well as general benchmark variables, and measurement of transaction costs. In terms of transaction costs, higher levels of interoperability are assumed to be associated with lower levels of transaction costs – collaborating agencies are performing more cost-effective when work processes are connected, knowledge is shared, value creation logic is linked, and strategies are aligned.

At level 1, organizational interoperability is concerned with coordination of work processes and other organizational matters needed to achieve desired level of cooperation. This is a question of strategy, strategic alignment and strategic positioning at the highest level and most advanced stage of organizational interoperability. The extent of interoperability will depend on the extent of strategic synergy between the cooperating organizations.

At level 2, we identify the value creation in organizations. Value chains, value shops and value networks have different value creation logic, drivers and performance measures. The role of information systems is quite different in each of these value configurations. While IT systems in value chains are successful if they contribute to efficient logistics and production, IT systems in value shops are successful if they add value at problem solving. In the value network, IT systems are successful if they operate efficiently while providing more services to more clients.

At level 3, knowledge is needed to exchange electronic information. There is a need for know-what, know-how and know-why. Know-what represents knowledge about what is going on in cooperating organizations. Know-how represents a deeper understanding on how work is going on in cooperating organizations, while know-why is the most fundamental source of knowledge, as it represents an understanding of causality.

Finally at level 4, the first level of organizational interoperability is concerned with work processes. Connecting work process in digital government enables seamless production of services based on output from several agencies.

REFERENCES

Anderson, S. W., Glenn, D., & Sedatole, K. L. (2000). Sourcing parts of complex products: evidence on transactions costs, high-powered incentives and ex-post opportunism. *Accounting, Organizations and Society, 25*(5), 723-749.

Bigley, G. A., & Wiersema, M. F. (2002). New CEOs and corporate strategic refocusing: How experience as heir apparent influences the use of power. *Administrative Science Quarterly, 47*(4), 707-727.

Buchholtz, A. K., Ribbens, B. A., & Houle, I. T. (2003). The role of human capital in postacquisition CEO departure. *Academy of Management Journal, 46*(4), 506-514.

Carpenter, M. A., & Wade, J. B. (2002). Microlevel opportunity structures as determinants of non-CEO executive pay. *Academy of Management Journal, 45*(6), 1085-1103.

Das, T. K., & Teng, B.-S. (2003). Partner analysis and alliance performance. *Scandinavian Journal of Management, 19*(3), 279-308.

Eisenhardt, K. M. (1985). Control: Organizational and economic approaches. *Management Science, 31*(2), 134-149.

Greiner, U., Lippe, S., Kahl, T., Ziemann, J., & Jäkel, F. W. (2007). Designing and implementing cross-organizational business processes - Description and application of a modeling framework. In G. Doumeingts, J. Müller, G. Morel & B. Vallespir (Eds.), *Enterprise interoperability: New challenges and approaches* (pp. 137-147). London: Springer Verlag.

Jensen, M. C., & Meckling, W. H. (1976). Theory of the firm: Managerial behavior, agency costs and ownership structures. *Journal of Financial Economics, 3*(4), 305-360.

Jensen, M. C., & Zajac, E. J. (2004). Corporate elities and corporate strategy: How demographic preferences and structural position shape the scope of the firm. *Strategic Management Journal, 25*(6), 507-524.

King, W. R., & Teo, T. S. H. (1997). Integration between business planning and information systems planning: Validating a stage hypothesis. *Decision Science, 28*(2), 279-308.

Koehler, J., Hauser, R., Sendall, S., & Wahler, M. (2005). Declarative techniques for model-driven business process integration. *IBM Systems Journal, 5*(2), 203-225.

Kutvonen, L. (2007). Interoperability knowledge management issues. In R. Gonzales, J. P. Müller, K. Mertins & Z. Martin (Eds.), *Enterprise interoperability II* (pp. 629-632). London: Springer Verlag.

Legner, C., & Lebreton, B. (2007). Business interoperability research: Present achievements and upcoming challenges. *Electronic Markets, 17*(3), 176-186.

Mason, J., & Lefrere, P. (2003). Trust, collaboration, e-learning and organisational transformation. *International Journal of Training and Development, 7*(4), 259-270.

McDonald, M. L., & Westphal, J. D. (2003). Getting by with the advice of their friends: CEOs' advice networks and firms' strategic responses to poor performance. *Administrative Science Quarterly, 48*(1), 1-32.

Porter, M. E., Lorsch, J. W., & Nohira, N. (2004). Seven surprises for new CEOs. *Harvard Business Review, 82*(10), 62-72.

Scholl, H. J., & Klischewski, R. (2007). E-government integration and interoperability: Framing the research agenda. *International Journal of Public Administration, 30*(8), 889-920.

Williamson, O. E. (2000). The new institutional economics: Taking stock, looking ahead. *Journal of Economic Literature, 38*(3), 595-613.

Chapter XII
E–Government Dynamics

1. E-GOVERNMENT DYNAMICS

It was Sterman's (2000) book entitled *"Business Dynamics: Systems Thinking and Modeling for a Complex World"* that introduced the term business dynamics. Business dynamics is concerned with learning in and about complex systems. Effective decision-making by growing dynamic complexity requires executives to become systems thinkers – to expand the boundaries of their mental models and develop ways to understand how the structure of complex systems creates behavior.

We start this chapter discussing how to overcome barriers to E-Government. Then we present a framework for assessment of E-Government projects. In the context of system dynamics, we discuss causal loop diagramming, modeling and organizational performance.

1.1 Overcoming Barriers to E-Government

In a study of the European Union, Archmann and Kudlacek (2008) identified the main interoperability barriers including sensitivity of data, cultural differences between government departments, issues of trust, timing, collaboration between agencies, organizational and technical problems, unsatisfactory workflows, convinc-

ing stakeholders of the importance of the system, legal issues and also the importance of political support and funding. On the other hand, they identified enablers
of improved interoperability, such as wide use of digital signatures, commitment
at all political levels to interoperability projects, engagement and involvement of
all stakeholders from the very beginning and time constraints.

In a research agenda for E-Government integration and interoperability, Scholl
and Klischewski (2007) suggest future research projects to study the foci and purposes, limitations and constraints, as well as processes and outcomes of integration
and interoperation in electronic government. In such future research projects, the
stages of growth models presented in this book might prove helpful in organizing
findings.

Progress towards realizing the full potential of E-Government – using digital
technologies to improve public services and government-citizen engagements – has
been slower and less effective than the technologies' take-up in spheres such as e-
commerce and e-business according to Eynon and Margetts (2007). They identified
seven categories of barriers to E-Government progression:

1. Leadership failures resulting in slow and patchy progress to E-Government.
2. Financial inhibitors limiting the flow of investment to E-Government innova-
    tion.
3. Digital divides and choices, where inequalities lead to differences in motiva-
    tions and competences that constrain and fragment E-Government take-up
    and fail to address particular user needs.
4. Poor coordination across jurisdictional, administrative and geographic bound-
    aries that holds back E-Government networking benefits.
5. Workplace and organizational inflexibility impairing adaptability to new
    networked forms of information sharing and service provision.
6. Lack of trust heightening fears about inadequate security and privacy safe-
    guards in electronic networks.
7. Poor technical design leading to incompatibilities between information systems
    or difficult-to-use E-Government services. Where such services lag behind
    innovative applications used by society more generally, government organiza-
    tions will find it increasingly difficult to address issues of interest to online
    communities, which will tend to have different communication channels and
    mechanisms for producing content.

The seven categories are broad and tied to a multitude of more specific barriers
relevant at different governance, institutional and jurisdictional levels. In addition to
the seven barrier categories, Eynon and Margetts (2007) explored eight legal areas
that provide important foundations for examining and identifying key barriers to

E-Government. Seven of the eight legal dimensions explored were of general applicability: (1) authentication and identification in online identity management, (2) intellectual property rights, (3) liability arising from a malfunction or inaccuracies in E-Government services, (4) privacy and data protection, (5) public administration transparency through the wide availability of public sector information, (6) reuse of public sector information, and (7) relationships between public administrations, citizens and other actors with a stake in E-Government services.

Eynon and Margetts (2007) suggest a range of organizational, technical and legal solutions to the barriers to E-Government for the future, among others:

- Creating a network of E-Government champions. This might compensate for leadership failures. Creating champions for E-Government across public administration is one way to ensure that the objective of making efficiency and effectiveness a reality is achieved, through the prioritization of E-Government issues at the highest levels of public organizations' strategies.
- Creating segmentation of citizens. This might compensate for digital divides and choices. Effective segmentation is going to be a key way of ensuring that no citizen is left behind.
- Working with chaotic co-ordination. This might compensate for poor coordination. Most of the solutions involving chaotic co-ordination are a question of best practice development.
- Encouraging an e-literate workforce. This might compensate for workplace and organizational inflexibility. An e-literate workforce is going to be vital in the future to maximize the benefits of E-Government and make efficiency and effectiveness a reality.

The future of electronic government is dependent on overcoming barriers by stimulating solutions to such barriers. In the US alone, there are over 600,000 E-Government Web sites. Barriers abound for those trying to do business with the government and the underlying issues have been studied for many years. To date, there are still no answers; however, if there were more interoperability between agencies and governments, perhaps some of these barriers would be eliminated. In order for that to happen, those that design the sites, those that work with the sites and those that use the sites must all be included in the process and integration. One of the issues that many system designers face is that they do not thoroughly study the end user and the situation. This issue must be addressed in order for E-Government interoperability to truly take place.

1.2   Assessment of E-Government Projects

The goal of E-Government is to capture benefits of the electronic economy. Esteves and Joseph (2008) developed a framework for assessment of E-Government projects. The framework includes *maturity level*, s*takeholder evaluation*, and *assessment level.*

Maturity levels are (1) innovative leaders, (2) visionary followers, (3) steady achievers, and (4) platform builders. At the national level, Canada, Singapore and USA were found at the highest maturity level of innovative leaders, as they provide innovative Web-based solutions for citizens and businesses. Norway, Australia and Finland were found at the next level of visionary followers, because they strive to improve sophistication and administrative simplicity. New Zealand, Hong Kong and France were identified as steady achievers performing steady improvements with less ambitious projects. Finally, Japan, Brazil and Malaysia were examples of platform builders representing new E-Government initiatives.

The second component in the assessment framework is stakeholders. A stakeholder represents any entity (individual, group, organization) that can affect or is affected by the organization's execution of its objectives. According to Esteves and Joseph (2008), the primary E-Government stakeholders are:

- **Citizens.** Citizens in contact with public administration, using public services exercising their civil rights, and participating in democratic processes.
- **Employees.** All categories of public employees, including politicians and various other public administrators.
- **Businesses.** Both for-profit and non-profit companies interact with government. Businesses are in contact with public administration in their compliance with taxes, social, and legal obligations. Many non-profits also seek and submit proposals for grants.
- **Governments.** In multi-tier systems, there is interaction among local, state, and federal levels of government.
- **IS/IT personnel.** E-Government solution suppliers from both the private and public sector. They are suppliers of solutions, know-how, advice, skilled resources, and hardware and software expertise.
- **Special interest groups.** Aggregated and organized citizens interacting in local communities to build their voice through examples such as non-government organizations and civil service organizations. Also included here are international organizations such as the European Commission and the United Nations.

Assessment level is the third and final component in the framework. Dimensions here include strategy, technology, organization, economy, operations, public services, and information services.

Esteves and Joseph (2008) suggest that an assessment of E-Government projects should not only add up "scores" according to the components. Rather, interaction effects between the components should also be taken into account.

1.3 Dynamic Business Performance

Business dynamics can be understood as the evolution of one single business as well as the evolution of businesses in an industry or in a region. In the latter meaning, Brandt (2004) studied business dynamics in terms of the creation of new businesses and the decline or market exit of less productive firms.

The creation and growth of new firms and the decline or market exit of old firms are often regarded as key to business dynamism and economic growth in OECD economies. New firms are thought to be especially innovative and to play an important role as job creators. Based on these ideas, policy makers often believe that institutions, which foster firm entry may ultimately enhance the overall economic performance of their country (Brandt, 2004).

According to Brandt (2004), it is frequently reported findings in the firm demographics literature that most new firms do not survive for long. Chances of survival are especially low for firms that start small, as they usually do. Two-year survival rates for firms born in 1998 do confirm that there is a high risk of newly created firms being forced to exit the market rapidly. Survival rates correspond to the number of firms of the same cohort that have survived a given number of years as a percentage of all firms that entered the same year with them. In Europe, between 12 and 38 per cent of all new firms had failed already after the first two years, as the survival rates varied roughly between 88 and 62 percent.

Firm survival can also be assessed on the basis of hazard rates, which correspond to the conditional probability of leaving the market after a certain life span. These are calculated as the share of exiting firms in the number of survivors of the same cohort as of the previous year. While survival rates decline with firm age by construction, a priori there is nothing that precludes hazard rates from being comparable at different durations. One- and two-year hazard rates reveal that while entry rates tend to be higher in services than in manufacturing, the risk that these new firms have to exit the market early in life is higher in services, as well (Brandt, 2004).

Similar to the study by Brandt (2004) is the study by Callejón and Segarra (1999) on business dynamics and efficiency in industries and regions in Spain. They studied business dynamics in terms of firm births and deaths. According to their approach, new firms are seen more as users of innovations than producers of innovations. The results showed that both entry and exit rates contribute positively to the growth of total factor productivity in industries and in regions.

Business dynamics as the evolution of one single organization is the perspective of Sterman (2000). He argues that effective decision-making and learning in a world of growing dynamic complexity requires us to become systems thinkers – to expand the boundaries of our mental models and develop tools to understand how the structure of complex systems creates their behavior. To make the firm survive and avoid being part of the hazard rate, management needs the skills required to develop systems thinking capabilities, how to create an effective learning process in dynamically complex systems, and how to sue system dynamics in organizations to address important problems.

Managers seeking to solve a problem sometimes make it worse. Executive policies may create unanticipated side effects. Attempts to stabilize the system may destabilize it. Executive decisions may provoke reactions by others seeking to restore the balance. Such phenomena are called the counterintuitive behavior of social systems. These unexpected dynamics often lead to policy resistance, the tendency for interventions to be delayed, diluted, or defeated by the response of the system to the intervention itself (Sterman, 2000).

The Internet is a classic example of business dynamics in information technology. The Internet was probably the biggest technological revolution of the latter half of the twentieth century, but (McCullagh, 2003, p. 10):

Remember the heady days of the dot.com go-go years, when every company had to have an Internet strategy? The dogma that sparked this search for new business models (or were they muddles?) was that the "Internet changes everything". If you are in the business of book retailing or you're running a travel agency, this doctrine may still hold water, but in the cold light of day, how big an impact has the Internet had on the business design?

Without doubt, e-mail has drastically reduced the time it takes to send a message or file, and the Web has enabled new e-business models. But, as system dynamics modeling so nicely can visualize and simulate, the interactions between business performance and information technology applications can over time create all kinds of business dynamics, from exponential growth to decline and collapse.

There are all kinds of dynamics in organizations and between organizations. An interesting example is power dynamics within top management. Power dynamics highlights interest conflicts and competition within top management. A primary cause of interest conflicts and competition among top executives lies in their desire for power and career advancement. Senior executives are ambitious individuals who have high needs for power and achievement. As they move up the corporate hierarchy, their desire to become CEO and run their own show becomes even stronger. The extraordinary prestige and material benefits associated with the CEO title provide further incentives for senior executives to challenge the CEO of their company and to participate in a power tournament in the firm's internal labor market (Shen & Canella, 2002).

In addition, the external labor market generally evaluates executives' talent on the basis of the performance of their employing firms. When firm performance suffers, so does each senior executive's reputation and value in the external labor market. Senior executives thus, even if not direct power contenders themselves, have incentives to monitor the CEO's leadership and join others in taking action against the CEO when they perceive him or her to be less than capable. This is an example of power dynamics, where the interest conflicts and competition between a CEO and other senior executives put the CEO at risk of power contests with senior executives followed by dismissal and inside succession (Shen & Canella, 2002).

1.4   Causal Loop Diagramming

Much of the art of system dynamics modeling is discovering and representing the feedback processes, which determine the dynamics of a system. Feedback is important in a variety of systems (Bordetsky & Mark, 2000). All dynamics arise from the interaction of just two types of feedback loops, positive (or self-reinforcing) and negative (or self-correcting) loops. Positive loops tend to reinforce or amplify whatever is happening in the system: The more information technology is used in the organization, the more IT skills do users develop, leading to even greater use of information technology in the organization, as illustrated in Figure 12.1.

The + signs at the arrowheads indicate that the effect is positively related to the cause: an increase in information technology user skills causes the use of information technology to rise above what it would have been.

Figure 12.1. A positive feedback loop in information technology

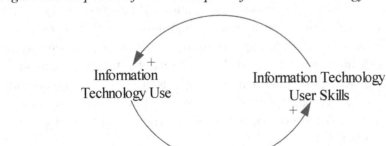

Figure 12.2. A negative feedback loop in information technology

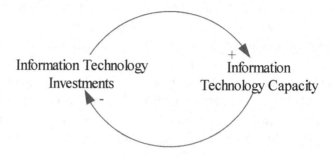

Figure 12.3. Dynamic system in information technology

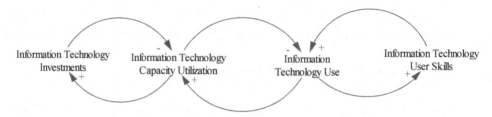

An example of a negative feedback loop in information technology is illustrated in Figure 12.2. The idea in the model is that more investments in information technology lead to higher information technology capacity. Assuming that the use does not change then capacity utilization drops, leading to lower information technology investments.

The negative minus (-) polarity for the link from information technology capacity means that an increase in information technology capacity leads to reduction in information technology investments. When the two loops are connected, we might find a dynamic system as illustrated in Figure 12.3. Here we have two negative feedback loops and one positive feedback loop.

From a management perspective, this figure can be interpreted in different ways. One simulation would be to focus on information technology capacity utilization. We might start with a high capacity utilization, leading to both higher investments and reduced use. After a while, capacity utilization drops as a consequence.

An example might be IT helpdesk. We can think of a staff of five persons working at the desk. Response times and service levels drop as a consequence of high capacity utilization. Another person is hired. At the same time, user stop contacting the help desk, leading to lower capacity utilization and the questioning of why this sixth person was hired.

Figure 12.4. Fluctuations in information technology capacity utilization caused by event-oriented investment decision-making

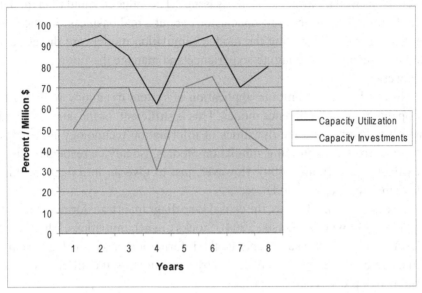

Another possible example based on the figure is illustrated in the next figure. As information technology capacity utilization increases, information technology investments increase, leading to a decline in capacity utilization. Since there are delays involved in decision-making, the firm might experience fluctuations and long-term decline in capacity utilization, as illustrated in Figure 12.4. While decision-makers probably don't like this development, they have themselves caused it by making information technology investment decisions based on events rather than an understanding of the feedback structure in Figure 12.3.

1.5   System Dynamics Modeling

System dynamics is a methodology for studying and managing complex systems, such as one finds in business and other social systems. It is used to address a variety of feedback systems. Feedback refers to the situation of X affecting Y and Y in turn affecting X, perhaps through a chain of causes and effects. The methodology identifies a problem, develops a dynamic hypothesis explaining the cause of the problem, builds a computer simulation model of the system, tests the model, devises and tests in the model alternative policies, and implements the best solution (System Dynamics Society, 2006).

The system dynamics methodology is an integrated multi-disciplinary modeling approach for identifying, conceptualizing, representing, and analyzing operational, tactical, as well as strategic business issues. The value of simulation models lies in its ability to help users draw conclusions about a real business situation or system by studying and analyzing the model. Simulation models are therefore tools for helping managers to imagine, experience and manage the future, before it arrives (Powersim, 2006).

In this book, we limit our application of system dynamics modeling to causal loop diagrams and reference modes. This is sufficient for the purpose of this book, which is to illustrate the dynamics of information technology management. For those interested in building simulation models, we advice readers to the standard textbook by Sterman (2000). However, just to give an introduction, this section describes the steps in modeling.

In the modeling process, the causal loop diagram is transformed into a stock and flow map (Moxnes & Saysel, 2004). Stocks are accumulations. They characterize the state of the system and generate the information upon which decisions and actions are based. Stocks create delays by accumulating the difference between the inflow to a process and its outflow.

Stocks and flows are familiar to management. While information technology capacity is a stock, investments in information technology is a flow. By investing more information technology (flow), management will cause an increase in information technology capacity (stock). Stocks characterize the state of the system and provide the basis for actions.

After turning the causal loop diagram into a stock and flow map, a simulation model is formulated. Formulation of the simulation model consists of specifying structure and decision rules, estimating parameters, behavioral relationships, and initial conditions, and testing for consistency with the purpose and boundary. The testing will consists of:

- **Comparison to reference mode:** Does the model reproduce the behavior adequately for management purpose?
- **Robustness under extreme conditions:** Does the model behave realistically when stressed by extreme conditions?
- **Sensitivity:** How does the model behave given uncertainty in parameters, initial conditions, model boundary, and aggregation?

When the model has successfully pasted these tests, then it can be applied for policy design and evaluation. Policy design means answers to questions such as: What new decision rules, strategies, and structures might be tried in the real world? How can they be represented in the model? What if something else happens? What are the effects of various policies? How robust are the policy recommendations under different scenarios and given uncertainties? Do the policies interact? Are there synergies or compensatory responses?

Many software packages are available for system dynamics modeling.Vensim from Ventana (2006) is a visual modeling tool that allows the model developer to conceptualize, document, simulate, analyze, and optimize models of dynamic systems. Vensim provides a way of building simulation models from causal loop or stock and flow diagrams. By connecting words with arrows, relationships among system variables are entered and recorded as causal connections. This information is used by an equation editor to help form a complete simulation model. The model can be analyzed throughout the building process, looking at causes and uses of a variable, and also at the loops involving the variable. When the model is built and tested, Vensim enables ways to explore the behavior of the model (Ventana, 2006).

An alternative software package is Powersim (2006). Powersim's approach to business planning involves the building of mathematical models (representations of the real situation or system) for computer simulation. The models are based on the system dynamics paradigm, which is the use of feedback theory to organize the system structure and the use of computer simulation to deduce the behavior of the business system.

System dynamics modeling has over the years been applied to a variety of business, regional, national, and global issues. One example is found in the Journal of Computer Information Systems where Chen (2004) presented a decision support system for tourism development. The model was developed to simulate visitor dynamics in response to different environmental changes and investment scenarios. The model is a system dynamics based interactive decision support system. It is designed in the Powersim program.

1.6   Organizational Performance

Despite the importance to researchers, managers, and policy makers of how information technology contributes to organizational performance, there is uncertainty and debate about what we know and don't know. A review of the literature conducted by Melville, Kraemer and Gurbaxani (2004) reveals that studies examining the association between IT and organizational performance are divergent in how they conceptualize key constructs and their interrelationships.

IT business value research examines the organizational performance impacts of information technology. Previous research has shown that information technology may indeed contribute to the improvement of organizational performance (e.g., Brynjolfsson & Hitt, 1996). The dimensions and extent of IT business value depend on a variety of factors, including the type of IT, management practices, and organizational structure, as well as the competitive and macro environment. Research also suggests that firms do not appropriate all of the value they generate from IT; value may be captured by trading partners or competed away by end customers in the form of lower prices and better quality.

Melville et al. (2004) developed a model of IT business value based on the resource-based theory of the firm that integrates the various strands of research into a single framework. The resource-based theory has been used to examine the efficiency and competitive advantage implications of specific firm resources such as entrepreneurship, culture, and organizational routines. It is also useful in the IT context, providing a robust framework for analyzing whether and how IT may be associated with competitive advantage.

Based on how Melville et al. (2004) modeled IT business value, we developed a causal loop diagram as illustrated in Figure 12.5. The locus of IT business value generation is the organization that invests in and deploys IT resources, which might be called the focal firm. But external factors also play a role in shaping the extent to which IT business value can be generated and captured. In particular the competitive environment, which surrounds the causal loop diagram in Figure 12.5.

In Figure 12.5, the information technology resources consist of the technological IT resource and the human IT resource. The technological IT resource can be further categorized into IT infrastructure, i.e., shared technology and technology services across the organization, and specific business applications that utilize the infrastructure, i.e., purchasing systems, sales analysis tools, etc. The technological IT resource thus includes both hardware and software. The separation into infrastructure and business applications is consistent with how companies view their physical IT assets. The human IT resource denotes both technical and managerial knowledge. Examples of technical expertise include application development, integration of multiple systems, and maintenance of existing systems. Managerial skills include the ability to identify appropriate projects, marshal adequate resources, and lead and motivate development teams to complete projects according to specification

Figure 12.5. IT business value model

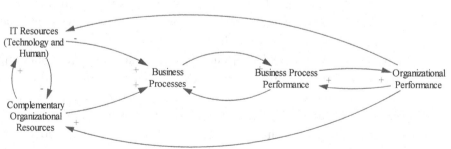

and within time and budgetary constraints. Although technical and managerial expertise are often intertwined, they are nonetheless distinct concepts, and their conceptualization as such is necessary for precision in describing IT investment impacts.

Although it is possible to apply IT for improved organizational performance with few organizational changes, successful application of IT is often accompanied by significant organizational change, including policies and rules, organizational structure, workplace practices, and organizational culture. When synergies between IT and other firm resources exist, we call the latter complementary organizational resources as illustrated in Figure 12.5.

Business processes in the figure are activities underlying value-generating processes (transforming inputs to outputs). Business process performance is the operational efficiency of specific business processes, measures of which include customer service, flexibility, information sharing, and inventory management. Organizational performance is the overall firm performance, including productivity, efficiency, profitability, market value, and competitive advantage (Melville et al., 2004).

Santhanam and Hartono (2003) applied the resource-based theory and tested empirically whether information technology capability influences firm performance. Their results indicate that firms with superior IT capability indeed exhibit superior current and sustained firm performance when compared to average industry performance, even after adjusting for effects of prior firm performance.

According to the resource-based theory, the benefits of superior IT capability must be sustainable over time. Sustained competitive advantage does not imply that the benefits will last forever, but indicates that it will not be competed away by the duplication efforts of other firms. The concept of IT capability was developed using the premise that while resources can be easily duplicated, a unique set of capabilities mobilized by a firm cannot be easily duplicated and will result in sustained competitive advantages. IT investments are often made with long-term goals, and there is a time lag in obtaining benefits. Therefore, the sustained effects of IT investments in terms of IT capability are important.

In their empirical study, Santhanam and Hartono (2003) found sustained effects of IT capability. The leader firms were identified as having superior IT capability. Similar results were obtained in another study by Ravichandran and Lertwongsatien (2005), who found that variation in firm performance was explained by the extent to which IT was used to support and enhance a firm's core competencies. Their results also support the proposition that an organization's ability to use IT to support its core competencies is dependent on IT functional capabilities, which, in turn, are dependent on the nature of human, technology, and relationship resources of the IT department.

Ravichandran and Lertwongsatien (2005) applied the resource-based theory and tested empirically the effect of information technology resources and capabilities on firm performance. They defined capabilities as socially complex routines that determine the efficiency with which firms transform inputs into outputs. IT capabilities are the routines within the IT department that enable it to deliver IT services to the organization.

While a variety of IT capabilities have been identified in the literature, Ravichandran and Lertwongsatien (2005) limit their focus to the capabilities in the core functional areas such as planning, systems development, IT support, and IT operations. Building on the notion that capabilities are determined by organizational routines, they adopted a process focus and defined IT capabilities in terms of the quality and sophistication of IT processes.

When measuring organizational performance, Ravichandran and Lertwongsatien (2005) distinguished between operating performance and market-based performance. Operating performance was measured using a four-item scale that assessed the extent to which the profitability, productivity, and financial performance exceeded those of their competitors in the past three years. Market-based performance was measured using a three-item scale that assessed the success of the firm in entering new markets and in bringing new products and services to the market during the past three years.

CONCLUSION

System dynamics is a methodology for studying and managing complex systems. In the context of system dynamics, a system might be a manufacturing company, a consulting firm, a government organization, an industry or some other part of the real world that has cause-and-effect relationships to be understood for decision-making. While in the context of system dynamics an information system has a different meaning, a system here is a set of organizational relationships to be explored as different system structures create different system behaviors. Using system dynamics modeling managers has a powerful tool for identifying, conceptualizing, representing, and analyzing operational, tactical and strategic business issues.

REFERENCES

Archmann, S., & Kudlacek, I. (2008). Interoperability and the exchange of good practice cases. *European Journal of ePractice, 2*(February), 3-12.

Bordetsky, A., & Mark, G. (2000). Memory-based feedback controls to support groupware coordination. *Information Systems Research, 11*(4), 366-385.

Brandt, N. (2004). Business dynamics and politics. *OECD Economic Studies, 38*(March), 9-36.

Brynjolfsson, E., & Hitt, L. (1996). Paradox lost? Firm-level evidence on the returns to information systems spending. *Management Science, 42*(4), 541-558.

Callejón, M., & Segarra, A. (1999). Business dynamics and efficiency in industry and regions: The case of Spain. *Small Business Economics, 13*(4), 253-271.

Chen, K. C. (2004). Decision support system for tourism development: System dynamics approach. *Journal of Computer Information Systems, 45*(1), 104-112.

Enyon, R., & Margetts, H. (2007). Organisational solutions for overcoming barriers to eGovernment. *European Journal of ePractice, 1*(November), 73-85.

Esteves, J., & Joseph, R. C. (2008). A comprehensive framework for the assessment of eGovernment projects. *Government Information Quarterly, 25*(1), 404-437.

McCullagh, K. (2003). Situating technological change within social and business dynamics. *Design Management Journal, 14*(2), 10-16.

Melville, N., Kraemer, K., & Gurbaxani, V. (2004). Information technology and organizational performance: An integrative model of IT business value. *MIS Quarterly, 28*(82), 283-322.

Moxnes, E., & Saysel, A. K. (2004). *Misperceptions of global climate change: Information policies.* Norway: The Systems Dynamics Group, Department of Information Science, University of Bergen.

Powersim. (2006). *Powersim Software* [Powersim Studio: User's Guide].

Ravichandran, T., & Lertwongsatien, C. (2005). Effect of information systems resources and capabilities on organization performance: A resource-based perspective. *Journal of Management Information Systems, 21*(4), 237-276.

Santhanam, R., & Hartono, E. (2003). Issues in linking information technology capability to organization performance. *MIS Quarterly, 27*(19), 125-153.

Scholl, H. J., & Klischewski, R. (2007). E-government integration and interoperability: Framing the research agenda. *International Journal of Public Administration, 30*(8), 889-920.

Shen, W., & Canella, A. A. (2002). Power dynamics within top management and their impacts on CEO dismissal followed by inside succession. *Academy of Management Journal, 45*(6), 1195-1206.

Sterman, J. D. (2000). *Business dynamics: Systems thinking and modeling for a complex world.* Boston: McGraw-Hill.

System Dynamics Society. (2006). What is system dynamics? *System Dynamics Society* Retrieved September 17, 2008, from http://www.systemdynamics.org/

Ventana. (2006). *Vensim: Ventana Simulation Environment* [User's Guide Version 5].

About the Authors

Petter Gottschalk is professor of information systems and knowledge management in the Department of Leadership and Organizational Management at the Norwegian School of Management. He is the author of several books on these subjects, and he has published in major journals. Professor Gottschalk earned his MBA at the Technical University Berlin, Germany, his MSc at Dartmouth College and Sloan School, MIT and his DBA at Henley Management College, Brunel University, UK. His executive experience includes CIO at ABB and CEO at ABB Datacables. See http://www.bi.no/users/fgl98023/ for a detailed description of education, publications and management experience.

Hans Solli-Sæther has a MSc degree from the University of Oslo and a PhD degree from the Norwegian School of Management. He has been the CIO of Norway Post and has several years of experience with outsourcing. Dr. Solli-Sæther has published several research articles and books on this topic. His current research interests are outsourcing and organizational interoperability.

Index

X

Y